The Transcendental and the Mundane

"Cho-yun Hsu is one of the best-known Chinese thinkers residing in the West, giving him a unique perspective from which to compare both civilizations. In this ambitious work, Professor Hsu synthesizes the essence of Chinese culture in order to offer solutions to the global crisis of faith and values. A work of passionate humanism, *The Transcendental and the Mundane* is a heartfelt call to the world to take seriously the best aspects of traditional Chinese culture in order to avoid a looming catastrophe. Now rendered into fluent and highly readable English by Professor David Ownby, one of the leading translators and analysts of contemporary Chinese thought, Professor Hsu's work will now find a new audience among westerners."

—**Ian Johnson**
Pulitzer Prize-winning author

"Professor Hsu is deservedly a legend in Chinese Studies, and this book only adds to a long and distinguished publication record by an innovative scholar who has contributed to an enormous range of disciplines, including the early history of the *shi* 士 (men in service), cultural geography, Han agriculture, and China in several global settings. Like all of Hsu's works, this can be read with pleasure and profit, as it is studded with insights drawn from antiquity to contemporary history. Hsu in addition brings to the feast his vast experience in promoting democratic transitions in Taiwan and elsewhere in the Sinosphere, and once again, we who have strong professional and personal commitments to a flourishing China find ourselves in his debt. Highly recommended."

—**Michael Nylan**
Sather Professor of History, University of California at Berkeley

"In *The Transcendental and the Mundane*, Professor Hsu undertakes a sweeping review of the beliefs, values, and visions that constitute Chinese civilizations from the ancient times to the present. Historically engaged and critically provocative, it is a must-read for anyone interested in Chinese Studies."

—**David Der-wei Wang**
Edward C. Henderson Professor of Chinese Literature, Harvard University

"This account of traditional Chinese ways of thinking and being by one of the world's most eminent Sinologists is an invaluable witness to lived Chinese cultural history and its overriding ideal of harmony. Drawing at once on his deep knowledge of Chinese history and literature and his personal experience of life in mainland China, Taiwan, and the USA, Professor Hsu describes Chinese values as rooted in a predominantly agricultural society composed of villages and suggests that, with the West in crisis, these values, 'centered on the person and on the idea of close, interdependent relations between humans and nature, might offer a solution.' His hope, expressed with great modesty and sincerity, is 'that humans might together build a world civilization without prejudice and conflict.' Not since Lin Yutang's *My Country and My People* has there been such an accessibly erudite tribute to one of the world's great civilizations."

—**John Lagerwey**
Research Professor of Chinese Studies, The Chinese University of Hong Kong

"Why do we study history?—A question frequently posed by general readers, but even the most professional historian may not easily offer a persuasive answer. If human behavior is determined by the culture in which they live, then it is just so inevitable that history is the most quintessential way to understand that culture. Professor Hsu's book shows exactly how this principle worked. It is a masterpiece that digs deeply into the roots of problems and their underlying values in modern Chinese society in a tradition that goes as far back as to the formative stage of Chinese civilization. While people who are striving to understand puzzles in their everyday lives can find lessons in times long past, people who are interested in the lasting impact of the Chinese tradition can be satisfied in seeing its outcome. Reading through the lines of the book, there is a deep sense of passion and concern for the future of the humankind."

—**Li Feng**
Professor of Early Chinese History and Archaeology, Columbia University

The Transcendental and the Mundane

Chinese Cultural Values in Everyday Life

Cho-yun Hsu

Translated by David Ownby

The Chinese University of Hong Kong Press

The Transcendental and the Mundane: Chinese Cultural Values in Everyday Life
By Cho-yun Hsu
Translated by David Ownby

English edition © The Chinese University of Hong Kong 2021

中國人的精神生活 © Cho-yun Hsu 2017
Originally published in Complex Chinese by Linking Publishing Co., Ltd. in Taiwan.
This English edition is published by arrangement with Linking Publishing Co., Ltd.,
through Ailbert Cultural Company Limited.

The publication of this book was generously supported by
Chiang Ching-kuo Foundation for International Scholarly Exchange.

ISBN: 978-988-237-212-2

The Chinese University of Hong Kong Press
The Chinese University of Hong Kong
Sha Tin, N.T., Hong Kong
Fax: +852 2603 7355
Email: cup@cuhk.edu.hk
Website: cup.cuhk.edu.hk

Printed in Hong Kong

Contents

Chronology of Chinese Dynasties

Dynasties	Years
Xia 夏	ca. 21st century BCE–17th century BCE
Shang 商	ca. 17th century BCE–11th century BCE
Western Zhou 西周	ca. 11th century BCE–771 BCE
Eastern Zhou 東周	771 BCE–256 BCE
Spring and Autumn Period 春秋	771 BCE–476 BCE
Warring States Period 戰國	476 BCE–221 BCE
Qin 秦	221 BCE–206 BCE
Western Han 西漢	202 BCE–8 CE
Xin 新	8–23
Eastern Han 東漢	25–220
Three Kingdoms 三國	220–280
Western Jin 西晉	265–316
Eastern Jin 東晉	317–420
Southern and Northern Dynasties 南北朝	420–589
Sui 隋	581–618
Tang 唐	618–907
Five Dynasties and Ten Kingdoms 五代十國	907–960
Northern Song 北宋	960–1127
Southern Song 南宋	1127–1276
Liao 遼	916–1125
Jin 金	1125–1234
Yuan 元	1271–1368
Ming 明	1368–1644
Qing 清	1644–1912

Translator's Foreword

By David Ownby

The coronavirus pandemic unfurled across the world just as I was beginning my sabbatical year in May of 2020, which left me with a fair bit of unexpected time on my hands. It was at this juncture that the Chinese University of Hong Kong Press asked me to translate Professor Cho-yun Hsu's *The Transcendental and the Mundane: Chinese Cultural Values in Everyday Life* into English. I accepted the challenge, and am very glad I did.

The Press contacted me presumably because for the last few years, I have been studying—and translating—Chinese establishment intellectuals, mainland Chinese figures who publish in China and in the Chinese language, and play by the Chinese rules established by the Chinese Communist Party without being spokespeople for the Party or the state or writing what we would call "propaganda." Their focus is inevitably on China's rise to great power status and how this "new China" will shape the world.

These writers are the product of China's reform and opening, now underway for some four decades, and their work represents a moment of great creativity in the history of modern Chinese thought. Between roughly 2000 and 2015, globalization, the rise of the Internet, and a relatively liberal domestic political setting came together to produce a diverse, pluralistic intellectual environment in China, where New Confucians debated Liberals who denounced members of China's New Left....Many of these figures sincerely believed that China's rise and America's decline meant that world history was at a turning point, and they put their talents and voices to work to try to understand that change and identify China's (and the world's) future direction. As you might imagine, much of this discourse was marked by a fair bit of flag-waving and chest-thumping, as China finally avenged its "century of humiliation" and reassumed its rightful position at the center of the world.

In this context, it was refreshing and perhaps even comforting to spend a few months with the reflections of Professor Cho-yun Hsu, who comes from a different world with different values.

Professor Hsu was born in China, left for Taiwan in the late 1940s, and subsequently had a long and successful career as a professor of Chinese history in the United States before returning to Taiwan after his retirement. Like intellectuals on the Chinese mainland, Professor Hsu is convinced that the world is at a historical turning point, but instead of chest-thumping and flag-waving, in this volume, Professor Hsu explores the spiritual life of the Chinese people and the spiritual values of Chinese traditional culture with an eye toward suggesting less "muscular" solutions to the problems of the world, solutions where man seeks a more harmonious relationship with nature, with other people, and with himself. Born in 1930, Professor Hsu writes with the wisdom of experience, while his Mainland counterparts often strut with the exuberance of youth.

Professor Hsu's book is a unique combination of scholarship—his specializations are in archaeology, sociology, and history—and memoir. Thus his chapters range from China's prehistory, through the dynasties and down to the present day, and are punctuated with charming personal memories from Professor Hsu's childhood in Wuxi, his experience in different parts of China as his family sought refuge during the Sino-Japanese War, and from his life in Taiwan. In explorations that cover topics as diverse as cooking and poetry, *fengshui*, and religion, Professor Hsu shows us another way of living, a way based on family and community (living and dead), grounded in concrete humanity rather than abstract concepts. Professor Hsu fears that this world is disappearing, eclipsed by the forces of urbanization and globalization, which lends his work a touch of nostalgia as well, but I highly recommend a visit.

This might be an opportune moment to thank colleagues who lent a hand when Professor Hsu addressed themes beyond my competence, notably Paula Varsano (Chinese poetry), Richard Smith (the *Yijing*), Raoul Birnbaum (Chinese Buddhism) and Michelle Thompson (Chinese medicine). I would also like to thank my friends and colleagues at the Press, particularly Minlei Ye and Wai Hin Justin Cheung. I have told them this by email, but it never hurts to see it in print: You are far and away the best I have ever worked with. *Hou hui you qi* 後會有期!

Foreword

By Ying-shih Yu

This book is an insightful and lively discussion of the spiritual life of the Chinese people. The author stresses that he has adopted "the perspective of the common people," which is not entirely true. The spiritual life as presented in this book is quite comprehensive, ranging from the cultural elite to the common people. It is true that in the past, philosophers' discussions of the spirit of Chinese culture were often expressed from the point of view of the elite, which made it difficult for the general public to understand, as we see in examples such as Feng Youlan's 馮友蘭 (1895–1990) *Purity Descends, Primacy Ascends: Six Books* (*Zhenyuan liushu* 貞元六書) or Tang Junyi's 唐君毅 (1909–1978) *The Spiritual Value of Chinese Culture* (*Zhongguo wenhua zhi jingshen jiazhi* 中國文化之精神價值). A major feature of Professor Hsu's new book is that it is an unprecedented—indeed pioneering—attempt to reach out to the general public. In the chapters of this book, the author covers all aspects of Chinese spiritual life, not only quoting from Confucian, Buddhist, and Daoist scriptures, as well as classical literature, as the starting point of his arguments, but also often providing philosophical discussions before returning to the viewpoint of everyday people. Therefore, his claim to merely present "the perspective of the common people" is to some extent an exercise in modesty.

The book's most important contributions can be summarized in the following three features.

The Use of Both Macro and Micro Perspectives

The author views the spiritual life of the Chinese as a multifaceted and interactive order, and therefore observes its manifestations from different angles and perspectives. However, the author does not forget his roots. Examining the microcosm of the local does not make him lose sight of the macrocosm of the whole. On the contrary, he highlights the inner connections and interactions between the global and the local, as well as the links among various "locals." This is why I call it the use of both macro and the micro perspectives. If we use the language of traditional China to express this, we would say that it is both "broad and subtle" at the same time.

Appeals to All Tastes

I mentioned above Professor Hsu's integration of the views of the elite and those of the common people, which suggests the work's broad appeal, but more needs to be said. Modern Western scholars of Western culture tend to emphasize the differences and even the conflicts between sophistication and vulgarity (their terms are "big tradition" versus "small tradition" or "elite culture" versus "popular culture"). However, the Chinese intellectual tradition tends to stress the mutual affirmation between the two instead of their differences. This is why the scholar Liu Xianting 劉獻廷 (1648–1695), who lived during the Ming-Qing transition, emphasized the connection between the classics and folk practices such as divination rituals, operas, and novels. This seems to be Professor Hsu's basic position throughout the book. What amazes me most is that, as Liu once pointed out, "There is no one in the world who does not believe in rituals and divination to appease the gods and demons, which is why the *Yijing* and the *Liji* exist to meet their needs." Chapter V of the book discusses the changes in the universe, beginning with the *Yijing* and extending step by step to various aspects of folklore, which can be seen as a comprehensive development of Liu's statement.

Linking Past and Present

Finally, it should be pointed out that the author is a historian who has always taken into account the factor of time in examining various features of Chinese spiritual life, especially the frequent linkages between past and present. His arguments often start from the latest archaeological discoveries, followed by historical texts and narratives, and then finally draw from his own personal experience. Therefore, the spirit of culture presented in this book is a reality that can still be verified today, and not some arid literary fiction. The author is also careful in his use of his personal experience, taking care to confirm the authenticity of the past and the present. So we find detailed accounts of his life in Wuxi as a child and his life in Taiwan as an adult (e.g., Chapters III, VII, and VIII), and he also includes accounts of overseas Chinese communities which he visited, though he did not dwell on them overmuch out of caution, as in the case of "virtuous families 義門" in the Hong Kong New Territories (Chapter IX) and ancestor rituals in Malacca (Chapter VI). All in all, Professor Hsu is a scholarly and thoughtful writer who has practiced a wide range of humanities and social disciplines over the course of his career. In writing this book, he has developed his extensive knowledge into a system of thoughtful analysis. In addition, he has made extensive reference to the relevant works of modern scholars, and in addition to Feng Youlan and Fei Xiaotong 費孝通 (1910–2005), who are mentioned repeatedly in the book, he also discusses other well-known viewpoints. Therefore, this book is not the product of a single person working in solitude behind closed doors, but rather the culmination and crystallization of many works. I believe that most readers will have no difficulty in identifying with the various aspects of culture discussed in this book. However, the author's final conclusions are not borrowed from others, but are instead based on the three-fold argument mentioned above, and this is where this book surpasses its predecessors.

As a work of scholarship, this book embodies the best of modern objective research. But the author's intentions go much further. He believes that modern civilization, dominated by Western culture, is already in crisis due to "the alienation between humans, and the separation between humans and nature," while Chinese culture is human-oriented, and humans and nature are interdependent. Therefore, he hopes that these features of Chinese culture can be used as a source of inspiration for other cultures to "solve the dilemma of modern civilization." The book's conclusion, "A New Life for Chinese Culture," is a powerful expression of a benevolent man's plea to save the world.

Gu Yanwu 顧炎武 (1613–1682)[1] once said, "The point of a gentleman's learning is to make clear the Way and to save the world." I respectfully recommend this work to the reader.

Ying-shih Yu is a preeminent historian of China, and is Emeritus Professor of East Asian Studies and History at Princeton University. He was awarded the John W. Kluge Prize for achievement in the study of humanity and the inaugural Tang Prize International Award in Sinology.

---

1   Gu Yanwu was a Chinese philologist, geographer, and scholar-official in the Qing dynasty. —Ed.

PREFACE

A Complex History: Theme and Variations

This book will address a very complicated question and is thus divided into 10 chapters that will discuss the spiritual life of the Chinese people from various angles, as well as an Introduction and Conclusion. Because of the number of the chapters, and the fact that they are linked together rather than being clearly separated, readers may feel a certain confusion when they begin to read. The point of this preface is to provide a bit of guidance and to help readers understand the relationships between the chapters, as well as to provide an overall description of the book.

In the Introduction, I begin by mentioning Feng Youlan 馮友蘭 (1895–1990) and Fei Xiaotong 費孝通 (1910–2005), two scholars who have already devoted a great deal of effort to this topic. Feng Youlan composed six works known collectively as *Purity Descends, Primacy Ascends: Six Books*,[1] the goal

---

1   *Purity Descends, Primacy Ascends: Six Books* (*Zhenyuan liushu* 貞元六書) is a collection of six related books written by Feng during the Sino-Japanese War. The books include *A New Philosophy of Principle* 新理學 (1939), *A New Treatise on Practical Affairs* 新事論 (1940), *A New Treatise on the Way of Life* 新世訓 (1940), *A New Treatise on the Nature of Man* 新原人 (1943), *A New Treatise on the Nature of Dao* 新原道 (1945), and *A New Understanding of Words* 新知言 (1946). These books have not yet been translated into English. —Trans.

of which was to seek to construct a modern Chinese view of the universe or a perspective on life after the chaos of the Sino-Japanese War. He worked as a philosopher, drawing on the history of Chinese thought and extending it to new concepts. By contrast, Fei Xiaotong began with observations based on his sociological fieldwork, bringing into focus how the structures of Chinese towns and villages came together to form communities. What I will attempt to do is to begin from the foundation established by these two scholars and seek to clarify Chinese ideas concerning the universe, human life, and nature, from traditional times down to the present day. These ideas influence how Chinese people organize their lives and sort out the problems of being human.

I look at these questions from the point of view of everyday people, which naturally gives us something quite different from the subtleties that would emerge from discussions with philosophers, thinkers, or theologians. Everyday people's ideas about spiritual life are largely inherited from tradition. In applying this inheritance to practical life, they may make their own choices or offer their own explanations. So the ideas of the everyday people cannot be grouped together with the exalted subtleties of the scholarly elite. Nonetheless, these general principles come together to form a whole. The culture that everyday people understand concretely and profoundly influences most Chinese people in terms of their relationship to nature, to other people, and to society as a whole. In Chapter I, I take pains to describe the life of the Chinese people, their life rhythm in this vast space defined by heaven, earth, and nature, and the relationship of this life to our culture and literature. This provides the macro-background necessary to understanding Chinese spiritual life.

In Chapter II, I argue that the spiritual life of the Chinese people revolves around ideas of being "human." This orientation of the Chinese cultural tradition is quite different from Western, Judeo-Christian culture, which is centered on "God." From this perspective, I hope that readers will also appreciate the many links between this chapter and Chapter III, which is devoted to "legends." The creation myth in Chinese legends— that of Pangu creating the earth and the sky—tells the story of a universe that generates itself, without a transcendent creator. As Pangu's body took form, it created the mountains and the rivers, and the heaven and earth Pangu carried on his head were our blue skies and great land. Pangu was not created, nor did Pangu continue to manage or rule the universe once it was created. The creator of the universe and the universe itself are coequal, and this distinction between China and the West determined that the standpoints of the two cultural systems concerning how to manage the world, how to manage people, and how to orient oneself in the world are all different. China takes "humans" as the subject while the West takes "God" as the subject.

Chapters II and III discuss the Chinese people's view of the universe. From the Spring and Autumn period, the axial age of Chinese culture which extended from roughly 770 to 476 BCE, this view of the universe combined worship of nature with worship of ancestral spirits, or in other words, it combined nature and human life in a spatial relationship, defined at the top by heaven, earth, sun and moon, and extending down to the human realm, and subsequently into the human body, forming a great four-level network. In terms of time, it saw past and present, and even human life before birth and after death, as a process of continuous flow. Space and time were linked together in a vast system where all elements engaged in multiple interactions; among these varied elements, there were both interactions at all levels of the structure, but also particular interactions among certain clearly identified factors, such as yin and yang, or the five elements, or similar variables, so that the vast universe became an order of interaction between each part and each element.

Chapter IV continues the discussion of this interactive order, which is in constant change, with change tending toward equilibrium, arguing that the universe is process and that the process is the universe itself—the two are inseparable. This complements the argument from Chapter III concerning the elements in constant change, arguing that the equilibrium achieved at each stage is only temporary; none of the variables can become either too strong or too weak. Similarly, change is continuous, and each phase takes form for a very limited amount of time. Hence, variation between stability and stagnation, change and vitality, occurs in time. There is never an eternal form, nor is there persistent change without direction. The ideas discussed in Chapter IV and Chapter V are all directly reflected in our everyday lives, so in Chapter IV, I use various examples drawn from topics such as food and medicine. In Chapter V, I explain the Chinese people's behavior through subjects like the Eight Trigrams, divination, fortune-telling, and *fengshui*,[2] illustrating how people attempt to acquire a certain agency or control in their dealings with nature through ways of thinking that are similar to science, or which imitate science.

Chapter VI, like Chapter I, focuses on life itself, its meaning as existence and in action. The focus of Chapter VI is on seeing life as made up of many lives, beginning from when my parents give birth to me, and continuing until after my death, and even my passage to another world— an after-life which, in fact, is an extension of the existing world: this is in fact a truer vision than what we think of as linear time. By contrast, in Chapter I, when I talk about aesthetics, my focus is on people's relation to nature in natural space, their "contract," their mutual engagement. The process of production in an agricultural culture must be in step with the seasons, and must coordinate with the natural environment. Given the intimate relationship between humans and nature, in legends, all things in the universe are seen as having life, and the mountain gods and river spirits, the snake spirits and fox fairies, are all reproductions of humans. Once they have breathed in the essence of heaven and earth, they can be transformed into human bodies.

---

2   The Eight Trigrams (*bagua* 八卦) refer to the hexagrams that appear in the ancient *Book of Changes* and which are used to predict the future. The word "divination" in the Chinese original is *zhanbo shushu* 占卜術數, a particular form of divination sometimes referred to as "Chinese astrology." "Fortune-telling" in the Chinese text is *xiangming* 相命, and can refer to any number to techniques, including face reading and palm reading. *Fengshui* 風水, or Chinese geomancy, seeks to use energy forces to harmonize people with their surrounding environments. —Trans.

Chapters VII and VIII are again linked together. What I talk about in Chapter VII is Chinese society—using the Taiwanese society with which I am familiar—and I explain how everyday people understand all kinds of natural phenomena through the act of offering sacrifices. In the past, all people who accumulated virtue became intimately connected with objects of worship. The subject of Chapter VIII is thus to take a look at institutional religions—the thought systems of Confucianism, Daoism and Buddhism, as well as some of their off-shoots—and examine how they interacted, how they coordinated, and how they continually absorbed elements from other beliefs. For example, ideas of karmic rebirth, salvation and revelation were ultimately absorbed into Chinese society in Taiwan and Hong Kong, becoming part of the secular life practice of the people.

Chapter IX begins with pre-war traditional Chinese society, and looks at how people dealt with matters in towns and villages so that they could help one another, take care of one another in times when aid from the state was not forthcoming, and thus assure the village's long-term stability. The commonly held values of the Chinese people, based in their spiritual life, facilitated the intimate, harmonious integration of an individual's values through the concrete practices of group life.

The final chapter begins with legends and aesthetics and continues on to a discussion of novels. This topic is slightly different from the basic focus of a book that examines the beliefs of the common people. Novels are works written by individual authors; and although not all of these authors belonged to the elite intellectual class, they still saw the world, human life, and human complexity from their own perspectives. Their viewpoints and arguments were their own, and not necessarily shared by the people at large. For this reason, I tried my best to choose popular works, such as *The Water Margin*, *The Romance of the Three Kingdoms*, and various crime novels, as well as a few well known works that are popular in opera and in the general culture. All of the works that I choose have been in circulation in Chinese culture for a very long time and have been enjoyed by many readers; their popularity can be considered the common property of popular culture. Thus while from this perspective the nature of the last chapter is somewhat different from the preceding chapters, and its appreciation of the nature of Chinese culture reflects that of particular intellectuals, at the same time this appreciation was also shared by everyone.

In the Conclusion, I share my thoughts that 21st-century Chinese people have been greatly influenced by modern, Western civilization, and yet remain outside of Western culture. At present, Western civilization itself, as represented by Europe and America, is on the verge of a great change. The problems they are facing, including various crises of alienation and separation from nature, are—in terms of their basic origins—problems for which Western civilization lacks the resources to arrive at a solution. Thus, in the Conclusion, I both sum up the various points discussed in the course of the book, and also propose that Chinese culture, centered on the person and on the idea of close, interdependent relations between humans and nature, might offer a solution. The idea is to integrate the features of Chinese popular culture into modern civilization to solve the dilemmas of this civilization. Can one person's humble opinions be of use? I don't know, but my dream is to act as the Chinese mythical bird who sought to fill the ocean with pebbles, or like the foolish old man who tried to move the mountain: they undertook such tasks even though they knew that success or failure is not decided by weighing the risks.

Acknowledgements

I would like to thank the Chiang Ching-kuo Foundation for International Scholarly Exchange for their generous support of this translation project, especially Professor Yun-han Chu for his care and concern. I am also extremely grateful to Professor Ying-shih Yu for generously writing a foreword to this book, and deeply indebted to Professor David Der-wei Wang for his stimulating advice on the book title and cover design.

I am very much thankful to the Director of The Chinese University of Hong Kong Press, Ms. Gan Qi, Acquisitions Editor Ms. Minlei Ye, Project Editor Mr. Justin Cheung, and the whole team of the press for their great efforts and thoughtful suggestions. I would like to give my heartfelt thanks to Professor David Ownby, who spent innumerable hours carefully and faithfully translating this book. I would also like to pay my regards to Roberta Raine, who copyedited the entire manuscript. A special thanks to Mr. Hei Shing Chan, who designed a brilliant book cover for me.

Last but not least, over the last half-century of life, Man-li, the dearest person in my life, has been by my side, sharing in the sweet and the bitter, caring for the family and raising our child. She has toiled to make a home, look after my disabled body, and comforted me when I am weary; we are one whole, without resentment or regrets, leaning upon each other in our old age. I sincerely dedicate this book, which may be my last work, to my wife Man-li, and I hope that the world will be at peace, so that we may live out our remaining years in tranquility. Thank you, Man-li!

The Transcendental and the Mundane

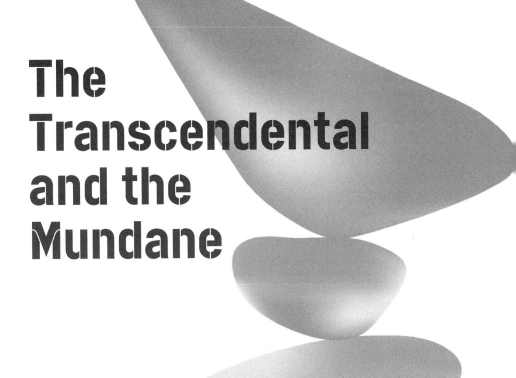

Introduction

Searching for the Spirit of Chinese Culture

The news we read every day is mostly about disasters and tragedies: countries attack other countries; people hurt other people. Believers in monotheistic religions criticize the followers of other faiths for believing nothing, and even within monotheistic religions, Muslims and Christians criticize and harm one another. In multi-ethnic countries, groups with different skin color, groups with different religious beliefs, even groups with different accents all ostracize one another. Refugees flee disasters in boat after boat, car after car, many dying violent deaths along the way. Other refugees flee hunger and poverty in the hopes of finding another place to live, an opportunity for a better life. Yet as they approach the frontiers of a better life, they are shut out, arrested and deported. Inequalities between rich and poor are also growing within countries. In times past, when inequality took the form of owning a lot of land or owning no land, the life-styles of the two groups remained roughly similar. Now, however, the rich in any country enjoy a lifestyle completely different from that of the middle class; and it goes without saying that the poor in the same country can barely make ends meet and have no hope of leaving poverty behind.

In the modern world, the industrial revolution has produced rapid increases in productivity. More recently, new advances in science and technology have yet again pushed the exploitation of our resources to another peak. Scientific exploration has brought us new understandings of the universe and of life; newly invented medicines can cure almost any illness, even if eternal life still is out of reach. In sum, people's lives are more comfortable and convenient than at any time in history. From another perspective, the improvement of public health conditions and the gradual elimination of contagious diseases has allowed the world population to balloon from 1.3 billion to 6.5 billion in the course of a mere century.

We are rapidly consuming the world's resources, despite the many new things we have discovered and invented, and the planet on which life relies will be unable to provide for the needs of the existing population, to say nothing of the fact that the population continues to grow. To survive, humanity will face even fiercer competition. There will not only be competition among individual humans, seeking to seize limited life-sustaining resources, but entire nations may enter a stage in which they seek to monopolize these resources. To create a more convenient life, humanity has altered the earth's climate, and the changes accelerating throughout the world threaten our planet with ruin. As the ancient adage puts it, "in the absence of skin, where will the hair grow?"[1] In the future, humankind may discover that the world they inhabit is no longer able to sustain their existence.

The 21st-century world seems to have parted company with the past history of humankind. Our progress seems to have boarded a deadly train that is speeding toward destruction. To quote Dickens from *A Tale of Two Cities*, "It was the best of times, it was the worst of times." Within this larger framework, the Chinese world is also facing changes. China's human-centered society, its order and ethics built out of human relationships, was once very different from the Western world based on the

---

1 The Chinese saying, "*pi zhi bu cun, mao jiang yan fu* 皮之不存，毛將焉附," comes from the Chinese classic *The Zuo Tradition* (*Zuozhuan* 左傳). The meaning is that things cannot exist without the basis on which they survive. —Ed.

premise of people competing against one another. More than a century ago, using its weapons and its economic power, the West established world supremacy. East Asia, with its nation-states enveloped in Chinese culture and existing as agricultural societies whose social goals were peace and stability, had no choice but to strive to emulate the West to ensure their survival. Within this larger East Asian world, Japan, following its slogan of "Leaving Asia Behind"[2], was the best student of the West; indeed, such imitation produced the arms and economic might that fueled Japan's later plunder and invasion of China.

Under the banner of modernization, the Chinese people went through three revolutions, as well as the New Culture Movement in the early 20th century[3], doing their best to turn themselves into Westerners. In the middle of the 20th century, China experienced an earth-shaking change, when a new political regime was established on the Mainland. However fearsome this earth-shaking revolution might have been, the changes wrought by the Cultural Revolution (1966–1976) were even more wrenching. Today's China should not be taken lightly in terms of its economic and military power. At the same time, in social and cultural terms, and especially in terms of personal behavior, it is completely different from traditional China. Motivated by practical considerations, many people blindly pursue their material interests. Chinese people are tough, which surely pushes economic development forward, but they often hurt other people without realizing it. The coldness and lack of feeling between people may lead to the division and collapse of Chinese society. In their interactions with the environment,

---

2   This reference is to a famous editorial by the Japanese intellectual Fukuzawa Yukichi (1835–1901), published on March 16, 1885 in the Japanese newspaper *Jiji shimpō* entitled "On Leaving Asia Behind," in which he argued that Japan should take immediate measures to reform its economy and society and hence "join the West." —Trans.

3   The New Culture Movement (*Xin wenhua yundong* 新文化運動) in the 1910s and 1920s criticized classical Chinese ideas and promoted a new culture based upon Western ideals like democracy and science. —Ed.

the Chinese people have the habit of overdoing things and cutting corners, of "pulling up the sprouts to help them grow," or of "draining the pond to get the fish," as two Chinese sayings have it, reminding us of the fact that one day, there may well be nothing left. If one fourth of mankind becomes a kind of savage, and a sixth of the world's land turns into wilderness, how will the Chinese manage? And how big a disaster will it mean for humankind?

Although Taiwan's Kuomintang government claims to do its utmost to protect Chinese culture, in fact, the rapidity and depth of the progress of Westernization have meant that the traces of Chinese culture remaining in Taiwan are increasingly rare. With the division between the Mainland and Taiwan, Taiwan's pursuit of autonomy, and the fear of what is happening on the Mainland, most people in Taiwan tend to be extremely opposed to the People's Republic of China (PRC). In this general climate of insecurity, most young Taiwanese are concerned solely with today's security and comfort, and have abandoned larger life goals. But a society that doesn't think about the future may well lose its way in a rapidly changing world.

Having gone through these political changes, especially the New Culture Movement and the Cultural Revolution, and the changes in cultural ideas wrought by these movements, a natural question arises: how is a Chinese person supposed to know how to act? This is especially true because today's West is also facing rapid changes. With the development of modern science and industry, modern society—originally defined by the Protestant ethic and the capitalism that grew out of this ethic—has gradually betrayed the basic spirit of these beliefs, and is now fueled by a new belief which consists solely of the pursuit of wealth and power. In the battle between capitalism and society, both will be destroyed. Modern society has already experienced an extreme change: as individualism surges, the distance between people grows and they care less about one another, at which point society sinks into disorganization and chaos.

The once gleaming Western world, the object that the Chinese have been emulating for a century, has now lost its way and is facing disintegration. What are the Chinese people to do? Yet the mode and direction of

Chinese development will also impact the future of the entire world. In this book, I will investigate the past and the present, and offer a number of questions that we should all reflect on. Perhaps it will be of some use as we probe ourselves and attempt to rebuild our societies.

This is an ambition that I have nourished for a long time, but I have never turned my hand to it until now. A work that inspired me long ago was Feng Youlan's *Purity Descends, Primacy Ascends*, a series of six related books composed during the Sino-Japanese War between 1939 and 1946: *A New Philosophy of Principle*, *A New Treatise on Practical Affairs*, *A New Treatise on the Way of Life*, *A New Treatise on the Nature of Man*, *A New Treatise on the Nature of Dao*, and *A New Understanding of Words*.[4] The aim of Feng's work was to try to "take the pulse" of China's cultural spirit, in the hopes of offering new solutions. The first of Feng's books was published in the third year of the Sino-Japanese War (1939), and the last in the year following the end of the war (1946). This period was one in which China was in a difficult life or death struggle, and ultimately triumphed with the national renewal following the end of the Sino-Japanese War. During this period of wartime difficulty and uncertainty, China's intellectuals, in part out of concern for the nation and for democracy, but even more to ensure the survival of Chinese culture, continued teaching and learning in air raid shelters, amidst the sound of alarms, or seated outside underneath the trees, hoping that the roots of Chinese culture would not perish in the conflict.

Feng Youlan was a professor at Tsinghua University who was deeply steeped in Chinese culture because of his family history; he also studied in the United States, specializing in Western philosophy, which meant that he was equally learned in Western studies. In these six books produced under the strains of war, Feng strove to revisit the origins of Chinese culture, at the same time seeking a way to connect Chinese culture with world

---

4   For the Chinese titles, please see Preface, Note 1. —Ed.

culture. Among the six volumes, *A New Philosophy of Principle*, *A New Treatise on the Nature of Dao*, and *A New Treatise on the Way of Life* more or less focused on reinterpreting the Chinese philosophical tradition and finding a way to combine Confucian, Daoist, and Buddhist thought in a way that would be both critical and innovative. *A New Treatise on Practical Affairs* and *A New Treatise on the Nature of Man* largely dealt with the ethical concepts that Chinese of a new age should possess.

At the time, Feng's work provoked considerable reaction, and academic philosophers criticized his comprehensive theory on the basis of the concepts and methodologies of their particular scholarly attachments. Most intellectuals, however, were profoundly moved, finding that Feng's work both incorporated the past and looked toward the future, and might well play an important role in China's eventual revival.

Yet very rapidly, following the changes produced by China's Civil War (1927–1949) and the change of regime to the Chinese Communist Party (CCP), Feng's research, based on his metaphysical standpoint, clashed with the materialism of the new regime. Under political pressure, Feng had no choice but to compromise and come up with a blend of materialism and idealism. This was, in fact, a difficult task, and the result did not convince Feng's readers. As a result, no one paid much attention to his original *Purity Descends, Primacy Ascends* collection. Elsewhere in China and abroad, Confucian scholars like Mou Zongsan 牟宗三 (1909– 1995) and Tang Junyi 唐君毅 (1909–1978) carried forward the original ideas of their teacher Xiong Shili 熊十力 (1885–1968), hoping to revive Confucianism, and people have paid more attention to them than to Feng's *Purity Descends, Primacy Ascends*.

In fact, questions like those raised by Feng are precisely what we should be thinking about now. This modest book of mine is just such an effort in this direction. The problem is that Feng's is a work in philosophy, and much of it is extremely subtle and abstract. He makes distinctions among different schools within the Chinese philosophical tradition, discussing differences between the School of Universal Principles (*lixue* 理學) and the Learning of the Heart and Mind (*xinxue* 心學)—as well as differences between Confucianism and Daoism—together with their mutual influence. As a scholarly investigation, such philosophical perspective is necessary, but the average reader has a hard time understanding it, much less applying it to his or her own thought. In terms of philosophy, I too am an outsider, and am not really qualified to join in the discussion. If I bring Feng up here, it is to remind us that to be able to produce such a work under the chaos of wartime conditions reflects the seriousness of such scholarly topics, even for Chinese people faced with extinction after a century of suffering.

At the same time, the era in which Feng lived and wrote is different from ours. From the perspective of the development of modern science, Feng's understanding was based in a cosmology of Newtonian mechanics; today, of course, science has moved on to relativity and quantum mechanics. In fact, compared to the certainties of the 19th and 20th centuries, scientific thought today seems better positioned to connect with traditional Chinese thought. In the past half century, the cultural globalization produced by economic globalization has also created a new situation. Compared to the nationalism of the 20th century, today's globalization is hungry for broader, global concepts to replace nationalism's tired focus on borders and territories. At the time, Feng Youlan was motivated by a strong sense of cultural nationalism, a natural concern at a time of national peril. One might even say that in submitting to the pressure of the regime, he was also submitting to the weight of "state" and "people," because he had no other choice. We can only feel compassion for the fate of this generation of Chinese intellectuals.

In the face of today's new circumstances, which suggest a completely different future, the direction sketched out in *Purity Descends, Primacy Ascends* and the new spirit for humankind that Feng proposes seem out of step with today's reality. How can I, as an amateur, hope to follow Feng's masterpiece with my little book? My humble wish, as the culture of the new world forces itself upon us, is simply to revisit the subject. My own training and research was not in philosophy; instead, my research fields, which I explored and accumulated over many years, were sociology, anthropology, and archaeology. These fields have to do with human beings' concrete lives and daily practices, and not with metaphysical reflections. When I was 15 years old, Feng Youlan's work had a deep impact on my thinking. Seventy years later, it still fills me with emotion. Still, I will seek out a path from within my own disciplines—looking not at philosophical debates but at how ordinary people think—as I revisit the subject of the spirit of everyday people in the realm of Chinese culture.

Wu Wenzao's 吳文藻 (1901–1985) contribution in establishing the field of sociology in China is inestimable. He had three disciples, all of whom wrote important books in the field. Fei Xiaotong created the notion of a "differential mode of association" to describe Chinese relationships: everyone has his or her own network of concentric circles, starting from the self and extending into various interpersonal relationships. Closely related to this was the idea of the interaction between the market and agricultural production developed in Fei's book *Peasant Life in China* (1939). In his work on lineage ties and inheritance, Francis L. K. Hsu 許烺光 (1909–1999) pointed out that the Chinese sense of temporal continuity centers on people and not on the gods. C. K. Yang's 楊慶堃 (1911–1999) work on popular beliefs focused more on the relationship between the people and the gods. He argued that the basis of this relationship was the individual, and that the spirit world was a reflection of the human world. His study of the continuities linking rural markets with cities is an important contribution to ideas about social space in Chinese life. Later on, the American scholar G. William Skinner (1925–2008) enlarged on this idea, and it became a famous school of thought for a time. C. K. Yang's work on the gods and the economy overlaps with and responds to the work of Fei and Xu mentioned above. This shows that Wu's students shared many points in common in terms of concepts and methodology.

In my study of ancient history, I made considerable use of the results of archaeological research. In this field, the relationship between the mode of production, productive capacity, and people's spiritual life is an important subject. Over the course of the long evolution of ancient history, archaeology supplied hints that revealed how people created different "spirit worlds." This process is something that neither religious believers nor philosophers have paid much attention to. Did humans create the gods? Or did the gods create humans? I suspect that only archaeology can provide answers to those questions. This is another aspect in which the search for spiritual life in this book differs considerably from a philosopher's perspective.

Toward the end of this book, I devote considerable time to the observations and theories of sociologists and archaeologists in an effort to develop my own thought. For this reason, my approach is quite different from Feng Youlan's metaphysics. This "humanistic spirit" is the foundation of this book. Moreover, when I talk about "humanity," I mean the common people, who might not have paid attention to the theories of the ancient scholars, but who nonetheless could not avoid building a social order and a human ethics on the basis of these theories. For this reason, in the course of my discussion I will spend some time revisiting Chinese traditional culture, but instead of citing the classics to discuss other classics, my approach will be to seek out the overall outcome of these classical thinkers and the impact of this outcome on the people's daily lives.

In the context of today's cultural environment, China cannot remain isolated from a world shaped by modern Western civilization, and by "China" I mean mainland China and Taiwan, as well as places like Singapore that represent the thinking of overseas Chinese—all of these Chinese societies are fully immersed in the environment of modern civilization. As already mentioned, an important part of modern civilization is a cosmology shaped by modern science. Another is the capitalist economy that emerged from the industrial revolution, as well as socialist opposition to this capitalism. This is an area where modern changes have been especially vast. Economic and social life are intimately linked, and urbanization is a universal development seen throughout the world. The economies of the past organized around herding and agriculture had a corresponding spiritual life. When we imagine the kind of spiritual life we should have now or in the future, we must bear in mind the huge changes that have already occurred.

Topics to be addressed in this book include the cosmological notions at the heart of Chinese traditional culture: questions of the internal order of the universe itself, and of how the balance is maintained between the universe and humans and between the static and dynamic modes of the order of the universe. Our spiritual life is often divided into sacred and profane aspects, but is this division antagonistic? Or is it rather interactive? Within the sacred realm, which concepts become "anthropomorphic" gods? How are hopes pinned on the gods dealt with in secular society? This is often revealed in the practice of rites and sacrifices. How do we arrive at a satisfying explanation both for the brevity of the life of an individual and the limitless universe? In other words, do life and death mark a genuine separation? Or are they linked? And how are transcendent sacred values expressed in the secular world in terms of modes of interpersonal behavior? How should we treat the natural parts of the universe—the mountains and rivers, the grass and the trees, the birds and the beasts? How should people treat one another? As individuals form groups, are all of the levels of society linked together? Or do the differences between the levels produce antagonisms? Some people are luckier than others, which means that there are those who are happy and those who are disappointed. How should the individual handle this? These are the topics that will be addressed in this book, through an examination of daily life (including eating, living, medical practices, poems and songs, art, literature, and so forth) and of "collective memory," such as legends, all of which will be treated as historical materials drawn from the lives of the common people.

In sum, my hope is that this book will present the uniqueness of China's enduring culture through a discussion of Chinese cultural ideals and life practices regarding heaven, humans, the group, and the individual. To my mind, the great Song Confucianist Zhang Zai's 張載 (1020–1077) description of the holism of culture in his "Western Inscription" (*Xi ming* 西銘) sums up my views quite well:

> Heaven is my father and Earth is my mother, and even such a small creature as I find an intimate place in their midst. Therefore, that which fills the universe I regard as my body and that which directs the universe

I consider as my nature. All people are my brothers and sisters, and all things are my companions. The great ruler is the eldest son of my parents, and the great ministers are his stewards. Respect the aged—this is the way to treat them as elders should be treated. Be compassionate toward those who are alone and weak—this is the way to treat them as the young should be treated. The sage identifies his character with that of Heaven and Earth, and the worthy is the most outstanding person. All those in the world who are fatigued, disabled, lonely, and widowed are my brothers who are in distress with no one to turn to.[5]

The opening lines of great Song-dynasty poet Wen Tianxiang's 文天祥 (1236–1283) "Song of the Spirit of Righteousness" (*Zheng qi ge* 正氣歌) simply yet forcefully convey the view of Chinese culture that the existence of the universe is the origin of all changes:

In the world there is the spirit of righteousness, taking many forms, bestowed on the ever-changing things. Below they are the rivers and mountains; above they are the sun and stars. With people it is called the spirit of honor and fearlessness, so vast it fills the universe. When the empire is tranquil, one pours forth harmony in the splendid court. When times are extreme, true fidelity is seen and goes down in history case after case....What is permeated by this spirit lives on forever revered. It links up the cosmos, so how can life and death compare in importance? The Corners of Earth depend on it to stand; the Pillars of Heaven depend on it to maintain their honor. The Three Relationships really do determine one's life; moral righteousness is the root.[6]

---

5   Translation taken from William Theodore De Bary, Wing-Tsit Chan, and Burton Watson, *Sources of Chinese Tradition*, vol. 1 (New York: Columbia University Press, 1960), 469, with modifications.

6   Translation taken from Feng Xin-ming, "The Song of the Spirit of Righteousness," 2008, http://tsoidug.org/Literary/Spirit_Righteousness_Comp.pdf.

In the context of this vast, ever-balancing universe, human beings—because they have rationality and conscience—can make their own minds shine forth, revealing the universe's "spirit of righteousness," which is the natural endowment of their existence. From the writings of Zhang Zai and Wen Tianxiang, we can understand that the culture that developed and evolved on Chinese soil—this combination of Confucian culture with the teachings of Buddhism and Daoism—from beginning to end understood and explained the universe itself through the lens of "humanity."

This introduction is different from ordinary prefaces, because its goal has been to convey my personal opinions, and my hope is that reading this may provide some assistance to the reader in understanding my purpose. My silent prayer is that the Chinese culture I am describing can continue to prosper and be of benefit to the future of the world, so that humans might together build a world civilization without prejudice and conflict. If this hope can be realized, then this book will not have been about summoning ghosts, but instead will greet the pioneers of a new culture.

I. Life Aesthetics in Time and Space

Chinese culture is a civilizational system based on agricultural production and village settlements. Since the beginning of the Neolithic period, China has practiced a settled form of agricultural production. After the Warring States period, this evolved in the direction of an intensive peasant agricultural economy. As explained in the Introduction, Chinese society was constructed on the basis of what the sociologist Fei Xiaotong called the "differential mode of association"—the idea that certain obligations and rights are part of interpersonal relationships. Similarly, because of Chinese society's base in agriculture, people's relationship with nature was also particularly intimate, and quite different from what we see in cultures based on hunting and gathering or nomadism. Nomads inhabit a mobile space in nature, unlike in settled villages, in which people develop close, lasting relations with the surrounding environment. In these circumstances, the relationship between humans and nature is to a certain extent interactive, and human settlements are largely inseparable from the nature around them. For this reason, in this chapter I will frame the discussion around the central topic of the relationship between people and nature.

The calendar created by the Chinese people displays a surprising consistency with periodic seasonal changes, a necessary phenomenon in an agricultural culture. In ancient Chinese writings we find the term "monthly ordinance" (*yueling* 月令), which was a kind of text describing the rituals, duties, decrees, and prohibitions of the government according to the seasons of a 12-month period. In surviving documents, the term appears in ancient texts such as the *Small Calendar of the Xia* (*Xia xiaozheng* 夏小正) and the *Book of Rites* (*Liji* 禮記), probably reflecting the situation from the Warring States period through the early Han dynasty, founded in 202 BCE. One work from the Han period that has been handed down—*Ordinances for the Four People* (*Simin yueling* 四民月令)—is a record of the development of the agricultural order in the Eastern Han. Generally speaking, these texts include astronomical observations for each month: for example, they note that a certain star will be visible at a certain position in the skies at this time. The texts also include meteorological phenomena, such as "cold," "freezing," "much rain," and "warming," as well as natural phenomena of a seasonal nature, answering questions such as "what will start to grow," and "what plant will ripen?" They even included things like "sparrows arrive," "swan geese depart," "otters catch fish," and "jackals hunt for food." For meteorologists and astronomers, these observations are original sources that help to understand the climate in ancient times, and offer a certain reflection of conditions surrounding agricultural production in North China around the period of the Han dynasty.

In ancient Chinese calendars we find the monthly organization of astronomical and seasonal natural phenomena, and the monthly ordinances in the *Book of Rites* is just such an agricultural calendar. Below are the entries from two months of the calendar, which will serve as an example:

> In the first month of spring the sun is in *Shi*, the star culminating at dusk being *Shen*, and that culminating at dawn *Wei*. The east winds resolve the cold. Creatures that have been torpid during the winter begin to move. The fishes rise up to the ice. Otters sacrifice fish. The wild geese make their appearance....In this month the vapors of heaven descend and those of the earth ascend. Heaven and earth are in harmonious co-operation. All plants bud and grow. The king gives orders to set forward the business of husbandry. The inspectors of the fields are ordered to reside in the lands having an eastward exposure, and (see that) all repair the marches and divisions, and mark out clearly the paths and ditches. They

must skillfully survey the mounds and rising grounds, the slopes and defiles, the plains and marshes, determining what the different lands are suitable for, and where the different grains will grow best. They must thus instruct and lead on the people, themselves also engaging in the tasks. The business of the fields being thus ordered, the guiding line is first put in requisition, and the husbandry is carried on without error.

In the second month of spring, the sun is in *Kui*, the star culminating at dusk being *Hu*, and that culminating at dawn *Jianxing*....The rain begins to fall. The peach trees begin to blossom. The oriole sings. Hawks are transformed into doves.[1]

In addition to the monthly ordinances, we also find a passage on the "seventh month" in the "Odes of Bin" (*Bin feng* 豳風) section of the *Book of Poetry* (*Shijing* 詩經), which illustrates the seasonal activities on a farm at that time through the example of a woman farm worker of the Spring and Autumn period. Here are the descriptions of three months:

In the seventh month, the Fire Star passes the meridian;
In the eighth month are the sedges and reeds.
In the silkworm month they strip the mulberry branches of their leaves,
And take their axes and hatchets,
To lop off those that are distant and high,
Only stripping the young trees of their leaves.
In the seventh month, the shrike is heard;
In the eighth month, they begin their spinning;
They make dark fabrics and yellow.
Our red manufacture is very brilliant,
It is for the lower robes of our young princes.

In the fourth month, the small grass is in seed.
In the fifth, the cicada gives out its note.

---

1   Translation taken from James Legge, trans., *The Sacred Books of China: The Texts of Confucianism, Part III: The Li Ki, I–X* (Oxford: Clarendon Press, 1885), 249–258.

In the eighth, they reap.
In the tenth, the leaves fall.
In the days of our first month, they go after badgers,
And take foxes and wild cats,
To make furs for our young princes.
In the days of our second month, they have a general hunt,
And proceed to keep up the exercises of war.
The boars of one year are for themselves;
Those of three years are for our prince.

In the fifth month, the locust moves its legs;
In the sixth month, the spinner sounds its wings.
In the seventh month, in the fields;
In the eighth month, under the eaves;
In the ninth month, about the doors;
In the tenth month, the cricket
Enters under our beds.
Chinks are filled up, and rats are smoked out;
The windows that face the north are stopped up,
And the doors are plastered.
"Ah! Our wives and children,
Changing the year requires this:
Enter here and dwell."[2]

In these three passages, we see a mixture of two different types of calendrical systems: references to the seventh month or the fourth month belong to the lunar calendar; while references to the "eleventh month" or the "twelfth month" belong to a lunisolar system that began the year in the tenth month and arranged the order of the months of the year in that manner, as will be explained below.

---

2   Translation taken from James Legge, trans., "Odes of Bin," Chinese Text Project, https://ctext.org/book-of-poetry/odes-of-bin.

Although these poems are works of literature, and the seasons appear in each poem in picturesque disorder, the depictions still allow us to understand the relationship at the time between the people and the natural, seasonal order. The poems also present the rituals and ceremonies that correspond to farm life, allowing us to feel the flow of time through the four seasons, and the relationship of this flow of time to the world of human affairs.

The Chinese calendar is a mixture of lunar and solar calendars. The year is the solar year, made up of 365.2425 days, each month containing 29.539593 days. When the 12 months are added together, it is slightly shorter than a solar year. Thus in a combined lunar and solar calendar, to respect the organization of the seasons, the full moon is treated as a "half moon" (i.e., the fifteenth day of the month), the new moon marks the first day of the month, and the moonless night is treated as the last day of the month.

The 24 "solar terms" of the Chinese calendar are determined by the length of the solar year, divided into 12 *jie* 節 and 12 *qi* 氣 (*jieqi* 節氣 is the word for "solar term.") This agricultural organization of the calendar is still in use, and the months are named as follows: Spring Commences, Spring Showers, Insects Waken, Vernal Equinox, Bright and Clear, Corn Rain, Summer Commences, Corn Forms, Corn on Ear, Summer Solstice, Moderate Heat, Great Heat, Autumn Commences, End of Heat, White Dew, Autumnal Equinox, Cold Dew, Frost, Winter Commences, Light Snow, Heavy Snow, Winter Solstice, Moderate Cold, and Severe Cold.

The arrangement of the 24 solar terms includes four principles:

The change of the seasons: Spring Commences, Vernal Equinox; Summer Commences, Summer Solstice; Autumn Commences, Autumnal Equinox; Winter Commences, Winter Solstice.

Changes in the climate: Moderate Heat, Great Heat, End of Heat, Moderate Cold, and Severe Cold.

Amount of precipitation: Spring Showers, Corn Rain, White Dew, Cold Dew, Frost, Light Snow, Heavy Snow.

Seasonal phenomena or agricultural chores: Insects Waken, Bright and Clear, Corn Forms, Corn on Ear.

In sum, everything revolves around seasons, the time sequence, and phenomena having to deal with farming and weather. These records are sufficient to show that the Chinese people took natural time as an important element in their lives. Today's urban life, by contrast, is a long way from farming, with its dense housing patterns and even air conditioning—the natural environment, climatic changes, seasonal changes in plant and animal life—none of this is part of our natural lives. As a result, people no longer feel a close connection to nature.

Thinking back to how we used to live, village life was lived in the fields. We set to work when the sun rose, and rested when the sun set, and the natural changes from dawn to dusk regulated our lives. The changes of the four seasons influenced how we farmed, as well as the entire economy of our village. People's existence was inseparable from the environment; at the break of dawn, the crowing of the cocks and the barking of the dogs got people out of bed; while working we would encounter flocks of birds—especially in North China, where there were crows everywhere; I still remember the huge flocks and their raucous calls. The farmland was full of all kinds of birds, animals, and insects, all within arm's reach. If the winter was warm, people were comfortable, but everyone worried that insects might ruin planting in the spring. If the summer and autumn were too dry, then everybody knew that the harvest would not be sufficient. When the day's work was done, the farmers would head home, sharing their observations about nature with their companions. If there were too many crows, would there be too few bees? What would this mean for our beans and melons? The cow has been breathing hard recently. It this because it's too hot? Maybe we should do the plowing in the evening and rest more at lunch? Village elders, even if they had already retired from field work, still often gave their opinions, making predictions on the basis of their experience about the climate's effect on farming. Talking about farm work was an indispensable part of village life.

In traditional Chinese society, there would have been gardens for flowers and vegetables even around the houses in the cities, and in the central courtyards of urban dwellings, most people would leave space to plant flowers, trees, and vines. Even today, in traditional houses in the old parts of Beijing, you find grape vines, flower pots, plum trees, plantains....My home in Wuxi was a traditional compound, with a huge mulberry garden with 800 mulberry trees, and clan members could have their own vegetable plot in the garden, where they grew melons, beans, and vegetables. There were ornamental plants in the four corners of our courtyard. Outside the windows of the parlor and the study, on one side there was an osmanthus tree that was hundreds of years old, and when it was in bloom, the roof was covered with brilliant red and the aroma was everywhere. On the other side was an old plum tree that grew as it could in its limited space, twisted and gnarled like a dragon.

Some of the little courtyards outside the bedroom windows were there only to let in the light, but even in these closed spaces, the walls were full of old climbing vine, twisting and turning as if in a painting. Even when garden space was lacking, some people would put rocks and potted plants on desks and tables inside the house, shrinking nature so that they could see it at all times. Sparrows came in the spring and departed at the end of summer. In the great Qing novel, the *Dream of the Red Chambers* (*Hong lou meng* 紅樓夢), the big purple sparrow that was dear to the main character Lin Daiyu's heart could be seen in the eaves of the houses in any traditional city. The line from Li Qingzhao's 李清照 (1084–1155) poem that reads "the foliage should be thick and green, with flowers blooming delicate and red"[3] was also something that everyone could see—the begonias, plantains, peonies, and bamboo growing in the courtyard.

---

3   Li Qingzhao was a poetess and essay writer, considered one of the greatest poets in Chinese history. The poem cited here is "As if in a Dream Made: Don't You Know?" which describes flowers in a courtyard after a rainstorm: "Sudden winds scatter last night's rain showers/Heavy sleep failed to clear my head of wine/I ask you as you're rolling up the blinds/But you say the crab apple is unchanged/Don't you know?/Don't you know?/By now the foliage should be thick and green/With flowers blooming delicate and red." Andrew Grimes Griffin, trans., "Translation of Li Qingzhao's 'As if in a Dream Made: Don't You Know?'" Tankawanka, May 7, 2016, https://tankawanka. wordpress.com/2016/05/07/translation-of-li-qingzhaos-as-if-in-a-dream-made-dont-you-know/. —Trans.

Traditional China was an agricultural society, and most of the time, more than 80% of the population lived in villages. The farmers organized their productive life by combining the solar and the lunar cycles. In addition to the lunar months and the solar terms, they also had to bear in mind the growing season of their crops as well as the dates when taxes were due—because after-tax income was what most agricultural families lived on. Hence there were a number of important dates, or junctures, over the course of the year, which marked communal obligations. The first was the spring harvest, celebrated with the Dragon Boat Festival on the fifth day of the fifth month in south and central China. This was the time to harvest the first crops—mainly vegetables, melons, and fruits. In the north, this was the moment to harvest the winter wheat.

The second juncture was the full moon of the fifteenth day of the eighth month, which is when the entire country would harvest the spring's planting. In addition, because the weather is dry at that time of year, the autumn moon is particularly bright, as it is unobscured by water vapor. At harvest time, after long days of work, families would happily gather under the crisp moonlight for the Mid-autumn Festival. This moment was also important for merchants in the cities and towns because some needed to ready the capital to buy agricultural products, while others calculated their receipts for the first half of the year.

The third juncture was the twelfth lunar month, which in ancient times was called *la* 臘, the name of a sacrifice that took place each year shortly after the winter solstice. In ancient times, each kingdom or dynasty had its own *la*: the *la* of the Han dynasty was in the tenth lunar month, but later on it was basically moved to the twelfth lunar month. *La* marked the beginning of the year in ancient times, because at this moment in the year, from the point of view of the government, it was possible to calculate revenues for the coming year—in other words, to establish the budget on the basis of the receipts for the entire past year. This is the same as what we now call an "accounting year," and the "eleventh month" and "twelfth month" mentioned above are the equivalent in accounting terms to the "first month" and the "second month" in a calendar that begins with the tenth month. Just as the government planned its budget, merchants also did their year-end accounts in the twelfth lunar month, after which they planned their commercial strategy for the coming year.

The winter solstice marks the day when the sun is at its furthest point from the Tropic of Cancer, and is the shortest day of the solar year. The harvest is basically completed at this point, and the fields have been cleared; what needed to be sold has been sold, what needed to be bought has been bought, and in a little more than a month, it will be New Year's. Hence, the winter solstice is a harvest season that also marks a break after a busy year. Next comes the first day of the year on the combined lunar-solar calendar, called the "New Year," or the "first month of the lunar year" (*xin zheng* 新正). Throughout China, with the exception of certain coastal provinces in the south—where there are no clear distinctions between the seasons—and in most regions, New Year's is the only time farmers can take a rest from field work. The Chinese arranged their lives year after year according to this calendrical cycle, and compared with today's industrial society, traditional agricultural countries were much more in sync with the natural environment.

Since the changes of the annual cycle determined their lives as they passed from one juncture to another, Chinese farmers had to be very sensitive to the order of time. In my memories, the Dragon Boat Festival on the fifth day of the fifth lunar month, the Mid-Autumn Festival on the fifteenth day of the eighth lunar month, and New Year's, were all times for family celebrations. Children working elsewhere came home, and those who worked in the fields could enjoy the fruits of their hard-earned labor. For Chinese people and other East Asians who use the same calendar, the meaning of these dates is much more important than Christmas or New Year's in today's world. I still remember, at a time when I could barely hold a writing brush, that on the winter solstice, every child who could read would be given a task called "9–9 days to live through the cold season," for which, beginning on the day after the winter solstice, the children would write, one brushstroke per day, each one of the nine characters that is composed of nine brushstrokes. When completed, the characters made up the sentence: "The weeping willow before the courtyard awaits the arrival of the spring breeze." Counting the winter days in this way taught children in traditional China to appreciate time.

Chinese people's sensitivity to time was a habit shaped in such an environment. Their sensitivity to seasonal changes likewise involved being attentive to seasonal changes in flowers, grasses, and trees, and to the movements of birds and animals. In this way, their feelings about nature became an inseparable part of life. In addition to the seasonal festivals already mentioned above, feelings about and reactions to nature are also an important part of literature and art. Below I will cite a few examples from Sikong Tu's 司空圖 (837–908) classic work, *The Twenty-Four Styles of Poetry* (*Ershisi shi pin* 二十四詩品).

The Graceful Style
Flower water gleams and gleams
And far-off spring is lushly blooming.
Deep in a serene valley,
Glimpses of a beautiful woman.

Emerald peaches. The trees are full.
A riverbank of wind, sun, and water.
In the willow shade a road zigzags.
Orioles pour forth with song, one next to the other.

Ride it far and it will take you farther.
The more you gaze, the clearer its truth.
If this style isn't to be exhausted
You must take the old and make it new.

The Potent Style
Green woods, a wild hut.
Setting sun in the transparent air.
I take off my headdressing, walk alone,
Often hearing the calling of the birds.

No flying swan brings me messages
From my friend traveling so far away.
Yet the one I miss *isn't* far.
In my heart we are together.

Ocean wind through emerald clouds.
Night islets and the moon, bright.
After one good line, stop.
A great river spreads across your path.

The Lucid and Rare Style

Through bright and slender pines
Shivering ripples flow.
Sunlet snow covers the strand.
Across the water, a fishing boat.

A pleasant person, precious as jade,
In clogs, seeks hidden landscapes,,
Strolling, then pausing,
As the sky's hollow blue goes on and on.

This spirit is ancient and rare
But so limpid it can't be held—
Like moonlight at dawn,
A hint of autumn in the air.

The Sad and Poignant Style

A typhoon rolls up the waters,
Forests are smashed.
This sadness feels like death.
You summon Peace. She doesn't come.

Centuries flow away
And wealth and nobleness are cold ash.
With the Dao fading day by day,
Who can be a hero?

A noble warrior wipes his sword.
His sorrow fills the world

As falling leaves sift and shift
And rain dribbles over dark moss.[4]

Sikong Tu was a Tang-dynasty poet who classified the styles and visual scenes of poems into 24 categories. He did not describe the nature of each category in prose, but instead used rhyme to set the scene, and used this scene to represent the style of a particular category. This mode of literary criticism also exists in the literature of other civilizations. For example, in the "Songs of Solomon" and the "Book of Psalms" in the Bible, some verses are quite similar to Sikong's approach. Yet in Chinese literature, rhymed verse can almost always make use of a scene in nature, or changes in the natural environment, to communicate the mood and feelings the author wants to convey. Su Dongpo's 蘇東坡 (1037–1101) famous comment on Wang Wei 王維 (699–759)—that he "had poetry in his painting and painting in his poetry"—completely captures the mutually sustaining relationship between poetry and painting.

The above explanation makes it clear that the Chinese people's sense of the relationship between nature and self is that the two are fully fused, so that inner feelings are inseparable from changes in the external environment. Time and space are similar, in that changes in time do not occur in isolation, but manifest themselves through changes of things in natural space. Hence, the three individual components of time, space, and humans are in fact integrated in a closely related whole. To make this point clearer, I would like to use the example of two poems from China's greatest poets to illustrate how they observe the natural world, how they deeply reflect on the vast universe, and how they make meaning of this.

---

4   Translation taken from Tony Barnstone and Chou Ping, trans., *The Art of Writing: Teachings of the Chinese Masters* (Boston: Shambala, 1996), 25–37, with modifications.

One of Wang Wei's couplets translates as: "Vast desert, lone spire of smoke stands straight/Long river, round is the setting sun." The first five characters (immense desert lone smoke straight) set the vertical against the horizontal; the second five characters (long river setting sun round) describe a great circle on the line of the horizon. The image of the desert is that of a vast space; the image of the Yangzi River is that of infinite movement through time. At the same time, if the smoke rises from the plain in a vertical cloud, it is because there is no wind, and the fact that it is dry already implies a seasonal description. The sun sets at dusk, a concrete image of a specific sunset within ever-flowing time. The implicit meaning of these 10 characters is elegant and powerful.

The final line of Li Bai's 李白 (701–762) "Remembering Qin E" (*Yi Qin E* 憶秦娥)—"Western wind and setting sun, the tomb of the Han dynasty"—contains only eight characters, yet is full of both time and space. "Setting sun" refers to the order of time within a day, "western wind" to seasonal changes, "Han dynasty" to the rise and fall of political regimes, and "tomb" to the difference between life and death. These scant eight characters link the progress of a single day to the passage from life to death, one a cycle, the other a finality. Li Bai was a masterful poet and Wang Wei was not without talent, and both succeeded in conveying deep feelings in simple and elegant poetry. Their works express the intimate relationship between time and space, situating images in time and space and expressing ineffable emotions.

Chinese poetry and songs are part of an extremely rich treasure house of literature. And because the Chinese language is made up of individual characters or two-character phrases linked together, writers can express their own viewpoints by the way in which these links form a whole. There is also a vast imaginative space between the writer and the reader in which each expresses his or her understanding of the time and space around him. Among the many examples that could illustrate this point, I choose the work of the Southern Song poet Yang Wanli 楊萬里 (1127–1206).

Among the cultural artefacts my father left me is a scroll of one of the Song-dynasty poet Yang Wanli's 11 four-line verses, in the calligraphy of

Shen Yinmo 沈尹默 (1883–1971). In my living room there are several prize examples of calligraphy whose beauty I can appreciate day and night as I enjoy the lines of the poems. Among these 11 poems, this one, "Crossing the Zhaoxian Rapids" (*Guo Zhaoxian tan* 過招賢灘), directly expresses his feelings about the environment: "Snow in the sixth month, who would believe it? I stand in front of the Zhaoxian rapids, observing the white foam." One more example, from another poem, is "The green mountains proudly display their dustless hue, eagerly reflected in the emerald stream throughout the day." Both of these couplets are direct observations, reflecting scenes and particularities revealed by nature. There is also another poem entitled "Spending the Night at Xiaosha Creek" (*Su Xiaosha xi* 宿小沙溪):

> The trees hold aloft the mountain mist, filling in gaps in the clouds.
> The wind rubs together flowers and rain to make a fragrant dust.
> The green hills know I hate walking in the mud,
> And sweep away the foolish clouds to indulge my lazy mood.

These two examples also illustrate Yang Wanli's style of anthropomorphizing nature, giving it feelings that it otherwise would not have. The poet thus speaks in the place of nature, projecting his own feelings onto time and space, as if he knew nature's thoughts.

Su Dongpo's remark about Wang Wei, that he "had poetry in his painting and painting in his poetry," can also be understood as meaning that our mindset frames how we view the world, or that we are moved by what we see. When Su composed his astonishing rhymed prose, "Ode on the Red Cliffs" (*Chibi fu* 赤壁賦), as well as his poem "Memories of Red Cliff" (*Nian nu jiao, Chibi huai gu* 念奴嬌 · 赤壁懷古), which reimagine a famous naval battle at the end of the Han dynasty, he was himself beside the Yangzi River, pacing back and forth under the moonlight, listening to the sounds of the weeping river. Looking at this scene, the poet not only thought about the great war that once occurred here, but went on to muse about the rise and fall of contenders in history, the success and failure of the heroes of the day, all of whom had since passed on. At this point, the ups and downs of his own life, together with the ever-flowing river, came together in a feeling like an eternal dream. Finally, in the last line of the poem—"One wine vessel, offer back a drink to the river-reflected moon"[5]—we see that the poem does not in fact rail against fate, perhaps because he had no choice, or perhaps because he freely accepted his destiny. He overcomes change, understanding that "change" is unchanging eternity. As Su said elsewhere: "If we look at things from the perspective of 'change,' then everything in the world is changing every moment; but if we look at the perspective of 'unchanging,' then everything and myself may last forever." This understanding is the essence of Chinese culture.

This kind of composition is the result of mutual illumination between humans and nature, a product of the blending of inner and outer. Wang Guowei's 王國維 (1877–1927) "Remarks on *Ci* Poems in the World" (*Renjian cihua* 人間詞話) discusses the difference between human beings being separate and not separate from nature, which is another way of saying that we are moved by what we experience, and that we should not remain separate from it. The category of "sorrowful" that we find among the categories of poetry enumerated in the above-mentioned *Twenty-Four Styles of Poetry* by Sikong Tu can be compared with the feelings we encounter in Su Dongpo's work, because both of them depict a bleak world.

Since we have already mentioned the notion of "paintings within poems," we might as well extend our aesthetic discussion of poetry to the world of painting. The Tang and Song eras were the most flourishing periods for landscape painting. This is especially true of Song landscapes, which represent the pinnacle in the history of Chinese painting. Guo Xi's 郭熙 (1020–1090) theory of landscape painting highlighted three principles:

---

5   Su Dongpo, "Su Dongpo: Memories of Red Cliff," LAC Poetry, April 1, 2017, http:// www.learnancientchinesepoetry.org/2017/04/01/su-dongpo-memories-of-red-cliff/.

horizontal distance, vertical distance and depth distance. A good painting should arrive at a harmonious presentation of these three angles. In his painting "Early Spring," the protruding peaks dominate the center of the painting, but there is an axis extending from the bank of the islet to the waterfall, and then turning toward a crack in the rock, and finally reaching the crags on the top of the mountain, all of which directs the viewer's gaze from the bottom of the mountain to the top. The two veins of spring water on the side of the mountain extend left and right, forming a plain. However, halfway up the mountain there are two footpaths, one visible and one hidden, that lead to the back of the mountain, directing the viewer's gaze to appreciate the view of the spring mountain.

This form of art does not follow the principles of perspective employed in paintings in general. The Chinese painter prefers to guide the

Fig. 1 "Early Spring" by Guo Xi
(Courtesy of NPM Open Data, National Palace Museum)

reader directly into the painting, following the landscape up and down. When enjoying this kind of painting, the gaze is mobile; there is no fixed point of perspective and viewers enter the painting where they wish, following their own preferences.

An even more concrete example is Huang Gongwang's 黃公望 (1269–1354) "Dwelling in the Fuchun Mountains" (*Fuchunshan ju tu* 富春山居圖). This is a long scroll that was once cut in two, with half in the Forbidden City in Beijing, and half in the Palace Museum in Taipei. In recent years the two halves have been joined together to form one complete painting. From right to left, the scroll follows the flow of the Fuchun River, offering the entire landscape to the gaze of the viewer. The viewers must imagine that they are on a boat, enjoying the view as they travel along, in an ever-changing perspective of sceneries.

Another example is Zhang Zeduan's 張擇端 (1085–1145) "Along the River during the Qingming Festival" (*Qingming shang he tu* 清明上河圖). This painting offers a vivid depiction of the Song-dynasty capital Kaifeng, starting from the paddy fields and willow trees in the suburbs, continuing into the city along the Bian River, and finally ending in the Jinming Pool of the Royal Palace. There is a bridge over the Bian River and boats of different sizes, there are many activities in the markets on the riverbanks, and many neighborhoods behind the markets, where we see shops and homes, and no fewer than 800 people. In this painting, there are no significant differences in size between the images of the people appearing on the river boats at the beginning of the painting and those at the markets, inside homes or living rooms, or working in the stores, who appear later on. The viewer of the painting seems to be suspended in mid-air, looking at the rooms behind the doors, and surveying the activities of the various participants. This painting makes no sense if considered in terms of perspective, because there is no one place from which you can see the activities over 10 miles and involving 800 people at a glance, and with no adjustment of the size of the figures. The only solution is to put oneself in the painting and follow the action, to add one's "self" to the cast of hundreds; this is the only way to appreciate the bustle of the imperial capital depicted by the painter.

Fig. 2 "Dwelling in the Fuchun Mountains" by Huang Gongwang
(Courtesy of NPM Open Data, National Palace Museum)

Fig. 3 "Along the River during the Qingming Festival" by Zhang Zeduan
(Courtesy of NPM Open Data, National Palace Museum)

Engraved illustrations sometimes appeared in traditional Chinese novels, and one might find images of maidservants (an example would be "The Night Revels of Han Xizai" [*Han Xizai yeyan tu* 韓熙載夜宴圖] by Gu Hongzhong 顧閎中), which follow similar principles of "the viewer entering the painting." In the activities revealed in those images, whether they be behind the door, in front of the courtyard, or in the parlor—viewers are required to put themselves in the scene to understand them. A table in the picture—which according to the rules of perspective should appear bigger in the front and smaller in the back—is presented in precisely the opposite way in these pictures. Once again, the painter is inviting the viewer to come into the scene; the background is slightly larger than the foreground, the principle of perspective being reversed to compensate for the gap in space.

Fig. 4
"The Night Revels of Han Xizai"
by Gu Hongzhong
(Courtesy of NPM Open Data,
National Palace Museum)

In sum, having read this chapter, I hope that the reader has understood that within Chinese culture, humans, time, and space make up a whole. People flow with time, and merge with space. People and nature are inseparable. It was such aesthetic principles that made Daoist thought possible: people are part of nature and cannot leave nature or put themselves outside of it.

II. The World of Heaven and Earth, Humans and Gods

Today's modern civilization has inherited the Judeo-Christian tradition, which explains humankind's origins with the story that, at the beginning, God created Adam and Eve. Immediately thereafter, Adam and Eve turned their backs on God's will by committing original sin, and their atonement could only be achieved through belief in God. In fact, people all over the world have their own mythological systems and there are different legends about the emergence of human beings. In this chapter, I begin with the story of humanity's origins in ancient Chinese legends to explain the position of humans and their uniqueness in the context of China's cultural heritage, a story completely different from that of God's creation of Adam and Eve in the West.

China is a big place, and legends concerning the origins of humans vary from region to region. Yet, at least during the Warring States period, the story of Pangu opening the heaven and Nüwa creating humans was largely accepted by everyone. The legend of Pangu and Nüwa probably traces its origins to the Yangzi River Delta region in central China, and to the ancient

Man 蠻 or Miao 苗 peoples.[1] But in the Warring States period, we find the story of the opening of heaven and earth and the origin of humans in Qu Yuan's 屈原 (340–278 BCE) poem "Heavenly Questions" (*Tian wen* 天問).

Before the opening of the heavens, the universe was in a state of primal chaos, shaped like a huge egg. The egg suddenly split apart and sitting in the middle was Pangu. Pangu raised his hand and pushed the lighter atmosphere upward, where it became the sky, and shoved the heavier elements downward, where they became the earth. Pangu's bones became the mountains, his blood became the rivers, his hair became the plants and the trees, and the world *was*. We can call this a process of "nothing" to "something." When the Daoist philosophers Laozi 老子 (6th century BCE) and Zhuangzi 莊子 (late 4th century BCE) argued that "Nonbeing is there prior to the state of Being," or when they said that "primal chaos" was our original state, it fit together with the Pangu story. This view of a natural evolution from "nothing" to "something" is truly a unique feature of Chinese culture. It is quite different from the cultural system appearing in the Middle East, and which later became the cosmology of the Judeo-Christian tradition.

Explaining the origins of the universe in this manner is more philosophical than simply summoning a God out of nowhere, because people are likely to ask: "Where did God come from, then?" When modern astrophysics discusses the origins of the universe, the basic premise is that the universe began from a point, and then exploded to become the universe. We might ask the same question: where did that point come from? In a mathematical sense, the point occupied no space, and hence was equal to zero. But again, how could a "zero" explode?

---

1   Ancient China, like modern and contemporary China, was made up of numerous ethnic groups. The dominant ethnic group in China is and was the Han people, whose origins can be traced to the North China Plain. Groups like the Man and the Miao were found further south, and ultimately retreated into the mountains as the Han migrated south over the centuries to eventually dominate most of today's China. —Trans.

In the Chinese myth of the creation of the universe, Nüwa comes after Pangu, and Nüwa simply stands for woman. In the Daoist system of gods, Nüwa is the same as Doumu 斗姆, the "Mother," which again is the same as the "primoridial venerable mother" (*xiantian laomu* 先天老母) in popular religion, all of which represent the origin of woman. It is also the same thing as Laozi's notion of the mysterious female (*xuan pin* 玄牝). Nüwa used mud and water to compose a human form and give it life, and people were created.

The character of Nüwa was not only the creator of humankind, but also the regulator of the universe. When the water god Gonggong got angry and broke the heavenly pillars on Buzhou Mountain, Nüwa melted colored stones on the ground to repair the hole in the heavens. When the great flood occurred, Nüwa piled up reeds and cinders to block the surging waters. From this perspective, the strength of Nüwa is that of earth, and complements that of heaven. Despite her godly power, Nüwa is not the spirit that controls the universe. She is not God, but simply represents the power of female and earth. Corresponding to her there is a male being with the strength of the heavens—he is known as Fuxi.

In stone engravings from the Warring States and Han periods, there are many images of Fuxi and Nüwa. They are depicted with human heads and snake bodies, their tails coiled around one another, symbolizing copulation. In the hand of one is a compass and in the hand of the other, a ruler, perhaps symbolizing that the heavens are dome-shaped (round) and the earth is square. To summarize, Nüwa created people and patched up the heavens, which simply symbolizes the primitive productivity of woman. The point of this legend is to signal that "humankind" is a product of nature, not a submissive child of God, and there was no point in turning their backs on any contract with God.

There is another way to tell the story: Nüwa's two great achieve-ments—patching up the heavens (the northeastern part of heaven, broken by Gonggong) through melting rocks, and blocking the source of the flood—might be metaphors for kiln-fired pottery and fine stoneware, two technologies that evolved in the Neolithic Age. Fuxi represents the nomadic era of cattle-herding and pairing him with Nüwa might well represent the combination of herding and agriculture, symbolizing the two distinctive modes of production in the Neolithic Age. These two images taken together convey the different stages of the evolution of humankind, as well as the concepts of yin and yang and copulation. It is likely that these legends were not particularly important in the spiritual life of the common people.

I will provide a fuller discussion of beliefs in ancient China in subsequent chapters. What I want to introduce here is the idea of the relationship between people and the sacred power of the universe. In the Neolithic era, all along China's Pacific coast—from Liaoning's Hongshan culture in the north to Zhejiang's Liangzhu culture in the south—we find a belief in the heavens symbolized by the sun. The sun, high in the sky, became the origin of China's "Great Heaven" (*haotian* 昊天). On mountains in the Hongshan culture area, a temple of goddesses, as well as tombs and altars dedicated to tribal chiefs and priests, were unearthed. Around the altars and tombs were numerous hollow, bottomless clay pots encircling the sacred area. Such an arrangement likely symbolizes the communication between heaven and earth, with the sacred space serving as the channel of communication. The tomb occupant was a respected figure, and was buried with a sorcerer's implements. He was perhaps a priest or a tribal chief, again responsible for communication between heaven and earth.

Excavations in Liangzhu uncovered a *cong* 琮, which is a square piece of jade with a round hole in the middle. Some people say that the *cong* has a round cover and a square base, which would symbolize the channel through which heaven and earth communicate. Another *cong* has an image of a flying figure engraved on it. Perhaps it is the god of heaven? Or the gods' messenger? Or a shaman whose responsibility was to facilitate communication between heaven and earth? We do not know. On yet another *cong* we find an image of a flying bird. In the legends of many places, flying birds are often seen as the messengers of the gods, and perhaps this is the case for these Liangzhu birds. In the ancient tradition of the Taihao 太昊 and Shaohao 少昊 cultures around the Bohai Bay, to the north of present-day Shandong, Taihao leaders were designated as clouds, while those in Shaohao were symbolized as birds. This arrangement may, again, reflect the fact that people had a certain role to play in the communication between heaven and earth.

There is a Han-dynasty silk painting from the Chu region in south-central China which, although it is rather late, may well have inherited these ancient legends. This silk painting, from the Mawangdui archaeological site in Changsha, Hunan, is divided into three levels: at the top is heaven, at the bottom is underground water, and the area between the two is the boundary between the living and the dead. In the painting there is a great tree whose roots extend into the lower level, while branches and leaves are in the upper level, with 10 birds perched upon them, perhaps the sunbirds of the era. In Sichuan, a bronze tree was unearthed at the Sanxingdui site, and there are many birds perched on the trunk too. This Heavenly Tree may be the same kind of tree as in the Mawangdui silk painting that connects heaven and earth. Again, this is a passageway between heaven and earth, and humans find themselves in the middle of the passage that leads up to heaven and down to earth. Historians of religion tell us that this notion of a tree extending to heaven is found in many places, and that the tree later on may have turned into a tower, as in the Tower of Babel in the Bible. So it seems that this ancient idea was not unique to China. But it is worth emphasizing that in China, humans always stood between heaven and earth.

The Chinese understanding of the human body was that it had a "round skull and square feet," symbolizing the round heaven and the flat earth—meaning that the human body was itself just like a universe. During the Warring States period, the Yin-Yang and the Five-elements masters,[2] representing two competing schools of natural philosophy, each offered their

---

2   These "masters" were members of loosely organized philosophical or cosmological schools, "priestly intellectuals" often respected by the elite and commoners alike.—Trans.

explanation of how the universe evolved. The Yin-Yang masters argued that there are two forces in the universe—yin and yang—and their interactions became the driving force of the universe. Everything in the universe contains both yin and yang; the two are not antagonistic, but complement one another. By contrast, the Five-elements masters ascribed the composition of the universe to five elements: metal, wood, water, fire, and earth. These five come together to produce all things, each of which has a specific mixture of the five elements, no more and no less. After the Qin-Han period, the marriage of the Yin-Yang and the Five elements schools made up the metaphysical basis for Chinese study of natural sciences.

The relationship between yin and yang of course also encompassed the relation between the genders and the process of the creation of life, which is why the life force was understood in terms of yin and yang. Neither of these elements could operate independently; with only yin no birth occurred, and with only yang nothing grew. This is why Nüwa and Fuxi had to exist at the same time. Yin and yang had to accommodate one another and not conflict; the two are in constant pursuit of equilibrium, and if one or the other is too strong or too weak, the entire mechanism falls out of balance, leading to disaster.

The five elements concept was very similar to the idea of the four basic elements found in the Mesopotamia-Greece area and in India. In the Mesopotamian four elements—earth, water, wind, and fire—each item is relative: earth is divided into dry desert and fertile land, water is divided into sweet water and bitter water, wind is divided into burning wind and gentle wind, and fire includes the fire brought by the burning wind and the fire that daily life must rely on. These dichotomies did not complete one another but were in conflict. In the Chinese notions about the five elements, we find on the one hand the idea that the elements gave rise to one another, and on the other the idea that they overcame one another: metal gives rise to water, water gives rise to wood, wood gives rise to fire, fire gives rise to earth, and earth gives rise to metal; metal overcomes wood, wood overcomes earth, earth overcomes water, water overcomes fire, and fire overcomes metal.

All of these concepts were the results of observations in daily life. That "metal gives rise to water" refers to the fact that metal, when heated, melts and becomes a liquid. That "water gives rise to wood" refers to the fact that without water, plants cannot grow. That "wood gives rise to fire" is very easy to understand, since we use bits of wood to build fires. That "fire gives rise to earth" is less obvious and that "earth gives rise to metal" refers to mining for metal underground. As for the idea of "mutually overcoming," the concept that "metal overcomes wood" refers to using a metal axe to chop wood; "wood overcomes earth" refers to the use of wooden tools to work, or break up, the soil in farming; "earth overcomes water" refers to building earthen dikes to prevent flooding; "water overcomes fire" requires no explanation; and "fire overcomes metal" again refers to melting metals at high temperatures.

This series of explanations illustrates how ancient people developed simple theories out of daily life. Any element or function was always conditioned by another element or function, and the coordination of the five elements was necessary to the construction of a complete life system. Similarly, within every element were strong and weak mutual constraints, because should any element become too strong or too weak, it could lead to disaster. For this reason, the five elements theory was like the ideas of yin and yang, and emphasized that all elements in the life of humans must be kept in equilibrium. Once balance was lost, life-sustaining resources not only might not be able to contribute to continued existence but might even hurt the environment on which existence depends.

Viewing the universe as ever balanced and dynamic clearly influences notions of time. In the view of modern science, time moves in a straight line. From the perspective of Christian theology, time began with God's creation of heaven and earth, and will continue until the final judgment day. Humankind's time on earth will be over, but time in the universe will continue. The Chinese conception of time is cyclical, forever seeking a "completion" conditioned by many factors; yet since these factors do not come together, the frontier of "completion" is difficult to reach. Notions of time within the universe of the Chinese people can be illustrated by the calendrical studies that developed at the end of the Han period following certain metaphysical reflections.

After a certain period of experimentation, the Chinese calendar—from the beginning of the Han period through the arrival of modern science in China—was a mixture of solar and lunar calendars: the length of a solar year was 365.25 days, and the length of a lunar month was 28.55 days. A year required 12 full moons, and every full moon had to occur in the middle of the lunar month, which required a fair bit of juggling just to meet this one condition. As discussed in Chapter I, in the Chinese calendar, every solar year was divided into 12 *jie* and 12 *qi*, and all critical points in the calendar represent important turning points in the continental climate of North China. The names of these solar terms were all related to climatic events important to the process of agricultural work—such as the Vernal Equinox and the Autumnal Equinox, at which moments the length of the day and the night were equal—or the Winter Solstice, the day with the least sunlight, the Summer Solstice, the day with the most sunlight, or Spring Commences, the start of the growing season. Each month was divided into two solar terms, and the start of each year had to be close to Spring Commences. When the math of the solar year and the lunar months didn't add up, a leap month had to be added to the calendar at the point where the extra days were needed, the month where its absence would have the most impact on patterns of daily life.

To this we need to add the astronomical ideas of the Chinese people: the universe is a vast ball composed of the sun, the moon, and the five elements, and each star's distance from us represents a layer of heaven. There are seven heavenly layers, which are concentric circles surrounding the earth. For the calendar maker, the ideal origin day for the universe would be when the sun and the moon are in harmony and the five stars in alignment. This day would be Spring Commences, which would fall precisely on the night of New Year's Day. The one time all these conditions came together was more than 27 million years before the reign of Emperor Ping (1–5 CE) of the Han dynasty, on a date called, in the technical language of calendrical studies, Utmost Beginning (*shangyuan* 上元). Yet even arriving at the end of such a vast period, time will not stop;

according to the Chinese calendar, the trajectories of the sun, the moon, and the five planets follow constantly changing patterns. Thus, after one long period, another new period begins, and time moves ever forward. Humans play the leading role in observing these changes, which means that the universe's perpetual balance is tied to their existence.

All things considered, the Yin-Yang masters probably emerged first— the appearance of the Five-elements masters would have had to await the Bronze Age or the Iron Age for the "metal" function to become prominent. The metaphysics of the yin and yang interaction is, of course, connected to Fuxi and Nüwa, discussed above, and has historical origins. In the Han dynasty, the Confucian scholar Dong Zhongshu 董仲舒 (179–104 BCE) synthesized Confucian ethics, integrating the theory of Yin and Yang and the Five elements, and organizing them into a theory of resonance between heaven and man. In his huge cosmic system, there are many layers of large and small universes, and the human body is also a self-sufficient mini universe. Resonance exists throughout, from the vast universe of heaven and earth, to the universe of the human order, and to the mini universe found in each person's body. It is not just that the large universe influences the small universes; changes in the small universes will also have an impact on the large universe and trigger corresponding changes. In these universes, no element can become too strong, suppressing the other elements; nor can an element become too weak, otherwise there will be no way to ensure the dynamic equilibrium of the whole.

From Han times onward, the homeostasis within the universe and among the universes accorded humans the same position in the vast universe as heaven and earth. Heaven, earth, and people were understood as the three levels of "power" or cai 才 in the universe. This is why, in Daoism, the traditional Chinese religion that appeared at the end of the Han dynasty, the primitive deity "officials" were identified as heaven, earth, and human; in the Eastern Han the human official was replaced by the water official. Humans remained, however, as those who named and interpreted things at all levels throughout the universe. An individual was not a living being required to submit to the natural order, but instead a cosmic component coexisting with heaven and earth.

In Dong Zhongshu's theory of mutual resonance between heaven and humankind, not only do changes in the heavens affect people, but changes in the human realm also affect heaven. Changes in the human realm, especially in terms of collective behavior, such as sudden changes in government policy or political institutions, can have an effect on the balance of the universe. Beginning in the Han period, official state histories often included a chapter entitled "disasters" or "auspicious omens" or "five elements," in which the historians recorded things like climatic changes and disasters, and these were often linked to the actions of the government, because the historians believed that it was human error that had led to climatic and other natural changes. For example, if the emperor relied too much on imperial relatives, or if there were despotic rule under a female ruler, this would be a case of an excess of yin, and could result in serious flooding.

Another example would be if the government practiced excessive torture or other measures of cruel government, this would give rise to a desolate sort of vital energy leading to a serious case of early frost in the autumn that would damage the harvest. Of course, such metaphysical mysteries strain our credibility, but such ideas truly influenced Chinese people's behavior in history, and remonstrating officials often used the occurrence of disasters to forthrightly criticize the errors in the government's ways. When the theory of heaven-human resonance appeared in the Han dynasty, intellectuals actually used the occasion of the occurrence of natural disasters to demand political reforms, sometimes even risking their lives by proposing that the emperor should step down. All of this reveals the close links between Chinese ideas about cosmology and human life. Within the universe, humans are not in a subordinate position, but as one of the three powers, they have their own right to take initiative.

Even today, Chinese medical theories are largely based on the idea of this resonance between heaven and humans, as well as the metaphysics of yin and yang and the five element theory, from which they derive ideas about the proper balance among elements within the human body, as well as about the interactive relationship between the corporal system and the system of the external great universe.

As for the human body, Chinese medicine sees it in terms of *jing* 精 (essence), *qi* 氣 (vital energy), and *shen* 神 (spirit), a theory that scholars of Chinese medicine trace back to the *Inner Classic of the Yellow Emperor* (*Huangdi neijing* 黃帝內經)[3] or especially the "Numinous Pivot" chapter that is part of that classic. But when you consult the *Inner Classic of the Yellow Emperor, jing, qi,* and *shen* do not appear as an isolated theory, but are linked to things like souls. *Jing* is life, or the essence of life; *qi* is life's motive force, and is dynamic; *shen* is the state produced by the operation of *jing* and *qi,* or to use of word frequently employed by Chinese medical practitioners today, *shen* is "capacity." The *jing, qi,* and *shen* within the human body are intimately linked to the world outside the human body. From the point of view of maintaining health, proper nutrition is a crucial step in nourishing *jing, qi,* and *shen,* but conditions in the external environment—cold, heat, dryness, humidity—also influence the balance among *jing, qi,* and *shen.* Extending this theory, we come to realize that the life of an individual is not an "object" that exists in opposition to the external environment, because this life is part of the vast universe, and individual agency can similarly positively or negatively impact the balance of the universe, meaning that a person is both object and subject. Humankind's dignity stems from the uniqueness described above, and an individual's rights, in the context of such theories, can also be understood as having been conferred by the heavens.

In the Introduction, I mentioned Feng Youlan's work entitled *A New Treatise on the Nature of Man.* Feng's view was that the broad realm of human life could be understood in terms of four dimensions: the

---

3 The Yellow Emperor was one of the legendary Chinese sovereigns and cultural heroes included among the mytho-historical Three Sovereigns and Five Emperors. He is imagined to have existed in the 24th or 25th century BCE, and several learned works, such as the medical text mentioned here, are attributed to him. —Trans.

primitive, the utilitarian, the intellectual, and the cosmic. In our primitive state, our biological nature will be the most prominent. But we should not be content with simple biology, and instead display desires and behaviors to exploit life to the fullest, which is the utilitarian dimension. Within this realm of utility, we also need to increase our rational knowledge, which is the intellectual dimension. The final realm is that of heaven and earth, where utilitarianism is sublimated, and we are in communication with the great universe. Feng believed that this gradual upward process was dependent on our "awakening." The word for awakening, *juejie* 覺解, is perhaps the same as the word "enlightenment" we encounter in the Confucian Learning of the Heart and Mind. Clearly the word Feng employed is also linked to words used to mean "enlightenment" in the Daoist and Buddhist traditions (*juewu* 覺悟 and *jietuo* 解脱, respectively).

Now I will leave philosophy behind, and return to the understanding of humanity within Chinese popular culture. Chinese medical ideas about the human body are representative of a body of medical knowledge applied to the study of humans in popular culture, and we see extensions of the ideas of *jing, qi,* and *shen* in popular customs and beliefs. During the Northern and Southern dynasties, Daoist alchemy grew out of the practice of refining medicine, the goal of which included both preserving health and pursuing eternal life—taking cinnabar was believed to prolong life or even grant eternal life. This belief in itself illustrates how much life was prized, in that it was worth extending indefinitely. Refining cinnabar led to the development of theories and methods of internal alchemy— including the belief that people could cultivate and transform their bodies by manipulating the "true fire" and "true water" already found within. At the highest level, the practitioner could further refine the central elements of *jing, qi,* and *shen* in the body's "internal fetus," converting them into his "original spirit" (*yuanshen* 元神). According to the mysterious theories of Daoism, the "original spirit" is our true self, and can live forever, setting aside the flesh-and-blood body, even becoming an immortal. And even without cultivating to the level of godhood, the "original spirit" can still leave the body for short periods of time and engage in activities. This idea of the "original spirit" almost says that the body can exist eternally. That an individual can reach such a level through his or her own efforts shows us once again how valuable humans are.

In the everyday life of the Chinese people, there are many strange stories of spirits, and most Chinese people have heard of snake-spirits, goblins, fox-fairies, and demons of all sorts. Most people believe that any ancient thing or animal can turn into *jing*, which at its highest state can evolve to take on human form, thus surpassing its original nature. People can become immortals, things can become people; in theory, spirits can become gods, and live forever. The "human" level remains higher than that of things, together with all life. Again we see how valuable a human being's position is; he or she is not a mere object of god's grace.

Feng Youlan's "awakening" is called "cultivation" in popular religion. Salvational religions from the Middle East entered China during the medieval period. At the outset, these religions remained true to their original nature, as in the cases of Zoroastrianism and Nestorianism. Later on, however, with the exception of Chinese Islam, which kept its original nature, the other salvational religions adopted important aspects of Daoist teachings, a synthesis that we see in many popular religious groups today, such as Yiguandao 一貫道,[4] which has carried forward many familiar popular beliefs from the past. To save themselves, they no longer rely on an external savior, but instead seek a salvation that can be reached internally through cultivation. The Yiguandao's "Eternal Venerable Mother" is a transformation of the Daoist idea of "evolution from nothingness." Achieving this level of enlightenment similarly involves purifying the contaminated parts of the body and the mind, gradually improving until

---

4   Yiguandao, often translated as "The Unity Way," became very popular in the 1930s and 1940s, attracting hundreds of thousands of followers throughout China. The group was suppressed by the Communists on the Mainland after the revolution, but survived on Taiwan and elsewhere in the Chinese diaspora. Following Taiwan's liberalization in the 1980s, Yiguandao was legalized, is an important force in Taiwanese society, and has even made inroads on the Mainland. —Trans.

enlightenment is achieved. Thus the "paradise" a person can reach does not require asking for heavenly grace, but is achieved through one's own efforts.

Certain non-salvational religions, like the cult of Mazu, the Chinese sea goddess, or the cult of the Plague God, use the gods' magic powers to remove difficulties and disasters from people's lives, and these same gods can lead believers to paradise after death. Yet the roles assumed by these gods are not solely instances of salvation through external magic. Those who are saved must also cultivate, at least in terms of their personal morality, otherwise the god will not intervene and help. Of course, there are any number of believers burning incense and making offerings at temple gates or leaving offerings at altars, but true believers will always tell us that solely relying on these gifts will not serve to accumulate the needed merit. Only if you cultivate your own heart and elevate your own moral character will the gods lead you to paradise.

Foreigners often think that the Chinese "purchase" the gods' favors through such acts as chanting Buddha's name or offering alms. And there are some unlearned believers who think that performing such meritorious acts can earn the gods' grace. The examples I have offered in this chapter illustrate that even within popular religion, the emphasis is on what an individual can do to achieve goodness. Through one's own efforts to achieve goodness, a person can attain enlightenment, and perhaps enter the realm of the sacred.

To sum up, from Chinese myths about the origins of the world through to today's popular religions, the position of humans within Chinese culture has been coequal with heaven and earth, and the three exist as a whole. I will discuss Confucian ethics in a subsequent chapter. What I have sought to illustrate in this chapter is that a person is sufficient within him/herself, and does not require external assistance to seek goodness or elevate him/herself or even to transcend the realm of biology or the limitations of physics. Clearly, this is an idealistic argument, but within Chinese culture, the influence of such a belief has been enormous and universal. Compared to the position of humanity within Judeo-Christian culture, Chinese "humanism" may have a clearer claim to the term.

III. Legends and Ghost Stories

The legends mentioned in this chapter are, of course, only some of the countless examples found in China's rich storehouse. The stories I have selected are basically of unknown origin and authorship, and have been handed down for a long time. I have tried to avoid including stories from literary works. However, if the plot of a literary work, such as a novel and or a play, has been retold so frequently as to become well known among the people, I have allowed myself to use it as a legend, something that reflects popular feelings.

In ethnology, legends customarily begin by recounting the creation of the heaven and the earth, the emergence of order, etc., because these legends also define a cultural system's interpretation of the universe and the surrounding environment. Before the initial unification of China by the Qin dynasty in 221 BCE, the broader Chinese culture developed in many different local cultures, each with its own myths and legends. It was more or less during the Warring States period that the cultures gradually merged into a fairly coherent system. In the Han dynasty, this integration proceeded even further. During the Warring States period, we can see the integration in two great works by the poet Qu Yuan—"Heavenly Questions" and "Nine Songs" (*Jiu ge* 九 歌)—which appear in a volume of poetry known as *The Songs of Chu* (*Chu ci* 楚 辭), grouped together with other poems of the Chu style. However, when these myths and legends became part of the cultural orthodoxy, they ceased to be recounted orally as part of folklore.

In "Heavenly Questions," which we will discuss further below, Qu Yuan first asks how the order of heaven and earth was established. What were the positions of the sun, moon and stars? How were they arranged? How was China's topography constructed in the creation legend? In the story of the great flood, what was the struggle of Gun and Yu? Then the poet brings up the creation myths of several dynasties and poses questions about the miraculous births of certain heroes. Finally, he asks about the early "dynasties" in history, their rise, fall, and changes: for example, how did Hou Yi usurp the power of the Xia dynasty? How did he discover that Chang'e stole the elixir? and so on. In Qu Yuan's other work, "Nine Songs," he specifically describes several important gods, their power and their character: Donghuang Taiyi[1]; the Lord of the Clouds, worshipped for rain and good weather; and the Lord of the East, the sun. He also describes water gods, the Lord and Lady of Xiang, both related to the Xiang River in present-day Hunan, their respective roles and relationships with each other.

And then we come to what I think is the most interesting chapter, entitled "The Mountain Ghosts," which are lovely spirits who toy with those walking in the forests, grasslands, and on tree-covered hillsides. It is only at the end that Qu mentions the ghosts of those who perished in battle: the "soldiers killed in war." These materials are indeed a treasure trove for us, helping us to understand the myths and legends of the time, even if the situation described is that of the southern state of Chu, which included most of the present-day provinces of Hubei and Hunan, where the mythic traditions are different from those of the central plains. However, as mentioned above, as time went on, these stories became literary treasures, and may not necessarily have been passed down among

---

1   This is a combination of two gods, the Lord of the East and the Grand Unity. —Trans.

the people. Therefore, in this chapter, I do not intend to give a detailed account of these stories, but only to remind readers of China's complex cultural heritage. This heritage draws on many sources, and some of the messages from ancient times are extremely beautiful and worthy of appreciation. Qu Yuan's "Nine Songs," with its mysterious forest spirits and the Lord of the Clouds, a handsome man who patrols the sky, is an excellent piece of literary imagination.

Since legends are passed down orally, they may, of course, vary in many details from place to place; written versions of legends are also often unique. For all these reasons, there is no standard book from which to cite legends. The legends mentioned in this chapter are in reality only approximations; many details have been omitted. This kind of history based on word-of-mouth recollections is not like normal historical sources, which can be cited.

I learned about these legends from my family, elders, and friends at various stages of my life. During the Sino-Japanese War (1937–1945), our family moved around a fair bit, sometimes staying in villages, sometimes in county towns, and while traveling I chatted with coolies, cart drivers, and boatmen, listening as everyday people retold some of the stories that have been passed down through the centuries. I am particularly grateful for having been in Huangjiaoya, a suburb on the south shore of Chongqing, the last stop in my family's refugee life. For two years, on Sundays, my parents worked in Chongqing city, and my brother and I stayed in the countryside and were cared for by Wang Sisan, an older gentleman. Wang, who hailed from the Huaixi region of Anhui, had been a wanderer all of his life. He was a rough and ready type, full of the spirit of righteousness and loyalty.

While my brother went to school, Wang carried me on his back (because of my disability) to a teahouse in the market, where we passed the time. There, as a member of the brotherhood of drifters like him, he had to "take care of business," as the saying goes. Local elders listened to the petty disputes of their neighbors, and rendered their verdict on the merits of the cases. On such occasions, in a teahouse in the countryside, I heard many stories that the Sichuan people used to tell when they were gossiping among themselves. That was 70 years ago, when I was only 13 or 14 years old, and I still remember Wang Sisan's personality and behavior. I would like to take this opportunity to commemorate this old friend of mine who was unfortunately killed in the 1950s during the campaign against "sects and secret societies."[2]

⁓

The first batch of legends are stories about the heavens: Let's start with the story of Hou Yi shooting the sun and Chang'e running away to the moon. It is said that Hou Yi was a divine archer who never missed a target. Hou Yi lived in the middle period of the Xia dynasty—China's first— which, according to Chinese dynastic calculations, would have been more than 3,000 years ago. At that time, the climate was changing dramatically, with years of drought and fires in the fields. (From today's archaeological data, it seems that there really was a period of very dry climate around 4,000 years ago, which led to great population movement at the end of the Neolithic era). According to legends, the drought was caused by the fact that all 10 suns came out at once. An ancient Chinese legend tells us that there were 10 golden birds on a great tree in the east, and one of them flew across the sky every day, which was the sun that people saw. For some unknown reason, at one point, the 10 suns appeared together, at the same time, the temperature shot up, and the ground was as hot as fire, with fields burning everywhere. This archer, Hou Yi, responding to the people's

---

2   This was an extensive campaign waged by the newly-established Communist govern-
    ment against what they labeled "reactionary sects and secret societies." These groups,
    now referred to by scholars as "redemptive societies," had spread widely in China
    during the Republican period; membership reached tens of millions, if not more. The
    Chinese Communist Party viewed them with suspicion both because of the "supersti-
    tious" nature of their teachings, and because of the political connections many of the
    groups had enjoyed with the defeated Kuomintang.—Trans.

entreaties, raised his bow and shot at the suns, bringing down nine of the birds, and leaving one in the sky as usual. The people were grateful and made him king.

However, as ruler he continued hunting every day, and given his skills, he killed almost all of the animals in the world with his bow. He felt that his merit was such that he deserved to live forever and procured the elixir of immortality from the Queen Mother of the West, the goddess who ruled over paradise. Hou Yi's wife, Chang'e, the eternal beauty, thought that if Hou Yi continued to hunt, he might begin to take human beings as his prey. So she deliberately hid the elixir from him, preventing him from taking it. Hou Yi continued searching for the elixir, and under pressure, Chang'e swallowed the medicine herself and fled to the moon. From that point forward, she endured eternal solitude on the moon in the Guanghan palace.

What is the meaning of this tragic legend? Perhaps it was that, caught between her love for her husband and her love for the people, the eternal beauty made the only decision that she could. The common people have recited this story for years, not necessarily because they really believe that there is a Chang'e in the moon palace, but simply to respect and commemorate her. Another story about the heavens is the legend of the Cowherd and the Weaving Maiden, who could only meet once a year. There are two constellations next to the Milky Way: one is the Weaving Maiden, made up of six stars suggesting the posture of a woman on her knees; the other, made up of seven stars, suggests the outline of a cow. It is said that the Cowherd and the Weaving Maiden, he being industrious in ploughing and she in weaving, fell in love, and the Heavenly Emperor made them husband and wife. After their marriage, they were so engrossed in their love that they neglected their work, and the emperor punished them by putting the Milky Way between them. The Heavenly Emperor finally took pity on the lovers, who greatly missed one another, and ordered the magpie to send a message to the lovers, allowing them to meet once every seven days. But the magpie got the message wrong, and said: "You may meet once a year, on the seventh day of the seventh month." From then on, the couple could only meet once a year on the bridge formed by the magpie's wings.

This love story has been handed down over the centuries, and all lovers, under the clear skies of summer, can promise that they will love each other forever. To this day, what some call Chinese "Valentine's Day" is unofficially celebrated on Taiwan on the seventh day of the seventh lunar month. In traditional Chinese society, love between a man and a woman was a very reserved and private affair. It is only by whispering such stories to one another that they could express their feelings for each other. At the same time, the actions of the Heavenly Emperor in the story represent the terrible authority of the father, and abuse of such power was quite frequent in the traditional Chinese family, another reason that even loving couples could only express their love for one other in the most private settings.

Another tragic love story is that of Lady Meng Jiang of the Qin-Han period, who wept at the Great Wall. Lady Meng Jiang's husband, Wan Xiliang, had been drafted to the north to build the Great Wall by China's first emperor, Qin Shi Huang. The newly married couple had not even enjoyed three days of happiness together, and when the husband left for distant lands, his wife decided to take him some winter clothes. It was the coldest months of winter, and ice and snow blocked the roads, so when Lady Meng Jiang arrived at the frontier stockades, Wan Xiliang and thousands of other soldiers had died of exhaustion in the frozen grottoes of the Great Wall. Lady Meng Jiang wept at the base of the wall, and the Great Wall fell to the ground. This story has been told for thousands of years, and in many dialects, there is a folk rhyme about "Lady Meng Jiang bringing winter clothes." The origin of this story is that in the state of Qi, during the Spring and Autumn Period, a certain Qi Liang was killed in battle under the shadow of the wall of Qi, and his wife, Meng Jiang, tearfully accompanied the casket on its return home. Compared to the original story, the legend is indeed more moving.

Another tragedy in which love does not go as planned is the Liang-Zhu story from the Eastern Jin period, composed in the early Tang dynasty. The "Zhu" in the story was Zhu Yingtai, a woman disguised as a man and studying in Hangzhou (because women could only study within the household), where she developed a deep bond with her classmate Liang Shanbo, who did not know that Zhu Yingtai was a woman. When it came time to return home from school, Zhu invited Liang to visit her family, at which point he finally discovered that she was a woman. The two pledged themselves to one another for all eternity, but when Liang approached Zhu's family about wedding arrangements, it turned out that Zhu's father had long ago promised her to another man named Ma Wenyuan.

Learning this news, Liang Shanbo was utterly heartbroken, and before long took ill and died. On the day that Zhu Yingtai married Ma Wenyuan, the wedding procession passed by the grave of Liang Shanbo, and a thunderstorm struck, preventing the boat from proceeding. Zhu Yingtai knew that Liang's tomb was there and left the boat to pay her respects, and at this very moment there was a peal of thunder and the grave split open. Zhu threw herself into the grave, which then closed over her. Henceforth, a pair of butterflies appeared, bearing the names Liang Shanbo and Zhu Yingtai, and they can still be seen today. It is said that the famous poet Xie Lingyun 謝靈運 (385–433) even wrote a special inscription to commemorate this unfortunate pair of young lovers.

This story, too, has its origin. In the old folk poem "Huashan ji" 華山畿 there is the story of a girl from Mount Hua who heard that a young man from a neighboring village had secretly fallen so deeply in love with her that he fell ill. The parents of the boy sent a matchmaker to discuss marriage with the girl's family, and the girl took off her under jacket and gave it to the messenger as a token of her love. When the messenger delivered the jacket to the young man, he clutched it to his breast and died. When the coffin passed through Mount Hua, the young girl welcomed the coffin by the roadside, singing, "Since you died for me, please open the coffin." With a peal of thunder, the coffin split open and the girl leapt in, and both were buried at the base of the mountain.

A similar story appears in the "Han Peng fu" 韓朋賦,[3] where it is recounted that during the Warring States period, King Kang of Song fell in

---

3   This is an ancient folktale included in Tang-dynasty Dunhuang manuscripts, which over time generated many new motifs and appeared in different forms. —Ed.

love with the wife of his palace secretary, Han Peng, whose maiden name was He. The king forced Lady He to enter the palace, and put Han Peng in jail. Han secretly sent a message to He to express his sadness that they would be forever parted. When He received the message, she put on rotting garments and committed suicide by leaping from the highest point in the palace. The maidservant standing next to her tried to grab her by her clothing, but since they had rotted away, the clothes gave way. Lady He had left a note, asking to be buried with Han Peng, but King Kang was furious, and buried them on opposite sides of a tall platform, so that they could see but not approach one another. Yet, before long, trees sprouted on each of the graves, and their branches and roots intermingled. A pair of colorful birds lived in the trees and flew together, and this tree is known as the "lovers' tree" (acacia or mimosa).

The story of Hua Mulan is slightly different from the love stories just recounted. "Tsiek tsiek and again tsiek tsiek / Mulan weaves, facing the door."[4] Probably all Chinese children read "The Ballad of Mulan" in middle school. Hua Mulan, a woman dressed as a man, took her father's place when he was called to fight in the war, and returned home in triumph after a 10-year journey through the mountains and passes, refusing imperial rewards to return home. Only after returning did she take off her soldier's uniform and dress again in woman's clothing, and her fellow soldiers who had fought with her for 12 years were shocked to discover that she was a woman. In the original version of this story, which probably dates to the Northern Zhou period, when the ruler, the Khan, discovered that Mulan was a woman, he attempted to force her into the palace, but she resisted and eventually killed herself. Her comrade in arms, General Liu, also died for this cause. These details do not appear in the Mulan poems circulating today. If we look at the original story, it resembles the preceding three stories of difficulties in love.

---

4   Translation taken from Han H. Frankel, *The Flowering Plum and the Palace Lady: Interpretations of Chinese Poetry* (New Haven: Yale University Press, 1976), 68–72.

All of these love stories are about a man and a woman who love each other, but are prevented from being together by outside forces. Of course, under the surface we find the common people's criticism of patriarchal and monarchical power.

Now let's look at stories about the land. The culture of farming has been deeply rooted in China for thousands of years, beginning with the Neolithic period. In China, intensive farming requires a proper supply of water to irrigate crops. It is probably against this background that the following story about flood management has been passed down continuously, developing into other, similar legends.

It is said that more than 4,000 years ago, China suffered a great flood.[5] An official named Yu, known as Yu the Great, and his father, named Gun, received an order from heaven to stop the flooding, which they did by diverting flood waters into new channels, allowing for the cultivation of the fields once again. In this story, Gun attempted to solve the flooding with dikes, but the more dikes he built the worse the flooding became, which led Emperor Shun to sentence him to death. Yu the Great subsequently took over the task, and ultimately succeeded through his strategy of canalization. Both Gun and Yu received the help of many gods in their efforts to stop the floods, including that of Nüwa, who gave them a special self-swelling soil that was meant to block the flowing water; there was also a divine tortoise, which indicated where to dig the canals to divert the flood waters by drawing lines in the mud with its tail. On one occasion, the Yu

---

5   Recent archaeological and geological explorations have revealed that some 4,000 years ago at Jishixia Gorge, on the upper Yellow River, there was a dam created by a landslide, but later the dam was washed away by a great flood some 40 or 50 stories high, which could have caused the subsequent catastrophe in the Yellow River basin. —Ed.

the Great turned himself into a great bear and was dancing to summon the magic spirits when his wife, Lady Tushan, came to bring him food. When she discovered that her husband had turned into a bear, she was extremely frightened and ashamed and ran away, never seeing him again. For the same reason, Yu passed by the door of his home without entering during the many years he spent traipsing around the country stopping the floods.

Another story of water management is the legend of Li Bing, who was the governor of Sichuan under the Qin. While serving in that position, Li diverted the Min River to irrigate the vast farmlands on the Chengdu Plain. According to the story, in order to open up a certain mountain pass, Li Bing transformed himself into a water buffalo and fought with yet another water buffalo, which was the transformation of the water god. He taught his followers to recognize which of the buffalos he was, which was the one with the white seal on its waist, the seal of his office. He had his followers help him by stabbing the incarnation of the water god, which ultimately allowed him to complete the work of dividing the river. His son Erlang, now known as the Erlang god, used the earth that he had dug up to help complete his father's work. According to the legend, his spade turned into the Erlang god's three-pointed, two-edged knife, which was fearsomely powerful and could defeat any evil spirit. Today on the beach at Dujiangyan, there remains a statue of a man in a short outfit holding a spade—Erlang the Water God.

The third story of flood management is that of Zhang Bo, the Great Emperor of Zhishan, in what is now Anhui and Jiangsu, who was a local magistrate in Gaochun in the Han dynasty. In this region, hills and ridges surrounded the valleys, blocking the flow of water and causing silting. Zhang Bo diverted much of the water into channels that fed the Yangzi River and Lake Taihu. In his flood stories, Zhang Bo also took on the form of a pig, or a pig-headed dragon (probably developed from the form of a large porpoise, a legendary animal). While he was digging a canal after turning himself into a pig, his wife, who was bringing him food, saw him and ran away and hid. In my hometown, Zhang Bo is called "Great Emperor Zhang," and his rank is equal to that of the "Great Emperor of the Eastern Peak." Every year during religious processions, gods and goddesses from various places will set out to pay homage to him.

In these stories, when the Great Emperor Zhang turns himself into a pig and Yu the Great turns himself into a bear, it is in fact the same metaphor. The people were grateful, and understood that those things that man's strength could not easily accomplish needed to be entrusted to the gods. Both Emperor Yu and Zhang Bo sacrificed their family life in exchange for the people's eternal gratitude. In Chapter VII, I describe how the two local officials in Wuxi—the Eastern Water God and the Western Water God— were worshipped by the people for their meritorious efforts in flood control. Stories like this can be found all over China, north and south. In order to meet the needs of agriculture, officials built waterworks for the benefit of the people, and for this reason, the people always honor them.

Since we are talking about the effect of the natural environment on human beings, we should note that the Chinese pay special attention to irrigation. In this context, we can also mention the legend of the "flood dragon," which is related to the concept of irrigation. *Jiao* 蛟 and *long* 龍, the two characters that make up the compound "flood dragon," are both fantastical animals in mythology. In Chinese legends, the dragon is a mythical creature with great power, and the emperor used the dragon as a symbol of himself, but dragons were basically found in water. *Jiao* is a step down from the dragon, perhaps the dragon's deputy, or a lesser divine creature. *Jiao* is generally found in flowing water. The following is a story about a dragon.

In Sichuan and in the Yangzi River basin, there is the legend called "Gazing at Mother Beach." According to the story, a mother and son lived in extreme poverty in a village next to the river. One of the son's chores was to go to the bank of the river and cut river grasses for them to eat as vegetables. One day he discovered an extremely fertile patch of river grass, which they found to be unusually tasty. He returned a second day, and then a third, and the patch of river grass remained undiminished. By accident, he also discovered a red pearl in the patch of weeds, which he brought home with that day's harvest of grass. They had almost finished eating one day's basket of grasses, but early the next morning the basket was full again. The mother and son put the red pearl in the rice jar, and the next morning the container was full of white rice.

The word got out, and all the villagers came to see the red pearl. The boy became alarmed, ran back to the riverbank with the pearl, and accidentally swallowed it. He immediately felt very thirsty and went to the river to drink. His mother saw him drinking mouthful after mouthful of the river water, and when the boy raised his head again, his head was that of a dragon, and his body was growing longer. Finally, he turned into a huge dragon and jumped into the river, and from the water he waved his head at his mother to say goodbye. In Sichuan, there are many places with names like Nine Eddy Beach, or 72 Eddy Beach, each eddy marking the movements of the son, transformed into a great dragon, bowing to say goodbye to his mother.

This story expanded to become many similar stories. The red pearl was transformed into a jewel that could be placed in any object, the number of which could be increased to infinity. The legend about becoming a dragon after swallowing a pearl is most widespread in the Yangzi River valley. In my opinion, the explanation for this is that the course of the Yangzi River is very torturous, and with every curve in the waterway, the water on the outside of the curve crashes into the river bank and destroys a part of the bank, which makes the curve even bigger. On the other side of curve, the water flows slowly back the other way, and mud and sand pile up to add to the river bank. The great *long* is in fact the flow of the river, powerfully majestic, subtly rising and falling, flowing inexorably toward the east.

Jiao are thought to reside in the Yangtze River Basin, especially in the Sichuan River, where there are often underground rushing currents flowing into the river; gazing from afar at the underground stream, it does indeed resemble a giant, twisting animal. The *jiao* might also have been imagined from the image of the "Yangzi sturgeon." In fact, all of these stories may come from people who live along the banks of the Yangzi transforming what they see in the river into *long* and *jiao* and worshipping them as water gods. From this basis, they evolved into the "dragon god of the four seas" and the dragon spirits found in large and small rivers throughout China.

"Dragons and snakes thrive in deep mountains and great marshes" is a typical saying in ancient China, grouping dragons and snakes together. The image of a dragon is an expanded and more complex image of a snake. If fact, the dragon was probably a giant snake. In ancient times, when vegetation was abundant, the snake was a constant danger to human beings. The snake moved silently and seemed to be everywhere, and poisonous snakes were a mortal danger. The snake is thus portrayed in Chinese mythology as an imperceptible danger. In pre-Qin texts, the word "nothing" (*wu ta* 無它), a variant of which is "no snakes" (*wu she* 無蛇), meant "no harm." Thus in daily life, this kind of creature also became a symbol for disaster that must be guarded against. The snake's habit of curling up its body, lifting its head, and flicking its tongue in all directions makes it look like it is taking breath from the heavens. In legends, the image is that of a serpent with its head held high, absorbing the essence of heaven and earth, and finally becoming a snake spirit capable of transforming itself into human form and participating in the world of humans.

Among stories of snake spirits, the most famous is that of the "white snake," one of the four great Chinese myths. This 800-year-old white snake, who cultivated himself through religious practices on Mount Emei, absorbed the essence of the heaven and the earth, the mountains and the streams, ultimately transforming itself into a beautiful woman dressed in white. The story of the White Maiden evolved gradually: it probably existed in the Song dynasty in embryonic form, but by the Ming dynasty, it had already evolved into the white snake legend that almost every Chinese person knows today.

In the story, an eternally sorrowful tragedy, this white snake spirit fell in love with a man named Xu Xian. Because of the snake's love for

Xu Xian, it decided to transform itself into a maiden and live as a human afterwards. However, a nosy monk named Fahai, who was also a toad spirit, wanted to break up their relationship. During her fight with Fahai to protect Xu Xian, the White Maiden used her powers to flood the temple. Thus the White Maiden, a righteous and compassionate woman, committed a great sin—flooding the Golden Temple, causing a great disaster. Thereafter, the White Snake was trapped under the Leifeng Pagoda until the West Lake dried up and the pagoda collapsed; only then could the White Snake return to the world.

I once visited Jinshan Temple, where the monk, a very decent man, led me to see the hole in the wall from which Xu Xian is said to have escaped, which is a legend that has taken root in the people's hearts. In the southern part of the country, autumn crabs are a seasonal delicacy. Each time we crack open the crab, the children try to find the tiny white bone between the crab's eyes, which is said to be Fahai. In the didactic reasoning of folklore, the monk who broke up the marriage bond was relegated to live in the crab shell for all eternity. In many Chinese regional operas, there is a version of the "Legend of the White Snake" in which the snake's son, who was born a human, passes the highest level of the imperial examination and returns to Leifeng Pagoda to pay homage to his mother. The mother and son can only meet briefly, and the part where the mother laments her life and her misery when trapped under the pagoda is very touching.

In folk tales, snake fairies are not always evil figures. The White Snake is a character that deserves our sympathy. In the Yangzi River Valley, and indeed throughout the entire southern region, snakes are common and rarely poisonous because of the lush vegetation and the abundance of water. For this reason, snakes are often regarded as deities that can protect families. In the house in Wuxi where I grew up, there was a big tree by the water, which reached higher than the second floor. There was a big hole in the upper reaches of the tree, the result of a big branch falling off. A big snake lived in the hole in the tree (I suppose it was actually a snake's nest) and we would occasionally see the snake on a branch high up in the tree. We didn't bother the snake and the snake didn't bother us, and most people generally saw the snake as the Hsu family deity. Snakes and swallows symbolize the rise and fall of a family's fortune. If the snake disappears and the swallow doesn't come back, the family will move toward decline. Therefore, on the first and fifteenth day of the first month of the Lunar New Year, my family's servants would put two eggs under the tree as an offering of thanks to the snake god.

The fox spirit is also a common theme in Chinese legends. The most common story is that the fox transforms into a woman and bewitches a young man, causing him to deplete his semen. The semen of these young men, however, nourishes the fox and deepens the spirit's powers. There are many variations on this basic tale, and some fox spirits are quite compassionate and do not endanger their lovers. The stories of fox fairies often have to do with borrowing their magical power, and the families that encounter them may become rich for a while, but good fortune conferred by a fox fairy does not last forever.

The fox earned its fame because of its beautiful, glossy fur and the shape of its eyes, which are slightly slanted, and are different from those of wolves and dogs. The fox's eye reminds us of a woman's teasing gaze. The fox moves at night, like the jackal, howling at the moonlit sky; this image has also been seen as the fox absorbing the essence of the sun and the moon. In fact, most of the villages in China are already densely populated and there are no wild animals around. Therefore, the story of the fox fairy may have been inspired by the weasel by mistake. Many literary scholars, such as Pu Songling 蒲松齡 (1640–1715) and Ji Xiaolan 紀曉嵐 (1724–1805), were good storytellers, and fox fairies appeared frequently in their stories. In fact, these stories are largely satirical in nature, and they are fables created by scholars, not legends cooked up by the people themselves.

To return to the human world: when people die, they become ghosts, and stories of ghostly souls naturally make up an important part of popular legends. To begin with birth, ever since the Buddhist notion of reincarnation entered China, the Chinese have imagined an underworld that exists outside the world of the living, and "rebirth" has meant a passage from this netherworld back into the world of the living. There is a common legend that when a woman is in labor, someone will see a dead friend or an enemy enter the room where the woman is giving birth, and after a loud cry, the baby will be born. The explanation will be that someone has come to repay a favor or to renew an old friendship, or in the case of the enemy, to collect a debt or exact revenge.

In my hometown there was a respected elder, Mr. Wu Zhihui 吳稚暉, who throughout his life never once celebrated his birthday. The story is that, before he was born, his father had a dream in which his deceased grandfather told him: "I bought you this child, which weighs seven pounds and twelve ounces, and he will be born tomorrow. This child has not been approved by the underworld. I bought him in secret. It is thus imperative that he never celebrates his birthday, so as to prevent the underworld finding out that we have smuggled someone into the world of the living." These kinds of stories are basically used to explain the reasons for the rise and decline of families. This is especially the case when a family has a child who is a bad seed, in which case they point the finger at poor behavior in a previous life, which has caused enemies to come and collect their debts.

Of course, ghosts who are unfairly wronged become powerful spirits that haunt the human world. In Chapter VI of this book, there is a story from the Spring and Autumn period about a man named Boyou 伯有 from the state of Zheng, who was killed while drunk, and whose wronged ghost sought revenge. Such powerful spirits not only seek personal vengeance, but can also cause widespread unrest throughout the area. Disease and war cause many deaths, and the souls of those who died unjustly have nowhere to rest in peace, and return to haunt the world. In times such as these, long periods of malaise may create emotional tension among the people, and suddenly stories such as "passing soldiers from the underworld" may appear.

I had a personal experience of this. In the second year of the Sino-Japanese War, the Japanese bombed many places in Sichuan. On one occasion, Wanxian, a medium-sized city, was flattened by Japanese bombs, leaving two-thirds of the city in ruins and countless dead. After the bombing, the people were much perturbed and the refugees, already homeless, slept in the open air or in the corridors of any shelter they could find. At that time, for about 10 very hot days, in the middle of the night the entire city took fright, everyone saying that they had seen "underworld soldiers" with severed heads and missing limbs walking down the streets in military formation. A phenomenon of mass unrest requires collective relief. Therefore, local religious believers asked Buddhist temples and Daoist monasteries to perform ceremonies to calm the souls of the dead and facilitate the passage of their lost souls, all of which eased the terror felt by the human world.

In Taiwan, the term "good brothers" refers to ordinary ghosts and spirits, while the terms *Dazhongye* 大眾爺 or *Yiminye* 義民爺 refer to those who were sacrificed in bitter feuds that marked earlier periods of Taiwan's history. There are small shrines and temples all over Taiwan where the good brothers are worshipped in order to prevent them from bringing harm to the world. Sometimes, other circumstances may lead the public to feel nervous, and they may still attribute the source of their anxiety to the disturbance of ghosts. When I first joined the Institute of History and Philology at Academia Sinica, there was a "pacifying the neighborhood" ceremony held in Nangang, where the Institute is located, and the Institute sent me to the ceremony as their representative, so I have seen with my own eyes the ritual process to appease the spirits: A medium casts divination sticks to find out the reason for the ghost's malaise; a Daoist priest sacrifices a document and a magic sword to mobilize the spirit soldiers; and the staff burns paper money and offers food and wine. Such is the combination of grace and mercy, of hard and soft measures, to settle the unhappy souls of the dead.

Among folk tales in Taiwan dealing with ghosts doing harm, the most famous is the story of Sister Lin Tou. Lin Tou was a woman from Tainan, a city in the south of Taiwan, who fell in love with a man surnamed Zhou, and they worked together to build a family while running their very small business. At one point Zhou returned to his hometown on the Mainland to do business. There, he had a change of heart and fell in love with someone else, and abandoned Sister Lin Tou and their children. Sister Lin was so angry that she hanged herself from a tree and died. Her angry ghost spirit lingered, hoping to take revenge on the man who had wronged her, but when attempting to cross the water to reach Zhou's hometown, her progress was blocked by the sea god. Later, with the help of a fortune-teller, she crossed the water with her ancestral tablet under an umbrella. In the end, Lin Tou's ghost found the culprit and exacted her vengeance. Another version has it that Lin took a chartered boat to the provincial capital, accompanying scholars who were to take the imperial examinations, and as they were under the protection of the deity of imperial examinations, the sea god did not dare interfere.

There is also a story about Zhou Cheng's trip to Taiwan. Zhou Cheng was a small businessman who left his first lover for another woman after crossing the sea. The woman in his hometown resented the unfaithful lover, and after she died, her ghost crossed the sea to seek revenge. The two stories are basically quite similar and probably share the same origin. The tragedies were caused by the separation of families and the fears of the Fujianese immigrants who came to Taiwan in frontier times, when the territory was being opened up. The famous Taiwan historian Lin Hengdao 林衡道 (1915–1997) believes that these stories are probably based on the theme of the "husband gazing rock,"[6] which is found everywhere in mainland China, with the addition of some details, thus giving us the stories we find on Taiwan.

People who have read Shi Nai'an's 施耐庵 14th-century novel, *The Water Margin* (*Shuihu zhuan* 水滸傳), all know the story of Song Jiang's concubine, Yan Poxi, who fell in love with Song Jiang's disciple, Zhang Wenyuan. This led Song Jiang to kill Yan Poxi, after which Song departed for Liangshan.

---

6   Rocks found particularly in China's coastal areas where wives would look out at the sea, hoping that the husband would soon return. —Trans.

Out of this evolved the legend called "Capturing Zhang San Alive." Death did not lead Yan Poxi to forget her lover, and her ghost strangled Zhang San (another name for Zhang Wenyuan) to death so that the two could live together in the underworld. This story is slightly different from the above-mentioned Taiwan legend. In the Taiwanese version, the unfaithful man was punished, while in the Mainland legend, there is some empathy for Yan Poxi and Zhang San, who were allowed to be together after death. All these stories reflect the experiences of the common people. In fact, they treat the soul after death as a continuation of the lives they had led, without mentioning Buddhism, or reincarnation, or karma.

The world is full of injustice, and we find unfairness everywhere. When ordinary people have been wronged, they always hope that someone will intervene and fix things on their behalf. This was the origin of a series of legends about "Lord Bao, the great Judge." The Song dynasty's Bao Zheng 包拯 (999–1062), commonly known as Lord Bao, was a famously honest official, impartial and incorruptible. According to the legend, as prefect of Kaifeng, he reversed the unjust punishments inflicted on the common people. The culprits at the roots of such injustices included relatives of the emperor, government ministers, rich families, and local tyrants. In the story, Lord Bao was able to intervene on behalf of the common people despite the power and influence of those who made them suffer. There are too many stories of this kind, so I need not go into detail, but the most widely told story is that of Chen Shimei.

Chen Shimei was born in poverty but eventually placed first in the imperial examination. The imperial family married Chen to the emperor's daughter and Chen was ennobled, becoming the emperor's son-in-law. Yet Chen had conveniently forgotten his first wife and the two children he had left in his hometown. His first wife went to the capital to look for her husband, but Chen Shimei refused to acknowledge her. Finally, Lord Bao made a fair verdict and executed Chen Shimei.

Stories like those of Lord Bao are found in every dynasty: Examples include Di Renjie 狄仁傑 (630–700) in the Tang dynasty, Hai Rui 海瑞 (1514–1587) in the Ming, and Shi Shilun 施世綸 (1659–1722) in the Qing

(1644–1912), all of whom are real life examples of "righteous officials" who often suffered for their insistence on justice. In addition to redressing the wrongs done to the common people, the stories also include the judgment of many strange cases, most of which are taken from Song Ci's 宋慈 (1186–1249) famous collection of cases, *Washing Away of Wrongs* (*Xi yuan lu* 洗冤錄). Taken together, these instances tell us that the Chinese people feel they have no recourse against the government, especially local magistrates, who accommodate the powerful and abuse their authority. The idea of these officials serves as emotional sustenance for the people, a symbol of hope in the midst of despair.

In this series of stories about Lord Bao, there is a group of rough and ready heroes who sometimes rob the rich to aid the poor, and sometimes help honest officials undo cases of injustice. Of course, this same kind of hero is also a theme in Chinese legends. In the Song dynasty the economy developed quickly, and with rapid urbanization, folk entertainment, such as storytelling and street theater, emerged in the cities. The stories told by these artists were often inspired by the heroes of the Five Dynasties period, when the world was in chaos and when "heroes made their marks with swords and cudgels." The "Peach Garden Oath," the "Uprising of the Wagong Heroes," and the "Story of Mount Liang" all build on these themes, as will be discussed in Chapter X. These stories often stress the formation of groups of swashbucklers with well-honed military skills, who come together out of a sense of justice and work outside the system, fighting injustice in the world. Some of them were even able to start their own kingdoms. Righteousness is a virtue prized above all others; for the sake of righteousness, they will sacrifice their life without regrets.

The origin and essence of these stories can be traced back to the knights and assassins described in *Records of the Grand Historian* (*Shiji* 史記) and to figures drawn from the Tang dynasty "tales of the strange." During the Ming and Qing dynasties, many gangs and brotherhoods emerged in the legendary world of rivers and lakes, as well among the people, and they also relied on chivalrous legends to solidify their groups around the basic spirit of "righteousness."

In this series of stories, we also see loyal martyrs who serve the country and its people, and who are often persecuted by treacherous ministers, sometimes losing their lives for the country. It was also during the Song dynasty that the story of the Yang family generals began to develop. Yang Ye 楊業 (923–986), originally a general in the Northern Han Kingdom, became a famous defender of the Shanxi frontier after surrendering to the Song dynasty, coming to be known as "Commander Lord Yang the invincible." In a battle against the Khitan Liao, Yang was asked to be in the vanguard, and the promised reinforcements were not forthcoming. He was defeated by the Khitan army and starved to death as a prisoner. His sixth son, Yang Yanzhao 楊延昭 (958–1014), also defended Shanxi and was a famous general for a time. These episodes evolved into a series of stories about the Yang family generals, interspersed with struggles between loyalists and traitors in the imperial court and conflicts between soldiers and civil officials.

In this series of stories, the Yang family becomes the generals who defend the country over generations, and generations of generals are either killed in battle or die of exhaustion, leaving a group of widows: a grandmother, She Saihua 佘賽花 (934–1010), and a granddaughter-in-law, Mu Guiying 穆桂英 (b. 982), led a family of widows and orphaned daughters, as well as the young descendants of the Yang family, to continue to serve the country. If we only look at the story of the Yang family, readers may have the erroneous impression that the Yang family was the sole protagonist in all of the foreign wars of the Song dynasty. In fact, after Yang Yanzhao, the only other important figure was Yang Wenguang 楊文廣 (1012–1074). Later on other figures who fulfilled the ideal of "exhausting loyalty to repay the country" included people like Zhang Xun 張巡 (709–757), Xu Yuan 許遠 (709–757), Yue Fei 岳飛 (1103–1142), Yu Qian 于謙 (1398–1457), and Yuan Chonghuan 袁崇煥 (1584–1630), soldiers who often suffered wrongful for their loyalty. The common people condemned the government and the monarchy for failing their generals, which led to protests against injustice.

The stories of the women generals of the Yang family are based on the deeds of Hua Mulan and Princess Pingyang's 平陽公主 army in the early

Tang dynasty, followed by the heroic deeds of Fan Lihua 樊梨花 (ca. early Tang), Qin Liangyu 秦良玉 (1574–1648), and others. The theme developed here is not so much an expression of the common people's appreciation of the status of women, or praise of their deeds, but rather their belief that a hero can be more than a bearded man.

Later on, the story of Lord Bao comes together with the stories of the "Yang Family General," to which are added the Eighth Virtuous Prince, Zhao Defang 趙德芳 (959–981) , the son of Emperor Taizu of the Song (a symbol of virtue), Kou Zhun 寇準 (961–1023) (representative of wisdom) and the Empress who returned to the palace from among the people (representing a maternal power who can overpower the emperor). These elements give Lord Bao, the embodiment of justice, the supreme power to punish imperial relatives, civil and military officials and the powerful and evil—the image of a protector that ordinary people can only dream of.

In Chapter VII of this book, I will talk about my hometown of Wuxi, where the objects of worship include Zhang Xun, Xu Yuan, Yu Qian, and in Yu Qian's temple, there is also a plaque dedicated to Xia Yunyi 夏允彝 (1596–1645) and his son. Yue Fei is also commonly worshipped in the Guan Yu temples in Taiwan. In the works of Jin Yong 金庸 (1924–2018), the master of modern martial arts fiction, the plot described in this chapter can be seen almost everywhere, one indication of the impact of this series of legends on the feelings of the Chinese.

This chapter has covered a seemingly chaotic range of topics, from the creation of the world to the heroes of the underworld, from love stories between men and woman to weird and wonderful phenomena of the ghost world. However, it also tells us about the likes and dislikes of the Chinese people in general, what they praise and what they criticize. Ordinary people seldom quote the classic Chinese books of learning, such as the Four Books, the Five Classics and the Twenty-four Imperial Histories, in their conversations. Their sense of history is a value system pieced together from the stories presented above. The values they recognize are that people should be fair to one another, that there must be justice among the people, and that there must be righteousness in the world. The contents of this chapter can be read in conjunction with the contents of Chapter VII on religion, and what I would like to underscore here is that the "humanization" and "secularization" discussed in the context of religion are equally present in the context of the conception and dissemination of legends and stories.

IV. A Plural, Interactive Order: The Five Elements, Chinese Medicine, and Chinese Cooking

Chinese culture has its own systems of classification. Chinese people are familiar with the five elements, the four seasons, and the three celestial bodies—all of which are categories—of which the five elements are the most representative. As early as the Neolithic period, in the Liangzhu culture of Zhejiang province, we find man-made earthen mounds that served as ceremonial or ritual centers. These were mountains of earth, topped by a platform made of sifted fine dirt, yellow in the center, and flanked by five colors of clay (green, red, black, white and yellow). This may be the beginning of the Chinese concept of the five elements: metal (white), wood (green), water (black), fire (red), and a central earth (yellow).

In the late Spring and Autumn and Warring States periods, there appeared a school of five element thinkers, who explained the many phenomena in the universe by reference to the characteristics of metal, wood, water, fire, and earth, and the relationships of the elements with each other. What was the relationship between this school of thought and the ancient tradition represented by the Liangzhu culture? We can't be sure. At the very least, this school, and another, known as the Yin-Yang school, both sought to explain and control all knowable phenomena by means of metaphysical constructs.

We will start by discussing the idea of the five elements. The "Hongfan" 洪範 ("great plan") chapter of the Confucian classic *Shangshu* 尚書 is based on the theory of the nine "Hongfan" categories described by the semi-legendary Jizi 箕子, the 11th-century BCE sage of the Shang dynasty, which illustrate how Shang civilization explained the operation of the world and the behavior of individuals by reference to certain patterns. Most of these nine categories are in groups of five: The first is the five elements, the second is the five human behaviors and abilities, the third is the eight objects of government, the fourth is the five modes of sacrifice, the fifth explains the five forms of good governance, the sixth is the three different types of personality, the seventh is the ten ways of divination and the laws explaining things, the eighth is the five ways of marking time, and the ninth is the five kinds of good fortune. These nine categories include political, social, and celestial relations in what is now known as the "realms," or what we would call "categories" in English.

In the history of Chinese culture, the Spring and Autumn period was an axial age, when humankind began to use abstract thinking and transcendental concepts to explain various phenomena around them. Axial ages have functioned similarly in other cultural systems. For example, Aristotle wrote a treatise precisely on the classification of things. Judeo-Christian scriptures are also often found to have various classifications of cosmic changes and human systems. In China some of the terms and concepts mentioned above were passed down from generation to generation over the centuries. To this day, traditional Chinese medicine (or what Chinese people simply call "Chinese medicine") and Chinese cooking often function on the basis of five elements ideas.

The five elements (metal, wood, water, fire, and earth) divide everything in the universe into visible natural elements. The appearance of "metal" indicates that China had already entered the Bronze Age when the classification system was invented, otherwise the concept of metal would not exist. In contrast to China, India's system of classification had only four elements: wind, earth, water, and fire, but no metal. In the "Hongfan" chapter mentioned above, the first of the nine categories follow the order "water, fire, wood, metal, and earth." Water is characterized by moisture, and water either flows or seeps downward; fire is characterized by flames rushing upward; wood is characterized by curves and straightness, but the curved parts can be straightened, and the straight parts can be bent; metal is constantly changing between solids, liquids, and gases; earth is the most important as the basic necessity for agricultural production.

In the "Hongfan" chapter, tastes are assigned to each of the five elements: water is salty, a concept probably derived from the salinity of seawater; fire is bitter, as the taste of charcoal is bitter; wood is sour, and while the origin of this is unclear, we might imagine that fruits are sour until they ripen; metal is pungent and offensive to the nose, perhaps because it gives off an acrid taste when it is cast in bronze; crops that grow out of the earth are our lives' most important resource, and both rice and millet have a sweet taste when chewed. The five elements not only give rise to one another, but also overcome one another, with water overcoming fire, fire overcoming metal, metal overcoming wood, wood overcoming earth, and earth overcoming water, all of which makes sense. The five elements can exist in harmony if they give rise to one another, overcome one another, and are compatible with each other (the similar phenomenon of succession and overcoming in the Eight Trigrams of the *Book of Changes* will be discussed in later chapters). However, in the mutual succession and overcoming, there are still differences in strength and weakness.

Ideally, strength and weakness would be present in equal proportions. For example, metal can produce water (for example, by digging wells), and strong metal requires water to cool quickly in order to create a sharp blade; metal overcoming wood has to do with an axe cutting wood, but cutting too deeply damages the wood; too much water and too little earth means flooding, and planting can only be carried out when water and earth are in proper proportions. Most of these explanations come from the experience of everyday life. In traditional China, the five elements were everywhere: earth is needed for farming and harvesting crops; houses are made of wood, tile roofs, and earthen walls; earthen dikes prevent floods and deep wells are used to fetch water; for everyday cooking, earthen stoves, charcoal, and iron pots are used to cook tea and rice. The sequence of daily life is in fact the interplay of the five elements.

In traditional times, the concept of the five elements was indeed intimately related to life. A few years ago, my wife, Manli, and I were relaxing at West Lake, and experienced ourselves the five elements. In a small cafe by the lake on Beishan Road, the owner had prepared a table and chairs for us. Water was boiling on a small charcoal stove, wine was warming in a copper pot, and the owner used a bamboo spoon to add boiling water to a small teapot to make tea. Wind chimes tinkled in the branches of nearby trees. These were simple pleasures involving all the five elements—metal, wood, water, fire, and earth.

By the Han dynasty, the concept of the five elements had clearly taken root in people's minds. Chinese characters are traditionally divided among six lexicographic categories, with most belonging to phono-semantic compounds. Such characters are made up of a radical which suggests something about its meaning and another element which is a guide to its pronunciation. Xu Shen's 許慎 (58–148) *Shuowen jiezi* 説文解字 is the first Chinese dictionary. In Xu's arrangement, based on the principle of "grouping [the characters] according to their characteristics," he created more than 200 categories to cover the entire body of characters. This dictionary is not only an orthographical dictionary, but also a concrete reflection of the cosmology of the time. In the characters having the "wood" (*mu* 木) radical, there are trees of all kinds as well as tools or implements made of wood; for those with the "water" (*shui* 水) radical, we find rivers, streams, lakes, ponds, as well as things in a liquid state, and phenomena related to water vapor. This makes sense; further details are not necessary. This may be a special characteristic of the Chinese writing system. If it was an alphabetic system, it would be difficult to present phenomena in terms of their concrete form.

In *Shuowen jiezi*, the percentage of phono-semantic characters is greater than that of the other five categories, surely accounting for more than 70% of the total. The Qing period's *Kangxi Dictionary* (*Kangxi zidian* 康熙字典), the last major dictionary in China compiled in the traditional way, contained

47,035 characters categorized according to 214 different radicals, most of which were phono-semantic characters. I did a little analysis of what the most important radicals were, and my results showed that the metal, wood, water, fire, and earth radicals—together with related radicals which are variants of these—account for a total of 12,791 characters. In other words, these 10 radicals, those of the five elements and their variants, which make up less than 4% of the total number of radicals, still account for a quarter of the total number of characters. Compared to radicals for cows, horses, sheep, fish, birds, grass, beans, and other common animals and plants, the number of words belonging to each radical is only a few dozen to a hundred. This is one way to gauge the influence of the concept of the five elements in the Chinese classification of things.

The concept of the five elements is still the most important metaphysical foundation for the theories of Chinese medicine today. *The Inner Classic of the Yellow Emperor* is the most important theoretical text in Chinese medicine, the main theory of which is to place the organs of the body and the strength of the various forces under the five elements, all of which can be represented as follows:

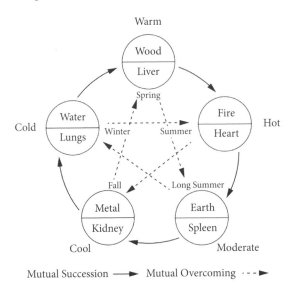

Fig. 5 Various Forces under the Five Elements

The liver, heart, lungs, kidneys, and spleen in the body are linked to wood, water, metal, fire, and earth, and their nature is described respectively as warm, hot, cool, cold, and moderate. Adding the four seasons and the four directions to this schema based on five categories is hard to arrange. Chinese medicine practitioners put an "earth" at the center of the four directions, which looks a little contrived; likewise, they added a "long summer" to the four seasons to get to five, which looks contrived as well. Equally contrived are the cold of winter, the heat of summer, the dryness of the fall and the warmth of the spring. Where do they go?

According to Chinese medical theory, the human body is actually a mini-universe, and the changes in the big universe outside have a certain effect on the small universe. These theories are used to explain that each organ has its own characteristics, and that the change of seasons will trigger changes in the organs themselves, changes which can sometimes result in imbalance, which can produce illness. In the cognitive system of Chinese medicine, spring makes one prone to the occurrence of "warm" diseases (the characters for "plague" 瘟 and for "warmth" 溫 in Chinese have similar elements). Summer is the time for heat illnesses, such as heatstroke, which is a common concept. Autumn is cool, winter is cold, and these are seasons when illnesses are common. In addition to seasonal changes, people's emotions, diet, environment, and other external conditions also vary, and the imbalances within the body caused by these changes are understood by Chinese medicine as causing illness. The basic principle of Chinese medicine is to correct the deviations that cause abnormalities: for those who are too cold, warmth is used to compensate; for those who are too hot, coolness is used to dissipate the heat, and so on.

The process of diagnosis in Chinese medicine involves looking, smelling, questioning, and palpitating; in other words, the Chinese medical practitioner will observe the patient's color, sniff the patient's breath, question the patient about the course of their illness, and take the patient's pulse in order to determine the internal deviations of the body. Chinese medicine is mainly herbal, supplemented by some natural compounds. Each medicine is classified by experience into five categories: warm, cool, cold, hot, and neutral. In the concept of Chinese medicine, every drug has certain characteristics; if used on its own, the medicinal properties may be too strong or too weak. A medicine that is too strong must be diluted somewhat by another; a medicine that is too weak must be strengthened by another: these two medicines are thought of as being like a "king" and a "minister," who are meant to complement one another. More herbs will have to be added in the event of an over-correction or deficiency.

The third complementary medication is referred to as the "assistant" and the last element of fine tuning, the "servant." In addition to the four types of medicine, namely, ruler, minister, assistant, and servant, there is also the medium, or the "vehicle," which is the water, oil, honey, wine, etc. used to administer the medicine. Let's take the example of Ephedra Soup from the popular late 17th-century *Recipes in Rhymes* (*Tangtou gejue* 湯頭歌訣) book of prescriptions. In this soup-based medicine, which treats chills, fever, headaches, and joint pain—or what we commonly call today a "bad cold"—ephedra is the "ruler" ingredient and promotes sweating; a cassia twig is the "minister" ingredient and assists ephedra in inducing perspiration; almond is the "assistant" ingredient, aiding ephedra to relieve asthma symptoms; and licorice root is the "servant" ingredient, harmonizing all of the others. The terms "ruler, minister, assistant, and servant" can also be called primary, complementary, adjuvant and priming herbs, and the adjuvant medicine is sometimes called the "second complementary."

Thus the ruler, the minister, the assistant, and the servant are four important aspects of prescribing in traditional Chinese medicine. Every Chinese medicine practitioner uses his or her own judgment in making prescriptions. There is no chemical analysis in Chinese medicine, which means that the strength or weakness of the medicines in a prescription can only be assessed by the practitioner based on experience and intuition. In traditional Chinese medicine, there is a saying that "healing is understanding." As a result, the formulas prescribed by each practitioner vary in terms of the specific ruler, minister, assistant and servant used; in addition, the fine-tuning process will not necessarily follow the four concepts, because some prescriptions require as many as eight ingredients.

For doctors who are particularly sophisticated in the use of drugs, both the "ruler" and the "minister" may be made up of four or five ingredients; indeed, the prescriptions of well-known doctors often include many medicinal herbs. Since the Tang dynasty, *The Divine Farmer's Materia Medica* (*Shen Nong bencao jing* 神農本草經)[1] has been viewed as an authoritative volume on the medicinal properties of Chinese medicines. Most of the medicines included in this volume are herbal, with some other supplementary medicines; the book is a taxonomic dictionary of medicines. By the Ming dynasty, Li Shizhen's 李時珍 *Compendium of Materia Medica* (*Bencao wangmu* 本草綱目) had become the most complete collection of Chinese pharmacopoeia, as well as a classic for discussing all the ingredients used in prescriptions.

In addition to the study of materia medica, Chinese medical textbooks also include what they called the study of prescriptions, which contain standardized prescriptions for various preparations. Some of the reference books for medical practitioners in the past were Ge Hong's 葛洪 (283–343) *Emergency Prescriptions Kept Up One's Sleeve* (*Zhouhou fang* 肘後方), Sun Simiao's 孫思邈 (581–682) *One Thousand Golden Remedies* (*Qianjin fang* 千金方), and Wang Ang's 汪昂 (1615–1694) above-mentioned *Recipes in Rhymes*, which was the most commonly used by folk doctors in the Qing dynasty. These tried and tested prescriptions are a collection of commonly used and effective remedies that can be found throughout the Chinese world. Every practitioner will refer to these formulas, employing and modifying them in daily practice, making notes about the results obtained. One tried and true prescription can in fact become a series of quite different prescriptions, as they are modified and added to over the generations. In traditional Chinese medicine, there are also some patented medicines, such as Po Chai pills and loquat syrup, among others. Their ingredients are very

---

1   This text is a compilation of oral traditions and is believed to have been written ca. 200–250. The original text no longer exists but is said to have contained 365 entries. —Ed.

complicated, with many medicines added and subtracted beyond those of ruler, minister, assistant, and servant. These additions and subtractions are all the result of the experience of doctors and the pharmacists.

The process is one of empirical development or, in today's jargon, a record of clinical practice. Traditional medicine, guided by the theory of the five elements succeeding and overcoming one another, employs a philosophical mindset that sees the human body as a mini-universe, corresponding with and parallel to the larger universe, to discuss illnesses and administer medication without any chemical analysis of the drugs in use. Therefore, traditional medicine cannot be considered a science. However, with the experience accumulated over a long period of time, it has developed into a medical practice with considerable efficacy, despite certain limitations.

Acupuncture is another practice existing in parallel with traditional medicine. As early as the Neolithic period, we find traces of the use of sharp stone tools as medical instruments. As part of our daily experience, most of us have felt the numbness that comes from hitting a sharp object somewhere on our body. This phenomenon, of course, is due to an accidental collision of a sharp object with the node of a certain nerve, causing pain or numbness. This may have been the origin of the study of acupuncture, which gradually evolved into a medical practice.

Although the study of acupuncture in China is grounded in the concepts of the five elements, its theoretical assumptions are based on the concepts of *jing*, *qi*, and *shen*, as discussed in Chapter II. Since time immemorial, there have been different understandings of these three terms. In his *Instructions for Practical Living* (*Chuanxi lu* 傳習錄), the Ming dynasty Neo-Confucian scholar Wang Yangming 王陽明 (1472–1529) argued that the three are different forms of the same thing: "When it is flowing it is *qi*, when concentrated it is *jing*, and when used with subtlety, it is *shen*." To put it simply, we can understand *jing* as the essence of life, *shen* as the rational and emotional spirit, and *qi* is the vital force, which some people call energy, which permeates the entire world. The physiological reactions of the human body and human behavior are in fact related to the nervous system.

On the other hand, blood and lymphatic fluid circulate throughout the body. The entire human body is a superposition of several large circulatory systems, the result of the coordination of many structural functions among various organs. In Chinese acupuncture, the main focus is to understand and control the various flows of *qi* energy. Most modern researchers of acupuncture today believe that the meridian system used in acupuncture has a close relationship with the nervous system; some scholars also argue that the flow of lymphatic fluid and blood can also be treated by acupuncture. We have not yet been able to ascertain whether these statements are true or not. This is especially the case because lymphatic fluid does not follow well-defined channels, making it quite difficult to know where it is and how it flows.

Chinese acupuncture focuses on finding and stimulating meridian points in order to regulate the body's functions. By the Han dynasty, acupuncturists had identified about 180 meridian points. As of today, there are more than 700. The number of meridian points grows through a process of random discovery followed by verification in a process of trial and error. Hence with time, the number of acupuncture points in the body increases.

There are more than 300 meridian points on the human body—from the "One Hundred Convergence" point on the top of the head to the "Gushing Spring" point on the soles of the feet—which can be found in today's medical books and on the "copper man diagram" (a model of the human form showing the meridian points, originally made in copper, or a diagram based on the model). The names of some points contain words like "pass", "door," or "mouth," while others have various names including words like "repository," "warehouse," and "sea", "marsh," or "pool." Linking these names together gives us the impression that the human body resembles a three-dimensional map: some of the meridian points house certain substances or energies, as suggested by their names, like the characters for "repository" and "pond"; others are gateways through which things pass, indicated by characters like "pass" and "mouth"; most of the meridian points are called "caves," which function as both storage locations and passageways. Inserting acupuncture needles at these inter-sections is equivalent to putting a lane change sign somewhere on today's highway system, diverting traffic to an alternate route. According to the science of acupuncture, blockage of *qi* energy will lead to disease. The cure is to find an alternative route so that the blocked blood can begin to flow. To extend the metaphor: where there is "traffic congestion" in the body, a planned approach to controlling the flow of traffic and relieving the congestion is another approach to finding relief.

Using this analogy, anyone who drives a car frequently will certainly be able to understand the theoretical basis of acupuncture, which is to take the human body as a mini universe, and extend the phenomena occurring in the macro universe to the flow of energy in the smaller universe. The fluidity and stagnation studied by the science of acupuncture may also occur due to external influences on the body, interfering with the original flow. For example, eating inappropriate foods creates an unhealthy ratio of nutrients within the body; inappropriate behavior can also affect the internal balance of the body. Any other external or internal reaction can lead to disorder and disease in various parts of the body. Acupuncture treatments can either unblock channels within the body, or use "capacity" stored elsewhere to transfer energy to the patient to adjust the imbalance.

This theory is grounded in the basic idea that the human body is a naturally balancing system. In the event of disorder, the body's ability to regain its balance is used to correct any deviations and resulting illnesses. Acupuncture, like traditional Chinese medicine, assumes that the human body is self-sufficient, and even in the event of external inter-ference, the body can adjust itself to eliminate the disease brought about by that interference. Chinese medical theories lack understanding of bacteria and viruses. As a result, Chinese medicine does not have good solutions for infectious diseases. In Chinese culture, the metaphysics of the mini universe and the macro universe are interrelated. This meta-physical theory affects Chinese people's minds and bodies, as well as their worldview.

The science of Chinese cooking is related to the theory of Chinese medicine. The Chinese culinary arts emphasize the coordination and balance of the "five tastes," which may have grown out of the concept of the five elements or could perhaps have been the result of direct experience. The "five tastes" are sweet, sour, bitter, spicy, and salty, and a good dish needs a balance of all five tastes. The five tastes represent the five elements, and indirectly explain the body's need for various nutrients.

We cannot live without salt. As early as the Neolithic Age, salt was a commodity that was transported from salt-producing areas to other locations. When humans lack salt, they often try to extract it from the blood of animals, showing that is the most important of the five flavors. In ancient China, sucrose was not used as a sweetener; it later came to China from India. In ancient times, honey was likely the main sweetener, but there were later other sweetening agents produced from grains, such as maltose and fermented rice. The earliest sour tastes probably came from plums and other acidic fruits, while bitter tastes were provided by plants such as dandelions (or tea).

Spicy flavors, which did not originally include today's chili pepper—which was cultivated in the New World and not introduced to China until the 16th century—were probably dominated by ginger, but may have included pepper plants as well. Sauces have only become popular in modern times. Especially important to this development were soya paste, soy sauce, and black bean sauce, all made from wheat and soy beans, which are used as salt additives. Grains are fermented and sweetened, becoming rice wine, which is further transformed into wine, and then into vinegar, through the addition of sweet, spicy, and sour ingredients. Pungent and spicy plants from elsewhere in the world have given the Chinese many choices other than ginger and pepper.

The Chinese culinary culture involves not only the harmonization of the five tastes, but also the interpretation and understanding of food in terms of four or five categories. Here, we will cite two passages to illustrate that this system of classifying ingredients or flavors, and the relationship between them, was already established in the Spring and Autumn and

Warring States periods. There is a passage in *The Zuo Tradition* (*Zuo zhuan* 左傳)[2] that contrasts cooking with the principle of governance, pointing out the importance of harmonizing the five tastes. The basic spirit of this system is to point out that the compatibility of multiple factors is far better than the exclusive focus on a single factor.

When the marquis of Qi returned from his hunt, Yanzi was with him in the tower of Chuan, and Ziyou drove up to it at full speed. The marquis said, "It is only Ju [another name for Ziyou] who is in harmony with me!" Yanzi replied, "Ju is an assenter merely; how can he be considered in harmony with you?" "Are they different," asked the marquis, "harmony and assent?" Yanzi said, "They are different. Harmony may be illustrated by soup. You have the water and fire, vinegar, pickle, salt, and plums, with which to cook fish. It is made to boil by the firewood, and then the cook mixes the ingredients, harmoniously equalizing the several flavors, so as to supply whatever is deficient and carry off whatever is in excess. Then the master eats it, and his mind is made equable. So it is in the relations of ruler and minister. When there is in what the ruler approves of anything that is not proper, the minister calls attention to that impropriety, so as to make the approval entirely correct. When there is in what the ruler disapproves of anything that is proper, the minister brings forward that propriety, so as to remove occasion for the disapproval. In this way the government is made equal, with no infringement of what is right, and there is no quarrelling with it in the minds of the people. Hence it is said in the ode: 'There are also the well-tempered soups,/Prepared beforehand, the ingredients rightly proportioned/By these offerings we invite his presence without a word;/ Nor is there now any contention in the service.' As the ancient kings established the doctrine of the five flavors, so they made the harmony of

---

2   *The Zuo Tradition* is a narrative history traditionally regarded as a commentary on the *Spring and Autumn Annals* (*Chunqiu* 春秋). It covers the period from 722 to 481 BCE, and focuses mainly on political, diplomatic, and military affairs. —Ed.

the five notes, to make their minds equable and to perfect their government. There is an analogy between sounds and flavors. There are the
breath, the two classes of dances, the three subjects, the materials from
the four quarters, the five notes, the six pitch-pipes, the seven sounds,
the eight winds, the nine songs; [by these nine things the materials
for music] are completed. Then there are the distinctions of clear and
thick, small and large, short and long, fast and slow, solemn and joyful,
hard and soft, lingering and rapid, high and low, the commencement
and close, the close and the diffuse, by which the parts are all blended
together. The superior man listens to such music, that his mind may be
composed. His mind is composed, and his virtues become harmonious.
Hence it is said in the ode, 'There is no flaw in his virtuous fame.' Now it
is not so with Ju. Whatever you say 'Yes' to, he also says 'Yes.' Whatever
you say 'No' to, he also says 'No.' If you were to try to give water a flavor
with water, who would care to partake of the result? If lutes were to be
confined to one note, who would be able to listen to them? Such is the
insufficiency of mere assent."[3]

The following passage in the *The Annals of Lü Buwei* (*Lüshi qingqiu*
呂氏春秋) is based on the theories of Yi Yin 伊尹 of the Shang dynasty,
which actually reflects the concepts about cooking from the Warring States
to the early Qin dynasty. This part of the text concerns not only about
harmonization of the five flavors, but also the characteristics of the ingredients themselves and their compatibility with each other. There is also
considerable discussion of the cooking methods already in use at the time.

When Tang got Yi Yin, he performed rites of purgation on him in the
ancestral temple, lighting a bundle of wood to eliminate noxious influences, and smearing him with the blood of a sacrificial pig. The next day

---

3   Translation taken from James Legge, trans., *The Chinese Classics, Volume V: The
    Ch'un tsěw, with the Tso chuen, Part II* (Hong Kong : Lane, Crawford & Co.; London:
    Trunbner & Co.), 684.

at his morning court, he gave an audience to Yi Yin with due ceremony. Yi Yin spoke to Tang about perfect flavors. Tang asked, "Can they be acquired and prepared?" Yi Yin replied, "The small size of my lord's state is insufficient to supply them. Only after he has become Son of Heaven can they be supplied. Now, there are three tribes of creatures: the water dwellers, which smell fishy; the carnivores, which smell rank; and the herbivores, which have a fetid smell. Although malodorous and evil smelling, they can be refined when each is properly used. As a general rule, the fundamental rule in preparing flavors is that Water is the first ingredient. For the Five Tastes and the three materials, as well as the nine simmerings and nine transformations, fire serves as the regulator. At times quick and at times slow, it eliminates fishiness, removes rankness, and eradicates fetidness. One must be sure that while these are overcome, one does not lose the inherent qualities of flavor. In the task of harmonizing and blending one must use the sweet, sour, bitter, acrid, and salty. The balancing of what should be added first or last and of whether to use more or less, is very subtle, as each variation gives rise to its own effect. The transformation within the cauldron is quintessential, marvelous, extremely fine, and delicate. The mouth cannot describe it; the mind cannot find an illustrative example. It is like the subtle arts of archery and horsemanship, the products of the mixing of Yin and Yang, and the different methods practiced in the four seasons. Thus, it keeps for a long time and does not ruin, is thoroughly cooked but not mushy, sweet but not cloying, sour but not excessively so, salty but not deadening, acrid but not caustic, mild but not bland, rich with fats but not greasy?"[4]

The foodstuffs listed in the following passage include some of the animals, seafood, fruits, and vegetables that are still around today. The text also mentions a few foods seen in legends—such as the phoenix

---

4   John Knoblock and Jeffrey Riegel, trans., *The Annals of Lü Buwei: A Complete Translation and Study* (Stanford, CA: Stanford University Press, 2000), 308–309.

egg—which we have omitted. On the basis on this passage, it is clear the range of goods eaten by the royal family at that time was far simpler than today. However, there are many ingredients, especially fruits, vegetables and condiments, that are still present in today's daily diet. The fact that wheat is not included as a staple food in the Chinese diet is a sign of the state of knowledge at the time, because while wheat, especially wheat flour, was known in the Han period, it became more common after the Tang and Song dynasties.

The finest of the meats are the lips of the *xingxing* ape; the feet of the *huanhuan* badger; the fleshy tail of the *junyan* bird; the paws of the shudang; the short tail the *maoxiang*....

The finest of the fish are the perch of Lake Dongting and the miniature fish of the Eastern Sea; a fish in the Li River called Pearl Turtle, which has six feet, has pearl-like nodules, and is jade-colored; and a fish in the Guan River called the "flying fish"; which is shaped like a carp with wings and which flies nightly from the Western Sea to the Eastern Sea.

The finest of the edible plants are the cress of Kunlun and the flower of the Longevity Tree; the leaves of the Vermilion Tree and the Black Tree that grow east of Zhigu in the state of Zhongrong; an edible plant colored like green jade, called the "lucky tree"; that grows to the south of Yumao, on a cliff at the edge of the southern limit; the fragrant cress of Yanghua; the celery of Yunmeng; the kale of Juqu; and a grass of Jinyuan called "flower of the soil."

The finest of the seasoning agents are the ginger from Yangpu; the cinnamon from Zhaoyao; the bamboo shoots from Yueluo; the vinegar made from Zhanwei sturgeon; the salt from Daxia; the dewy waters from Zaijie, which have the color of white jade; and the eggs from Changze.

The finest of the grains are the millet of Dark Mountain; the foxtail millet of Mount Buzhou; the panicled millet of Bright Mountain; and the black glutinous panicled millet of the Southern Sea.

The finest of the fruits are those of the Shatang tree; the hundred fruits eaten by all the Sovereigns, which grow north of Mount Chang, atop the Tou Gorge; the sweet berries found east of Mount Ji, in the nesting place of the Azure Bird; the tangerines from the banks of the

Yangzi; the pomelos of Yunmeng; and the stone ears from the banks of the Han River.[5]

From the above discussion, we can see that the classifications in culinary culture attempt to merge classifications based on "five" and "four." As mentioned, the five-based divisions are related to the five elements of metal, wood, water, fire, and earth, while the four-based divisions are closely related to the spatial and temporal divisions of the four directions and the four seasons. In the above quotations, the merger of the two systems is not yet altogether clear. In culinary texts of later generations, as well as in the texts of some modern food writers and what are called food therapists, the two classification systems are presented in parallel in the discussion of the characteristics of ingredients.

Since the Qin and Han dynasties, there have been so many texts discussing culinary culture that we cannot list them all. Here we will only introduce the concepts of dietary therapy advocated in the Yuan dynasty text *Dietary Principles* (*Yinshan zhengyao* 飲膳正要) and in modern Chinese medicine. Generally speaking, dietary therapy classifies food ingredients into four categories: hot, warm, cool, and cold. The occurrence of these four characteristics is correlated with seasonal climate changes throughout the year. For example, according to Chinese medicine, grains, fruits, and vegetables have characteristics of the seasons in which they come to maturity: wheat that ripens in early spring has the characteristics of spring, being "warm;" sorghum and corn that ripen in summer are "hot"; rice that ripens in autumn is "cool"; late-ripening beans are "cold." The characteristics of ingredients described in this classification are not really related to the four starch-based foods mentioned above. Such a classification, therefore, can only represent a metaphysical idea, not a conclusion based on empirical experience.

---

5   Knoblock and Riegel, trans., *The Annals of Lü Buwei: A Complete Translation and Study*, 310–311.

Following the same principle, traditional food science classifies fruits into four or five categories of color, depending on when they ripen, to determine their characteristics. The plum has the "warm" character of spring, the apricot has the "hot" character of summer, the peach has the "cool" character of autumn, and the chestnut has the "cold" character of winter. Similar classifications can be applied to five types of animals: chicken is "warm", lamb and beef are "hot", horse meat is "cool," and pork is "cold." An even stranger classification is one by color. Tangerines, oranges, and grapefruit ripen at the same time, and should thus belong to the same category. But because oranges are red, they are classified as "warm"; white grapefruits are "cool," while light yellow tangerines are neutral. These classifications, which are clearly arbitrary, do not exactly fit the characteristics of these foods.

The classification of animals, when describing the characteristics of chickens, cows, sheep and pigs, is completely different from the other classification systems already discussed here. In terms of Chinese ideas about diet, meat is often classified into two categories: land animals (chickens, ducks, geese, cows, sheep and pigs) and seafood (fish, shrimp, turtle and crab). Land-based products are seen as "warm" and seafood as "cool." There are two types of land animals: deer and sheep are kept in the mountains and are hot; cattle are neutral and pigs are warm; geese and ducks are mostly kept in the wild and are hot; chickens are kept at home and are mild. Obviously, these distinctions are entirely subjective, based on the seasons and growing conditions rather than on empirical evidence. In summary, I believe that Chinese food therapy and medical science are closely related to the classification of the characteristics of various foods, and there is no theoretical relevance to the concepts of fat, fiber, sugar, vitamins, and so forth studied today from a biochemical perspective. These notions, rather than being a traditional ecological concept in Chinese culture, are opinions rather than the result of academic research.

These classifications can be seen in everyday life and reflect the fact that a set of metaphysical concepts has become deeply rooted in people's hearts and become part of everyday experience. Similar concepts can also be found in eating habits. When older people, like my elders and those of my generation, go to a Chinese restaurant, they are accustomed to ordering four dishes, fairly evenly distributed among the four categories of meat, vegetables, land-based products, and water-based products. At the same time, there is a set of taboos regarding daily diet, especially for the sick, for pregnant women, and for women who just gave birth.

Prior to the Sino-Japanese War, Chinese traditional culture had not completely disappeared, and the general living conditions had not been destroyed by wars and revolutions, so the middle and upper classes were able to eat properly. In my memory, home-cooked meals did follow the custom of four dishes and one soup, with an even distribution of meat and vegetables, land-based and water-based foods. More formal banquets required at least two sets of four dishes and one soup, or four stir-fried dishes and four main dishes, that is, eight dishes and one soup—all of which could be expanded to fit the size of the banquet. In addition to the distribution of meat and vegetables, there are also the considerations of different cooking methods—steaming, boiling, stir-frying, and quick-frying.

Cooking with heat can be done directly by using fire (grilling, baking, roasting, smoking, broiling); indirectly using water (steaming, boiling, simmering, stewing); by using oil (frying in shallow oil, stir-frying, quick-frying, deep-frying, searing), and indirectly in clay pots (braising, simmering). Cooking also may occur through the processes of salting and marinating (pickling, soaking in wine, vinegar, molasses, sauces, spices, etc.). The use of condiments adds complexity, because with more choices comes more combinations. Generally speaking, a variety of condiments is used in the preparation of any dish, in particular soy sauce. There seems to be a distinction between primary and secondary cooking ingredients: salty and sweet complement each other, as do sour and spicy, and spicy and bitter—which might remind us of the role of ruler, minister, assistant and servant in the medical world, the point being to achieve perfect harmony and taste. These different approaches are individually compatible with the already discussed concepts of warmth, heat, coolness, and coldness.

Chinese culinary culture is one of the most complex and sophisticated in the world. Part of the reason for this is the accumulation of history, in addition to the fact that products from different parts of China vary greatly depending on climate, water, and soil conditions. Today, some say there are four major cuisines, while others identify eight, or even more by province or region. China is in constant contact with other cultures from all over the world, often importing and assimilating foreign ingredients and cooking methods, accumulating more experience, and integrating them into a complex Chinese culinary culture. In this integration process, due to the mutual mapping between the large and small universes of Chinese medical culture, the categorization theory described in this chapter has become the metaphysical support for the organization of Chinese culinary culture.

In summary, whether it is medicine, acupuncture, or cooking, Chinese culture has developed into a complex dynamic system based on the interaction and cross-fertilization of a variety of factors or ingredients based on groups of four or five elements. These are areas in which Chinese people experience diverse and interactive changes in their daily lives. This is the cosmic outlook and attitude to life that is characteristic of Chinese culture—an outlook and attitude that are very different from other cultures around the world.

V. The Ever-Changing Universe

This chapter is based on the world presented in the traditional Chinese classic *The Book of Changes* 易經 (*Yijing*) and explores the Chinese concept of a forever-changing universe. The *Yijing* is a book that has a special place among China's 13 classics. Although Confucianism treats the *Yijing* as a Confucian classic, written by King Wen of the Zhou dynasty and interpreted by Confucius himself, the divination methods discussed in the *Yijing* actually have a much longer history. Students of ancient Chinese history know that in the Shang dynasty there was a method of divination that involved burning cracks in ox scapula or the undershells of tortoises to predict the future. The physical evidence for this method are the inscriptions on the many fragments of oracle bones that continue to be found in Shang dynasty sites. However, as we know from frequent passages in ancient texts like *The Zuo Tradition* and the *Discourses of the States* (*Guoyu* 國語)[1], divination through oracle bones was only one of the

---

1   This ancient text is a collection of speeches attributed to rulers and other men from the Spring and Autumn period. —Ed.

methods of foretelling the future; another method, presented in the *Yijing*, uses the stalks of the yarrow plant. The two forms of divination were seen as complementary, one confirming the other. Between the two, oracle bones seem to have been more authoritative, whereas the written prophecies produced through the yarrow stalk divination leave more room for detailed interpretation.

In my view, these two methods of fortune telling may represent divination methods developed by two different cultures. Stalk divination perhaps emerged outside of the Shang dynasty, as its language suggests a landscape with high mountains and valleys—not low-lying canyons, but rather swampy, stagnant grasslands. Phenomena mentioned in the *Yijing* hexagrams include welcoming the bride with horses and wagons, and cooking sheep for food. The landscape and cultural images may well come from the region now known as Shaanxi and Gansu provinces, where there are towering snow-capped mountains and grasslands formed by melting snow flowing onto the plains. Since the Neolithic era, this region has had a unique culture, and maintained an agro-pastoral lifestyle for a long time. This is the very region where the Zhou and their ally, the Jiang people, were found. Since the relationship between King Wen of Zhou and the *Yijing* is now acknowledged to be a legend, it is not necessary to consider him the author or compiler of the work, but we may well consider *Yijing* divination as the type of prophecy that developed in northwest China.

The *Yijing* divination method divides 49 yarrow stalks into two separate heaps three times in a row, in manipulations that result in three bundles of stalks which are then assigned either an odd or an even number. (In today's divination, some Chinese people use bamboo blocks or coins instead of stalks, with the "heads" or "tails" of the blocks or coins representing odd and even numbers). The odd and even numbers are arranged together to form the images we see in the *Yijing*. The odd number is represented by an unbroken, or *yang*, horizontal line, and the even number by a broken, discontinuous, *yin* horizontal line, and the lines are subsequently assigned one of four numbers: six, seven, eight, or nine.[2] There are eight possible configurations of trigrams made up of these two types of lines, hence the name of the Eight Trigrams.

The eight basic trigrams mentioned above are: *qian* 乾 (heaven), *kun* 坤 (earth), *zhen* 震 (thunder), *xun* 巽 (wind), *kan* 坎 (water), *li* 離 (fire), *gen* 艮 (mountain), and *dui* 兌 (marsh). *Qian* and *kun* represent, respectively, yin and yang, positive and negative, active and passive. At the same time, pure *qian* represents men and pure *kun* represents women. (This concept, of course, is a phenomenon that emerged in a male-dominated society and is no longer relevant). In addition to *qian* and *kun*, other opposing pairs include *gen* (mountain) and *dui* (marsh), *xun* (wind) and *zhen* (thunder), and *kan* (water) and *li* (fire), all of which are polar opposites. Yin and yang, however must be in harmony to achieve unity. Fire and water can both complete and overcome one another. Wind and thunder are opposed, as thunder rises from the ground, while wind descends from above—imagine a vast plain where the climate has changed dramatically and a hurricane comes down with a bolt of lightning, as if the sky and the earth were fighting. When wind and thunder come together, rain comes down in torrents, another example of conflict and mutual benefit. The mountains are high and mighty, while the marsh forms a broad base below; without the low level of the marsh, the mountains would not be high enough, and without the high mountains, the marsh would not be able to accumulate as much snow melt from the mountains. These four pairs of mutually opposing and completing elements can continue to be combined in infinite variations.

---

2   The result of the four operations is that any given line will have a numerical value of either nine (an "old" *yang*) or eight (a "young" *yin*), or seven (a "young" *yang*) or six (an "old" *yin*), and that a "old" line indicates a change into its opposite. What this means in practice is that if one or more lines appear in a hexagram, the result will be the production ("derivative" might be a better word for it) of another hexagram with the changed lines supplanting the original ones. Generally speaking, this second hexagram also has to be taken into account in any divination. —Trans.

In terms of mechanics, as understood in modern physics, the two pairs of trigrams *qian* (heaven)/*kun* (earth) and *gen* (mountain)/*dui* (marsh) possess potential energy: changes in their positions can produce energy and bring about change. The trigram pairs *zhen* (thunder)/*xun* (wind) and *kan* (water)/*li* (fire) possess kinetic energy. When combined with other trigrams, they too can produce change. The arrangement of the eight trigrams will reveal 384 different "scenarios," each with corresponding individual changes.

In Figure 6, you can see the names of the eight trigrams (the characters nearest the circle), as well as their composition. Moreover, if you combine the eight trigrams with one another in all possible combinations, you will have a total of 64 hexagrams, each composed of six broken and unbroken lines, which is a much larger taxonomic group.

The key to *Yijing* divination is to find the appropriate line among the six to serve as the basis for the prognostication: the group from which to choose is made up of the 384 broken and unbroken lines found in the 64 hexagrams. The significance of the *Yijing* is to use these 300-odd phenomena, combined with more specific information, to provide an explanation, an answer, and advice. The explanations interpret each line of the hexagram, providing clues about the question you have asked. Proceeding through the six lines of the hexagram, from the bottom to the top, can illustrate how the future will develop, what trends are likely. Another means of divination involves splitting the hexagram into two halves, the upper and the lower, and then seeking out their intersection in a chart designed specifically for that purpose. The chart leads you to fuller interpretations of the hexagram and of individual lines within the hexagram and to other references. In other words, it is a binary number, not like the decimal system we are used to, but it is quite consistent with the way computers work today. Three hundred and eighty-four different phenomena can indeed encompass many possible situations in human life.

The *Yijing* is a classic that discusses change, and since ancient times, there have been three interpretations of the word *yi*: one is the book itself; another is that it means "change"; and the third is that it means

Fig. 6 Eight Trigrams (Later Heaven Sequence)

"changeless," the idea that while everything is constantly changing, this phenomenon—of constant change—is itself eternal. Scholars of the *Yijing* often say that the original meaning of *yi* was "chameleon," the small reptile that is constantly changing colors, an apt metaphor for the phenomenon of change described in the book.

Broken and unbroken lines like those found in the *Yijing*'s hexagrams also appear in the designs found on Neolithic pottery. The Chinese historian and paleographer Zhang Zhenglang 張政烺 (1912–2005) thought that these symbols were meant to convey certain meanings and he spent nearly 20 years of his life trying to decipher them, without success. Do these symbols represent a metaphorical code, or a series of numbers? And what would the numbers mean? We still don't know. The reason I bring up the phenomenon of the divination, which Mr. Zhang has been puzzling over throughout his life, is my hope that one day we will be able to interpret these codes. All we can say at this point is that the messages in the *Yijing* are simple and ambiguous, leaving a lot of room for readers to interpret the hexagram themselves.

Let's take the hexagram *Qian* 乾, for example. *Qian* is the first hexagram in the *Yijing*, made up of six unbroken lines, divided into two identical trigrams. The following is an explanation of the *Qian* hexagram:

> Qian represents what is great and originating, penetrating, advantageous, correct and firm.[3]
>
> The judgement says: Qian. Grandly supreme. Font of matter, Master of Heaven! The clouds pass, the rains fall, the array of matter flows into form. Crystal Comprehension of end and beginning. Each of the six places comes in its true time. Each of the six dragons rides heaven in due order. The Dao of qian is transformation, change. To things it gives their true nature, their true life-destiny. It preserves the great harmony. This profits, this is steadfast, the head raised high above the multitude of things. The myriad kingdoms all at peace."[4]
>
> On the image of the hexagram: "Heaven in its motion (gives) the idea of strength. The superior man, in accordance with this, nerves himself to ceaseless activity. The dragon lies hidden in the deep; it is not the time for active doing. The dragon appears in the field; the diffusion of virtuous influence has been wide. Active and vigilant all the treading of the proper path over and over again. He seems to be leaping up, but is still in the deep; if he advances, there will be no error. The dragon is on the wing in the sky; the great man rouses himself to his work. The dragon exceeds the proper limits; there will be occasion for repentance, a state of fullness, that is, should not be indulged in long. The same NINE (undivided) is used (in all the places of this hexagram), but the attribute of heaven should not (always) take the foremost place."[5]

---

3   James Legge, trans., *I Ching, Or The Book of Changes*, Kindle Edition, published by the Library of Alexandria. Originally published 1882, also available online as part of the Chinese Text Project, https://ctext.org/book-of-changes/yi-jing .

4   John Minford, trans., *I Ching (Yijing) The Book of Changes* (New York: Penguin, 2014), Kindle Edition.

5   Legge, trans., *I Ching*.

1. In the first (or lowest) NINE, undivided, (we see its subject as) the dragon lying hid (in the deep). It is not the time for active doing.
2. In the second NINE, undivided, (we see its subject as) the dragon appearing in the field. It will be advantageous to meet with the great man.
3. In the third NINE, undivided, (we see its subject as) the superior man active and vigilant all the day, and in the evening still careful and apprehensive. (The position is) dangerous, but there will be no mistake.
4. In the fourth NINE, undivided, (we see its subject as the dragon looking) as if he were leaping up, but still in the deep. There will be no mistake.
5. In the fifth NINE, undivided, (we see its subject as) the dragon on the wing in the sky. It will be advantageous to meet with the great man.
6. In the sixth (or topmost) NINE, undivided, (we see its subject as) the dragon exceeding the proper limits. There will be occasion for repentance.
7. (The lines of this hexagram are all strong and undivided, as appears from) the use of the number NINE. If the host of dragons (thus) appearing were to divest themselves of their heads, there would be good fortune.[6]

Reading the lines of the hexagram from the bottom to the top, the *qian* hexagram throughout represents firmness and strength, or, as the text itself said, "The superior man nerves himself to ceaseless activity." Reading the judgment, the lines of the hexagram also show a gradual progression from the dragon now hidden, now in the field, and now in the deep abyss, good things happening along the way, with the help of important people. By the fifth line, the dragon is already soaring across the sky in a display of extraordinary energy. However, in the sixth line, the haughty dragon begins to regret, which is a way of saying that when you achieve the maximum you may be too strong, too successful. There is no more

---

6   Ibid.

room left at the top, and the only way to go is down, which is a dilemma. The general understanding in China is that when a person is in an advantageous position, everything they do works out, yet when they arrive at the peak of success, they wish they could start over, because from the peak, the only way to go is down. So, the conclusion is not to be the leader of the pack. Let there be many dragons competing, without a clear winner. In the Chinese mind, the *qian* hexagram is a warning to an aggressive character, reminding us of what happens at the peak.

Now let us look at the 23rd hexagram, the *bo* hexagram. The *bo* is a very unlucky hexagram, in which *yang* strength is almost completely eclipsed, and the strength of *yin* dominates throughout, so that no progress is made without a struggle. What is described is a failure: the mountains have fallen, the foundation will not hold. Yet when things reach their nadir comes the moment to turn things around, because they cannot get any worse. The gentleman (or woman) seizes this moment, and as a useful person they know that they cannot relent or give in to despair but instead must cling to the Way of righteousness and exploit the opportunity. With persistence, the next step will lead them to the following hexagram, *fu*, which means "returning." Finally, arriving at the top line, we have our conclusion: the gentleman has a carriage, a usable vehicle, and can continue onward, leaving behind the difficult spot where he found himself during the bottom five lines. In other words, after repeated failure, progress. The meaning of this hexagram is precisely the opposite of that of the *qian* hexagram, and is to remind people that at the worst moments, there will be opportunities to turn things around.

The arrangement of the 64 hexagrams can be organized into a polygonal pattern. It would seem that in earlier times, the hexagrams were arranged in pairs, with hexagrams that opposed or completed one another placed diagonally. For example, *qian* was placed in the northeast corner on the upper right, and *kun*, which is considered *qian*'s partner, is placed in the southwest corner on the lower left. This arrangement was known as the Fuxi sequence (Fuxi being a mythical character believed by some to have invented the hexagrams), which later evolved to become to the King

Wen sequence (King Wen was believed traditionally to have compiled the *Yijing*), both emphasizing the dialectic between the opposite and the complementary. Later, the arrangement was changed and the hexagrams were arranged in an anti-clockwise direction, each hexagram followed by its opposite/complement, the whole arrangement illustrating the alternating of good and bad fortune, success and failure. For example, *qian* and *kun* are opposites/complements, as are *bo* and *fu* (hexagrams 23 and 24), and *sun* and *yi* (hexagrams 41 and 42), representing the ups and downs that we all know in our daily lives.

The arrangement as a whole illustrates the direction of change. In the image reproduced above, we see the two forces of yin and yang displayed in the *taiji* image (inside the circle), which looks like two fish chasing one other; this fully expresses the idea of ever-changing movement. Moreover, it is impossible to clearly tell which half of the image is black and which half is white, and if we imagine drawing a line from the center of the circle to a point on the circumference, and then moving the line around the entire circle, at no point will the line be either completely black or completely white. This means that the change from black to white is not sudden and abrupt, and that there is white in black and black in white. Such is the function of a two-dimensional dialectic. The changes from black to white are both hidden, yet announced before the change occurs.

The name of the *Yijing*, as mentioned earlier, means change or eternal change. There is not only variation between the hexagrams, but inside each hexagram, the six lines contain an alternance of yin and yang, expressing the constant transition between the two elements and illustrating the tension between the two poles.

The hexagrams in the *Yijing* were originally used for divination, and the situations described in the various hexagrams are perhaps examples of things that had occurred in the past, and thus serve as symbols representing the phenomena and situations described. The point of divination is to seek an answer to a question, and the situation symbolized in the *Yijing* hexagrams can serve as a reference, or even as evidence of what the outcome may be. This approach is what is called the study (or school) of "image and number" (*xiangshu zhi xue* 象數之學), a way of using the *Yijing* that is largely uninterested in the text, except to the extent that the structure of the hexagrams and the line relationships can be made to sound as if they explain it. Another approach is to summarize the many successes and failures of the past and come up with a set of choices that an individual should approach or avoid: this is what is known as the study of "meaning and principle" (*yili zhi xue* 義理之學). The study of the *Yijing* has always been comprised of these two approaches. Because the point of divination in ancient times was truly to foresee fortunate and unfortunate outcomes, the study of image and number came first and was more primitive. The study of meaning and principle was a later development.

Alongside the *Yijing*, other fields involving divination include geomancy—often called *fengshui*—and *qimen dunjia* 奇門遁甲 (lit. "mysterious gate escaping technique"), a form of divination based on the arrangement of numbers. We might see these as a kind of thinking that was practiced before the development of true science. Some people call them "pseudoscientific," but I think it might be more appropriate to think of them as "proto-scientific."

Let's start with geomancy, which is the art of bringing geographic forms together with human life, which we may call the primitive science of geographic placement. China's geographical location on the planet earth, together with its specific topography, determine the way human beings can live in harmony with nature in order to be safe and comfortable. China's geographical location is in mainland East Asia, with the northern and western parts of the country being high above sea level, and the east and the south descending to levels closer to sea level. The cold northwesterly winds that come in autumn and winter, especially in winter, bring cold weather to northern China. The monsoon winds from the southeast in spring and summer bring moist air. The climate in the south of China is mild and the north gets enough rain for plants to grow. The topography of China slopes from northwest to southeast, with highlands on the southern and eastern sides of the slope blocking the cool air, making the living conditions more comfortable. Rains in spring and summer can cause flooding in areas too close to the river. With these two conditions in mind, the Chinese built their houses and even their villages and markets on the east and south of the mountains, on the banks of rivers and lakes higher up from the water.

Archaeologically speaking, Neolithic sites in the Yellow River valley are usually found where two rivers meet or where the river bends, and are built on the two-level platform slightly above the water level. The position of the structure has its back to the northwest and faces the southeast. This kind of knowledge of geographical conditions must have been accumulated over a long period of time before the ancients understood how to find a suitable location for building a residence. On the northern loess plateau people lived in caves, almost all of which were dug out of the loess soil on the southern slope. Outside the door of the cave, facing south or east, there would be a relatively flat area, which was a space for activities, as well as a farmyard for growing fruits and vegetables. These considerations are, in fact, the original practice of the science of geomancy.

The first tangible manifestation of this experience in classical literature is in the *The Book of Poetry*:

> Of generous devotion to the people was duke Liu
> [His territory] being now broad and long,
> He determined the points of the heavens by means of the shadows;
> and then, ascending the ridges,
> He surveyed the light and the shade,
> Viewing [also] the [course of the] streams and springs.
> His armies were three troops;
> He measured the marshes and plains;
> He fixed the revenue on the system of common cultivation of the fields;
> He measured also the fields west of the hills;
> And the settlement of Bin became truly great.[7]

---

7   James Legge, trans., "Book of Poetry," Chinese Text Project, https://ctext.org/book-of-poetry.

The poem describes a setting prior to the Western Zhou conquest of the Shang, when they chose a suitable place to live and built the Zhou kingdom in the vicinity of present-day Luoyang. The location of the land is close to the water, and there is high ground to shield it from the cold wind, providing shelter for acres of fields.

Historically, the palaces in the imperial capitals were all constructed on a north-south axis, and the further north the palace was, the higher it had to be, the buildings gradually descending towards the south, one after another, until reaching more level ground. For the same reason, the entry gate was located on the south side, while the tall northern palaces could keep out the cold wind. The same principles governed the construction of imperial tombs. The Thirteen Tombs of the Ming dynasty near Beijing were grouped together in a valley with their backs to the northwest and facing the southeast. The Western Tombs of the Qing dynasty were in a valley surrounded by mountains, and the entrance to the valley was a narrow path between two overlapping hills. Once you snake your way into the narrow valley surrounded by the broad mountains, you find that all the cold winds are kept outside. The flowing water from the surrounding mountains fills the valley, which is why the trees are lush and green.

All these considerations are, of course, left to the *fengshui* experts to choose the right location and plan the best living conditions. Their theory is that the earth and mountains are organic life forms: the mountains are seen as subtly twisting dragons, rivers are in constant flow, and the combination of mountains and rivers, like the mutually completing yin and yang, can form an excellent balance. The study of geomancy emphasizes the subtle continuity of the dragon's veins, because even when portions appear to be missing, they are hidden and unbroken, meaning that the dragon's "vein" is alive, with a certain vitality and energy. The same applies to rivers. The flow of the river must be stable, neither overflowing nor drying up. Here we should also note that the south is yang and the north is yin, the north is high and the south is flat.

Given these considerations, we can readily understand why a city or village would be located at the juncture of water and mountains. Natural conditions permitting, the orientation should face south, or if this is impossible, east. If the ground on which the settlement is constructed is relatively flat—plains or terraces, with no significant mountain ranges to rely on—then often people will dig ponds or pools close to the houses to serve as water sources for a village or will dig a large well to serve as the center of village life. The houses will be built around the water source to create a space respecting yin and yang. Rural villages in southern Anhui are quite representative of this arrangement. The Hakka farms in the Taoyuan area of Taiwan are all dotted with ponds and clusters of farming communities, making for a unique living environment. This harmonious arrangement of water and soil is in fact a clever design to protect the natural environment.

When choosing a burial plot—the final resting place for the deceased— you must not only consider its above-ground location, but also whether it is dry or stable below ground. Therefore, when choosing the conditions for a tomb, we should consider factors such as *luan* 巒 (mountain range), *sha* 沙 (subsoil), and *shui* 水 (underground water) in order to choose the best *xue* 穴 (grave site). Tomb sites should be selected in such a way that the peace of the deceased will not be affected by water seepage or collapse. In addition to the hope that the occupant of the tomb will rest in peace and be free from disaster, today's geometric considerations believe choosing an optimal tomb site will also benefit future generations. Therefore, *fengshui* masters often use specialized terms such as "the land where the cows sleep" or "the phoenix crying to the sun," which are only metaphors for the idea of future genera- tions enjoying good fortune, which is a matter of assigning a "good omen" to the topography of a particular place as a reason for choosing the location.

Modern people live in cities and high-rise buildings, making it difficult to choose a house using the *fengshui* methods of the past. Yet a modern practice of *fengshui* has nonetheless developed among the people. The *fengshui* master will look into the location of the company or home, and pay particular attention to "road rush" (meaning that the building should not be facing the direction of the road so that the traffic does not come toward it) or "back-facing" (meaning to avoid enclosing the back of the building, blocking contact with the outside world). Inside the building, the *fengshui* master will also advise the homeowner to pay attention to the direction of the "flow," the so-called "moving lines." Basically, their consideration is to make internal arrangements smooth and harmonious. The location of a desk, for example, should not be facing the door, nor should it face the back of the room. If it faces the door it is "exposed," but if its back is to the door the passage between inner and outer will be "blocked," and so on. There are a few other little tricks: shops or restaurants should have a fish tank with a goldfish, as the flow of water is an attraction to fortune and a goldfish is a symbol of money. Some shops in Guangdong may put a pot of small orange trees indoors for auspiciousness.

The most common suggestion from *fengshui* masters is to hang a bamboo flute inside a room, beside a door or behind a window to achieve "harmony." These considerations have in fact deviated from the basic numerical and pictorial concepts of the eight trigrams and geomancy. Instead, this is a commonsense approach to setting up a more peaceful and quieter environment under the pretext of respecting *fengshui*. As noted above, the directions east, south, west, and north all have a specific meaning in terms of orientation. On the compass *fengshui* masters use for choosing directions, the eight directions of the eight trigrams are: east, south, west, north, northeast, northwest, southeast, and southwest. Therefore, in the process of developing the art of geomancy, or the science of geographic orientation, the eight trigrams became a very convenient symbolic tool.

As for the study of *qimen dunjia*, since ancient times it has been regarded as a mysterious magic, used for prognostication and possibly also for planning various events. Since I'm not familiar with *qimen dunjia*, I discussed it with Peng Yoke He 何丙郁 (1926–2014), a famous historian of science, who informed me that *qimen dunjia* is related to the "magic square" (similar to the modern-day Rubik's Cube). It is true that anything written on *qimen dunjia* begins its explanation with the "Nine Palaces" "magic square" of the *Luoshu* 洛書 (a book much associated with prophecy in Chinese history), a diagram showing the numbers one to nine on a magic square, like our tic tac toe game, where the three numbers across, down, and diagonally add up to 15 (see Figure 7). This diagram is a very clever arrangement in a decimal-based numbering system. The Chinese numbering system is based on the decimal system, but there are also the eight trigrams arranged in a binary system. Since the *Luoshu* can accommodate both binary and decimal systems, as well as multiplication of three by three in a nine-square system, we might conclude that this diagram can accommodate almost all combinations of numbers within the decimal system.

When mathematical concepts were still in their infancy, human beings could be entranced by the subtle relationships between numbers. As we all know, in the West, there was the "Da Vinci Code," with two positive triangles superimposed on each other to form a hexagonal figure with six sides on the outside and six sides on the inside. This symbol, which originated in Mesopotamia, is based on the senary (related to the number six) numeral system consisting of one, two and three. The Christian Church inherited this ancient mystical symbol, which is believed to have miraculous properties of its own. For another example, Greek geometry's Pythagorean theorem—"$a^2 + b^2 = c^2$"—led to later developments in the study of mathematics, geometry, and circumference. But in the time of Pythagoras, the Pythagorean Theorem itself was regarded as a gateway to the mysteries of the universe.

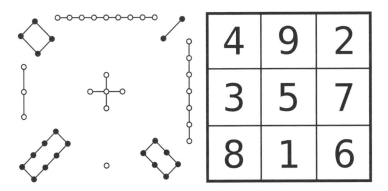

Fig. 7 "Magic Square" of the *Luoshu*

The Chinese "Rubik's Cube," like the two above examples from Middle Eastern and Western ancient cultures, has its place in the history of Chinese science, but it has similarly been trapped in a pre-scientific state for a long time.

Although the "Nine Palaces" in the *Luoshu* is a square, because of the influence of the eight trigrams and the *taiji* 太極 (the yin-yang symbol), the circle came to be the most common way to express these ideas. One can rotate the circle, and the position of the Nine Palaces inside can also be moved. Thus, using the form of the circle transforms the fixed square into a sphere of infinite changes. The ingeniousness of *qimen dunjia* lies in the fact that the whole and the inner mechanism are constantly changing. Mr. Peng Yoke He once overlaid the Chinese calendar and the pattern of seasonal changes onto the *qimen dunjia* to understand how various long and short cycles were arranged in traditional calendars, and he uses this simple pattern as a tool to retrieve data and calculations.

Traditionally, the science of *qimen dunjia* could be used in strategy for combat planning. In the popular Chinese historical novel, *The Romance of the Three Kingdoms* (*Sanguo yanyi* 三國演義), the author Luo Guanzhong 羅貫中 (1330–1400) describes the main character Zhuge Liang 諸葛亮 (181–234) as a wizard-like strategist whose strategies and tactics are unpredictable. Beginning with that book, Zhuge Liang is portrayed as a warlock wearing an eight trigrams robe. He arranged the Eight Trigrams Formation, which according to legend possessed a magical function through which a few piles of stones could be turned into a magic pit that could trap thousands of troops. Luo's novel married the image of the warlock to *qimen dunjia*, obscuring the "proto-scientific" characteristics of the latter.

Let's go back to Zhuge Liang's military strategy and try to reconstruct the meaning of the so-called "eight trigrams formation" from the beginning. Several ancient Chinese military manuals, including *Six Secret Teachings* (*Liu tao* 六韜) by Jiang Ziya (11th century BCE) and *Methods of the Sima* (*Sima fa* 司馬法) (4th century BCE) discuss the functioning of armies, both in terms the relationship between the various fighting units when in camp, and after the fighting has begun. All movements in and out of camp and in and out of battle must be carefully planned, at the same time leaving plenty of room for change. According to the *Romance of the Three Kingdoms*, after the death of Zhuge Liang, a general named Sima Yi 司馬懿 (179–251) inspected the camp he left behind and was impressed by Zhuge Liang's arrangements, and appreciated his talent.

From this point of view, we can perhaps understand that a "Nine Palaces" eight trigrams formation might have had the main force in the center, with the vanguard, rearguard, left and right wings arrayed according to the four directions, and the four corners being the roving units led by subordinate generals. In a camp, there are pathways connecting the units, but these can be closed at any time to intercept intruding enemies. When the troops move onto the battlefield, they need not employ the same point of entry; they can divide and attack from three or four different directions to carry out their assigned tasks.

In Zhuge Liang's time, the components of a battle were no longer individual soldiers, nor individual units fighting alone, but the entire army instead fought as a whole, with many different varieties of combat formations fighting as an integrated entity. For example, Zhuge Liang once invented a powerful crossbow that could shoot dozens of arrows in a single shot—such a weapon required a vehicle as a launching pad, and the vehicle had to be manned and protected by infantry. Each of the three types of combat units, chariot drivers, cavalry, and infantry, had a certain position, and each had its own role in covering and coordinating with the others when fighting. These needs of "quiet" in camp and "movement" in battle could be achieved jointly with the eight trigrams formation.

Zhuge Liang's complex military strategy was regarded as a marvelous use of troops during his time and later. And according to legend, *qimen dunjia* was the basis of Zhuge Liang's military strategy. *Qimen dunjia* is a body of knowledge that can be used for ruling a country as well as for running a business. In fact, both ruling a country and running a business are like a "battlefield," both requiring the coordination of various factors involving "quiet" and "movement" to maximize the effectiveness of various resources. From Zhuge Liang's tactics, it is possible to derive many other strategies. In sum, *qimen dunjia* in and of itself represents a sort of "proto-scientific" exploration, because it focuses on the superposition of various changes, one on the other, but it also gradually developed into a certain kind of mathematics or strategy.

Later, *qimen dunjia* developed into a Daoist art for composing talismans. This "talismanic" school of Daoist priests often claims to be able to use such symbols to block or send spirit troops and to manipulate demons. Among the many talismans employed, a common one was based on the magic square of the Nine Palaces: a simple pattern, from one to nine, is drawn into a series of cursive shapes, which the priests believe has the same mystical power as a magic cube. The nine palaces and the eight trigrams of the formation can also be used as forces to expel spirits and demons, with the help of various Daoist instruments and symbols to fill out the army, placing the gods and generals to form a cosmic net to capture the enemy. The most used gods and generals are also arranged according to the eight trigrams, with the gods and goddesses of the four directions and the stars of the 28 constellations part of the display, each with their own mission.

A powerful Daoist priest can use this mighty battlefield to ward off disasters and keep the peace of the people. When I was a teenager, the Daoist temple in my hometown held a joint festival every year, which became a sacrifice intended to protect the country and the people. The biggest one I can remember was in 1946, the year after the victory over Japan, when we longed for a period of stability. In Wuxi, not only did the local Daoist temples participate, but also many masters of the Maoshan monastic school were invited and a grand ceremony was held. My most unforgettable memory is a performance of the "ten great songs," which may be the last time that the folk Daoist religion included ancient music in their religious rituals. There is no telling if any of these old songs are still around today. Of course, these religious rituals absorbed elements of the surrounding cultural heritage, and culture is merely an adjunct to folk beliefs.

Even today, it is still a common practice in Chinese folk religions to try to predict the future by casting lots. This religious belief is related to the role of the shaman, and almost every temple has a bamboo tube with divination sticks, which believers use to tell their fortune. As the world is so complicated and there are many possible directions of development, how can we get the answer simply by an oracle or by throwing divination sticks?

In terms of the *Yijing*'s predictive function in ancient times, there are 23 historical cases recorded in *The Zuo Tradition* and the *Discourses of the States*, together with the predictions made by divination and the actual outcomes. Looking at these cases, one may see that the prophecies did not match the actual developments. For instance, *The Zuo Tradition* records that in the seventh year of Duke Zhao, in the state of Wei, two sons of the duke were possible successors to the throne. The divination was positive in the case of both, but only one could occupy the throne, so one of the predictions had to be wrong. In another instance, *The Zuo Tradition* records that in the sixteenth year of the reign of Duke Cheng, a war broke out between the states of Jin and Chu. The Jin state's divination foresaw Jin's victory, but they lost. According to the interpretation of the official scribe of divination, the "auspicious omen" actually meant "victory" for the opposing side. But rereading the results in such a way surely defeats the original purpose of the divination. This would seem to mean that if half of the prophecies over time have been true, then this is not so bad; however, playing fast and loose with the truth like this is not what made the *Yijing* a Chinese classic.

Folk practices at the popular level of traditional Chinese society combined the numbers and images such as yin and yang, the eight trigrams, *fengshui* and *qimen dunjia* into a cosmic pattern. This model reflects traditional society's understanding of the universe: a huge system with numbers and graphs inside, making up its constituent elements and the links between these elements. Such a system is constantly adjusting the relationship between its internal elements and coordinating with the three external systems of heaven, earth, and human beings. The process of change creates "fortune" and "potential," forces that can affect our lives. Therefore, such folk beliefs tend to seek the roots of these mysterious powers, being hypothetically demonstrated as numbers and shapes, in order to achieve maximum well being in a life shaped by fortune and potential.

These concepts are based on faith instead of rational theories. There is a great difference between this feature of Chinese folk belief and the Judeo-Christian attribution of all changes in the universe to the will of God. God in the Judeo-Christian faith has a will of his own to govern the universe; no mortal can know God's will, and he or she owes perfect faith and obedience to Him. From the Chinese perspective, the "fortune" and "potential" of the universe depend on the interaction within and between reality and people's wishes. If human beings can grasp and follow the general direction of fortune and potential, they will be able to obtain the maximum benefit from the energy of the universe and avoid possible disasters caused by ignoring the dangers. As mentioned above, this way of thinking is "proto-scientific" or at best "pseudo-scientific." The behavioral basis of folk beliefs is quite different from the metaphysical arguments of the theories of yin and yang and the eight trigrams.

From the perspective of the "study of meaning and pattern," we should truly be cautious about success and failure in the world. The overall picture presented in the *Yijing* allows us to realize that success doesn't last forever, and there is always a chance to recover from failure. The individual's own actions will determine the direction of success or failure in the future. It is said that in his later years, Confucius was particularly interested in the *Yijing*. His understanding of the *Yijing* seems to have been a reminder to people concerning the phenomena of success and failure: some behavioral patterns lead to good outcomes, while others lead to failure.

In the *Xici* 繫辭 commentary on the *Yijing* (one of the major commentaries, which are collectively known as the "ten wings"), Confucius explained that after King Wen composed the *Yijing*, he chose nine hexagrams among the 64, to teach people to cultivate their own virtues so as to prevent troubles before they arise. These nine hexagrams were: number 10 (*lü*), number 15 (*qian*), number 24 (*fu*), number 32 (*heng*), number 41 (*sun*), number 42 (*yi*), number 47 (*kun*), number 48 (*jing*), and number 57 (*sun*). Confucius explains the meaning of these nine hexagrams in his "The Great Treatise" commentary (part 2): "Therefore (the 10th diagram), Lu, shows us the foundation of virtue; (the 15th), Xian, its handle; (the 24th), Fu, its root; (the 32nd), Heng, its solidity; (the 41st), Sun, its cultivation; (the 42nd), Yi, its abundance; (the 47th), Kun, its exercise of discrimination; (the 48th), Jing, its field and (the 57th), Xun, its regulation."[8] In *The Correct Meaning of the Five Classics* (*Wujing zhengyi* 五經正義, a Tang dynasty commentary), it is noted that the point of this passage is to "illustrate that all of these hexagrams are useful in the achievement of virtue." In Han dynasty studies of the *Yijing*, the "school of image and number" was quite successful, but after Wang Bi 王弼 (226–249), the "school of meaning and pattern" became the mainstream. Confucianism reminds us to face victory with modesty and prudence, and to face adversity with perseverance and patience, in accordance with the direction of trends in the world.

In contrast to the Confucian understanding of the *Yijing*, Daoism offers a different idea. Daoists believe that grasping the principle of everlasting change should be the first step in reflection. As for the Confucian discussion of "virtue"—as in "cultivating virtue," or "ritual" models that develop out of "virtue"—Daoists believe that all of this is an extension of the Way. Therefore, Chapter 38 of Laozi's *Daodejing* 道德經 says:

> Hence when the way was lost there was virtue;
> When virtue was lost there was benevolence;
> When benevolence was lost there was rectitude;
> When rectitude was lost there were the rites.[9]

An old friend of mine, Pei Dekai 裴德愷, chose 10 quotes from the *Daodejing* and used them to study Daoist attitudes toward living in the world, and as pointers for behavioral patterns. The 10 quotes are:

---

8   Legge, trans., *I Ching*.
9   D. C. Lau, trans., *Tao Te Ching (A Bilingual Edition)* (Hong Kong: The Chinese University of Hong Kong Press, 2007), 23.

1. A Dao that may be spoken is not the enduring Dao. A name that may be named is not an enduring name. No names—this is the beginning of heaven and earth. Having names—this is the mother of the things of the world.

2. What is and what is not give birth to one another, what is difficult and what is easy complete one another, Long and short complement one another, High and low incline towards one another, Note and noise harmonize with one another, Before and after follow one another.

3. Governing a large state is like cooking a small fish.

4. Disaster—good fortune adheres therein; good fortune—disaster lurks therein.

5. The difficult undertakings of the world are all arise from simple situations, and the greatest undertakings in the world all arise from small details.

6. Men emulate earth; earth emulates heaven (*tian*); heaven emulates the Dao; the Dao emulates spontaneity.

7. Highest good is like water: water benefits the things of the world and does not contend. Dwell in places that the masses of men despise.

8. The Dao gives birth to one; one gives birth to two; two gives birth to three; three gives birth to the ten thousand things. The things of the world bear Yin on their backs and embrace the Yang. They exhaust their qi in harmony.

9. There is no calamity greater than not knowing what is sufficient; there is no fault greater than wishing to acquire. Thus the sufficiency of knowing what is sufficient is eternal sufficiency.

10. He who knows men is wise; he who knows himself is enlightened. He who conquers men has strength; he who conquers himself is strong.[10]

---

10   Ibid.

The sixth and seventh quotes are precisely the explanations of how the *Yijing* takes imagery from nature; the eighth is almost a description of the two elements of yin and yang, which are then combined into the three lines of a trigram, which then form hexagrams and represent all kinds of phenomena. As for the other quotes, especially the second, fourth, fifth, ninth and tenth, they summarize very concretely the attitudes that we find in the *Yijing* in relation to success and failure.

In my view, Laozi's explanation of the transformation in the *Yijing* from "image and number" to "meaning and principle" is even more fitting than in the case of Confucianism. According to Laozi's *Daodejing*, the Dao should represent the principle of change; virtue should be an attribute of all changing factors. It is the combination of the two that gives rise to the phenomenon and process of change, which is the main message conveyed by the *Yijing*. Laozi's status is said to have been that of a royal archivist, or an official scribe. There are more than 20 texts in the *The Zuo Tradition* and *Discourses of the States* that discuss *Yijing* divination, and almost all of those who joined in the discussions were ritual officials involved with ancestor worship, diviners, and scribes. If Laozi were an official scribe, he would have been familiar with *Yijing* divination and its interpretation, which would explain the considerable similarities between Laozi's *Daodejing* and the *Yijing*.

Zhuangzi's writings represents another school of Daoism, and the core ideas of the book *Zhuangzi* 莊子 can be summarized in the ideas of two chapters entitled "Discussion on Making All Things Equal" (*Qiwu lun* 齊物論) and "Free and Easy Wandering" (*Xiaoyao you* 逍遙遊). He also observed that everything in the world is in a constant state of flux. However, his argument is very different from Laozi's. Laozi focuses on the dialectical relationship between the positive and negative, so that the weak overcomes the strong, and that "nothing" appeared before "something." Zhuangzi, arguing from the theory of the unity of all things, believes that while the strange and unusual appearances found after the completion of any change would be different, many of these differences would be smoothed out if viewed from different angles. In this light, therefore, the pleasure taken by a giant bird in a thousand-mile flight is the same as that of a sparrow jumping on a branch in the backyard. There is little difference between the soaring Mount Tai and a little hill at the base of the mountain; it all depends on the distance from which you regard them. A mushroom that lives and dies in a day is not necessarily different from an 800-year-old tree if you take into account ways of measuring time.

Zhuangzi created a number of "deformed people," such as Crippled Shu in "In the World of Men," (*Renjian shi* 人間世) and Ai Taituo, Wang Tai, and Shushan No-Toes in "The Sign of Virtue Complete" (*De chong fu* 德充符) all of whom are ugly, virtuous characters. One description reads, "there's Crippled Shu—chin stuck down in his navel, shoulders up above his head, pigtail pointing at the sky, his five organs on the top, his two thighs pressing his ribs."[11] In real life, it is difficult for us to understand what kind of handicap or deformity is being referred to. Another example is Ai Taituo, an "ugly man" from Wei, who was "ugly enough to astound the whole world." Zhuangzi stresses the serious imbalance between form and spirit. The text continues: "Therefore, if virtue is preeminent, the body will be forgotten. But when men do not forget what can be forgotten but forget what cannot be forgotten—that may be called true forgetting." His attention is on the compatibility of the Dao and the spirit, and not on the physical form. This argument, too, is based on the standpoint of "making things equal." Supreme wisdom and the ugly image can coexist in one thing.

Zhuangzi also argues that wisdom comes from the senses, but the senses themselves have their limitations. In his prophecy, *hundun* 混沌 (primal chaos) is the primordial state, as we see from this passage from "Fit for Emperors and Kings" (*Ying diwang* 應帝王):

---

11   Burton Watson, trans., *The Complete Works of Chuang Tzu* (New York: Columbia University Press, 1968). Available online at https://terebess.hu/english/chuangtzu. html#4.

The emperor of the South Sea was called Shu [Brief], the emperor of the North Sea was called Hu [Sudden], and the emperor of the central region was called Hundun [Chaos]. Shu and Hu from time to time came together for a meeting in the territory of Hundun, and Hundun treated them very generously. Shu and Hu discussed how they could repay his kindness. "All men," they said, "have seven openings so they can see, hear, eat, and breathe. But Hundun alone doesn't have any. Let's trying boring him some! Every day they bored another hole, and on the seventh day Hundun died.[12]

Thus, Zhuangzi argues that one can have senses and wisdom, and still lose the original truth. Zhuangzi's argument seems to be even more nihilistic than Laozi's. At the same, it obscures the phenomenon of change in "making things equal."

Another classic of Daoism, the *Huainanzi* 淮南子, in the "Among Others" chapter, tells the fable of the old man at the border and the lost horse:

At the near frontier, there was a [family of] skilled diviners whose horse suddenly became lost out among the Hu [people]. Everyone consoled them. The father said, "This will quickly turn to good fortune!" After several months, the horse returned with a fine Hu steed. Everyone congratulated them. The father said, "This will quickly turn to calamity!" The household was [now] replete with good horses; the son loved to ride, [but] he fell and broke his leg. Everyone consoled them. The father said, "This will quickly turn to good fortune!" After one year, the Hu people entered the frontier in force; the able and strong all stretched their bowstrings and fought. Among the people of the near frontier, nine out of ten died. It was only because of lameness that father and son protected each other. Thus, good fortune becoming calamity, calamity becoming good fortune; their transformations are limitless, so profound they cannot be fathomed.[13]

---

12 Ibid.

13 John S. Major, et. al., ed. and trans., *The Huainanzi: A Guide to the Theory and Practice of Government in Early Han China* (New York: Columbia University Press, 2010), 728–729.

This story truly affirms Laozi's statement that "disaster and good fortune complement one another," and takes us back in the direction of the *Yijing*. The Chinese idiom of "the celebrants are rejoicing in the hallway, but the mourners are at the door" surely comes directly from the *Yijing* tradition of caution and fear.

To sum up the differences between Confucianism and Daoism on the *Yijing*'s theory of change, the basic Confucian stress is on activism. At the same time, the Confucians also discovered in the changes of the *Yijing* the dialectical relationship between disaster and good fortune. Using the same dialectic, Laozi affirms a principle and a variation of properties in harmony with each other, but Zhuangzi strays further from the tradition of the *Yijing*. Let me borrow the term "Mr. More or Less" coined by the New Culture Movement figure Hu Shih 胡適 (1891–1962) in the 1920s, which might be said to describe Zhuangzi's theory of making things equal. Under the "more or less" principle, arguments for and against something become unclear, after which attitudes of caution and fear have nothing to attach to.

Even today, the traditions of the *Yijing* still permeate popular customs. Almost all temples in Taiwan are set up to practice divination. The historian Lin Hengdao 林衡道 (1915–1997) came from the richest family in Taiwan, the Banqiao Lin family, but he was not like the sons in other rich families who simply enjoy their wealth; instead, throughout his life he studied what interested him, which was Taiwanese folk customs. In the 1960s, he took me and a few friends from the Department of Anthropology at National Taiwan University on a tour of temples around Taipei City. The divination tools available in these temples revealed their connections to the *Yijing* tradition. Although they used "moon blocks" instead of yarrow sticks, the fortune sticks inside the bamboo container were called the "Zhuge Eight Trigram Divine Numbers."

Usually there are 64 or 128 sticks, representing 64 hexagrams, or a multiple of 64. (If the design were based on the number of 384 individual lines of the 64 hexagrams, I'm afraid that the weight of the sticks would make the container unshakeable.) The person seeking to know his or her fortune shakes the canister until one stick falls out, after which he or she takes the number on the stick and reads the corresponding message in a temple book (sometimes the messages are hanging on the wall rather than in a book), and a temple attendant will interpret the prophecy. The wording of these messages is no longer the original text of the *Yijing*, but in almost every message we find the notion of the interdependence of blessings and misfortunes, stating that good fortune is coming soon, or reminding us to be aware of the bad fortune behind it. This tradition is deeply rooted in the hearts and minds of the people, whose plans for their own careers and peace of mind are very much influenced by the prophecies of such messages. The traditions of the *Yijing* have penetrated deeply into the spiritual life of ordinary people through this folkloric practice of casting fortune sticks.

Caution and fear in the face of the evolution of things is a unique phenomenon in Chinese culture. In the context of Western capitalist culture, Max Weber argued that, since the Reformation, Protestants considered their success as a manifestation of God's grace, and God's grace was an inscrutable gift of God, which could not be secured by human means. The only answer was to work ever harder, assuming the resulting success was evidence of God's grace. This dynamic forward motion has been the main driving force behind the expansion and growth of Western capitalism and imperialism over the past 300 years. Receiving God's grace is an extremely serious matter, and a good Christian, on the one hand, is grateful for that grace and, on the other hand, must always be careful not to make a misstep. That defense against the original sin in one's heart is what is called a "dark consciousness" in theological theory. Trying to avoid the effects of original sin is the Chinese equivalent of caution and fear.

This Protestant ethic is fading in the face of capitalism's present development. Having lived in the United States for decades, I have seen the norm: a company is so successful that it expands and expands to such an extent that it collapses. The powers of the world, one hegemon after another, have reached the limits of their expansion and are crumbling. The West's aggressive spirit is a powerful force, but the Western spirit has lost the "dark consciousness" of self-preservation. In this way, they often ignore the source of the problems that have been buried for a long time; they do not even look for the roots of the problems, but only deal with the existing manifestations.

As mentioned above, the Chinese are cautious and fearful, as reflected in certain Chinese idioms: one ant hill in a 1,000-foot long dyke can cause its collapse; a magnificent building can be destroyed by fire because of a tiny crack in an exhaust pipe. Returning to Zhuge Liang, his life was characterized by an attitude of "detachment and tranquility, allowing one to fix goals and achieve ambitions," a wisdom gained only after seeing through all of the changes, an attitude of "everything always changes and there's nothing strange about it."

On the other hand, there is the saying that "Zhuge Liang's life was defined by caution," meaning that he was extremely careful. I once heard former Taiwanese President C. K. Yen 嚴家淦 (1905–1993) elaborate on the word "prudence." He said that prudence means to be cautious, that is, to be aware of small pitfalls when they appear. Those who are truly capable of doing great things can seize the critical moments of change and grasp the opportunity to push them forward or correct them. In the history of China, we can see such behavior displayed by both public and private figures. They can do great things because they notice small changes. Such a spiritual outlook might be said to be a combination of the two philosophies of Confucianism and Daoism. This is also the direction in which the *Yijing* points for productive thinking: on the one hand, be aggressive, and on the other hand, be cautious and prudent. The two complement each other, reflecting an internal tension in the world of Chinese entrepreneurship.

Weber's theory is that there is an internal tension in the doctrine of Protestantism, and that this tension became the impetus for the capitalist's lifelong devotion to his or her enterprise. Chinese Confucians, including both scholars and the common people, in fact share the above-mentioned tension between positive, aggressive behavior and impulse toward caution. In his discussion of Chinese merchants, Professor Ying-shih Yu 余英時 also saw them as possessing a Weberian spirit, by which he meant this same internal tension, which we might see as the ego letting itself go but at the same time monitoring itself. There is a couplet used by Tong Ren Tang, a Chinese pharmaceutical company, which translates as: "Though no one sees the medicine being made, heaven naturally knows what to do with it." Here, heaven refers to the supervision of one's own conscience. The folk beliefs mentioned in this chapter are in fact a mechanism built into Chinese society to manifest the rituals and behaviors of faith and to remind everyone of them at all times: heavenly principles, the law of the country, and human emotions are parts of the order of the universe, and everyone must uphold them at all times without fail.

This mentality is reflected in the lessons Chinese elders often dispense to their children and grandchildren concerning clan and family traditions. Our family's ancestral motto is: "In times of good fortune do not be indulgent; in times of poverty do not lose your confidence." My father amended it to: "When things go your way do not be indulgent, and when things do not, do not lose confidence." This sets up the contrast between wealth and poverty as the calm that reigns over "getting what you want" and "being disappointed," which reminds us of Zhuge Liang's attitude of tranquility. My mother also mentioned the motto of the Zhang family, as told to her by my uncle: "People fear three forces in life: the will of Heaven, the words of man, and the weight of conscience." Conscience is what watches over our own actions. Such caution and fear permeate the spiritual life of the Chinese. Even when the Chinese are being aggressive, they tend to pull back at a certain point because of such fears. Perhaps the Chinese do not have the same drive and motivation as we see in today's Western culture; however, the Chinese can find some peace and calm in their mind of self-surveillance. With China having become so deeply Westernized, I hope we can still retain the posture of introspection and caution, so that the Chinese people can retain some clarity and rationality at a time of widespread anxiety in the world.

VI. The Meaning of Life

In any cultural system, "where does life come from and what happens when it's over?" is an important question. This subject has long been one of the main issues concerning philosophical and modern ethnological inquiries of peoples and their cultures: Where does life come from? Where does each group of people think they come from? Is life individual? Or rather collective? And when we talk about life, we must also ponder death. After death, does life simply disappear? If not, where does it go? With the advent of modern technology, and in particular, with increased knowledge of genes and the evolution of living organisms, we have been able to uncover certain evolutionary trajectories and patterns of the human body. At the same time, we have also attempted to explore the concept of life, discussing the spiritual aspects separate from the observable life of living organisms, although the topic remains elusive. At the end of physical life, the material part of the body finally breaks down into its original chemical elements, but are the memories left in the world a part of life or not? This is series of questions I wish to raise in this chapter. The concept of "life," however, is too complex and too mysterious for me to expect that the views presented in this chapter will provide satisfactory answers to these questions. I only hope to pique readers' curiosity and stimulate further thoughts on the subject.

The discussion of life and death in this chapter is, of course, not in the biological sense, but in the realm of belief, a proper area of concern for a book focused on spiritual life. In his *Religion in Chinese Society* (1961), Professor C. K. Yang points out that the biggest difference between Chinese religious beliefs and Western Judeo-Christian beliefs lies in the fact that the Chinese integrate religious feelings and the rituals associated with them into their daily lives. Mircia Eliad once pointed out that the separation between the sacred and the profane is an important consideration in discussions of religion. Yet, as Professor Yang pointed out, the Chinese combine the sacred and the profane in their everyday life. Of course, we must understand that China is not without institutionalized religions; Buddhism, which came from abroad, and Daoism, which is native to China, as well as Christianity and Islam, which came later, are all institutionalized religious systems. Diffused and indigenous religions were blended throughout time and space, together with systems of popular beliefs, which are their own kinds of institutionalized religions. However, when it comes to questions of life and death, the Chinese combine social ethics and spiritual beliefs into one, creating the fusion that Professor Yang identified.

I once defined Chinese religious beliefs as being focused on two main themes: gods and ancestral spirits. In matters of life and death, the ancestral spirits are probably the more important of the two. For another perspective, however, let's return to a primitive era, and take a brief tour of the Neolithic cultural site of Hongshan. On a mountain ridge at Niuheliang there is a temple to a goddess, inside of which are large and small icons of women, combining in one form the three stages of womanhood—girlhood, motherhood, and growing old—and representing the power of procreation. A little further down the mountain, there is a three-storied platform with a square superimposed on a circle, which was surely a site for sacrifices to heaven. Nearby are the graves of those who must have been community leaders. Both the tombs and the altar are surrounded by bottomless ceramic pipes, which I believe symbolize the connection between heaven and earth. The ritual paraphernalia found at the Niuheliang site combines the worship of heaven with the belief in the spirits of ancestors. The coexistence of the two, in fact, has never been completely separated through the ages. As discussed below, scrolls found in Han dynasty tombs address issues concerning both the continuity of life and death and the connection between the gods and the soul.

Returning to the subject of life and death, the Chinese character for "life" (*sheng* 生) evolved into the character for "sex" (*xing* 性) and the character for "surname" (*xing* 姓). This is something that can only be seen in pictographic languages; in alphabetic languages you have to beat around the bush to express the dual meaning of life in both the collective and individual sense. In Chinese, however, the character for "surname" combines the two components meaning "woman" and "birth," illustrating the collective meaning of kinship in life. An expression meaning "the common people" in China refers to the "hundred surnames;" of course it is not simply a question of "one hundred" (i.e. numerous), nor is it simply a question of "surnames" (i.e. kinship groups), since we have clans as well, which are sub-branches of surnames. The earliest surnames, as my teacher Professor Li Xuanbo 李玄伯 (1895–1974) pointed out, had much the same meaning as the totems of the Native Americans, indicating some common characteristics of the group. For example, some Native American tribes called themselves bears and others eagles, believing themselves to be descendants of the heavenly bears and eagles, and hence these tribes also endowed these totems with the divinity of the symbols of the sacred creatures.

As far as ancient Chinese surnames are concerned, the surnames of the Taihao and Shaohao (legendary sovereigns from the Bohai Bay region) were, respectively Feng 風 (鳳) and Zhi 摯 (鷙). Both surnames refer to birds—Feng is "phoenix" and Zhi is "hawk"—and these birds can be considered their totems. Hence it is noted in *The Zuo Tradition* that in the seventeenth year of the reign of Duke Zhao, Tanzi told the Duke that in the era of Shaohao, to which he traced his ancestors, all of the officials and tribes were named after birds. Later on, the surname of the Shang people was Zi 子, the image of a child being born. The myth of the Shang's creation is that "heaven commanded a mysterious bird to descend to earth and give birth to Shang," which meant that they were the descendants of a mysterious bird (a swallow). In fact, the Gwanggaeto Stele in the ancient Korean kingdom of Goguryeo (37 BCE–688 CE) records the origin of its ancestors as being sunlight and bird eggs. The legendary ancestral origin of the Manchu people is related in the story of three nymphs swimming in a pond, one of which swallowed a vermilion fruit from the mouth of a flying bird and then gave birth to Bukūri Yongšon, who was the legendary ancestor of the Manchu people.

The ancient Chinese surnames Jiang 姜, Ji 姬 and Si 姒 have similar meanings. As for the Ji surname, found in the Zhou kingdom, their female ancestor, Jiang Yuan 姜嫄, stepped in giant footprints and became pregnant, giving birth to Qi 棄, the founder of the Zhou people. Later on, certain totems were transformed into tribal names, and the tribe inherited the characteristics of the totems. Of course, the meaning of the totem was completely different from today's genetic concept of surname and family, but it does no harm to imagine that the transformation of a totem into a surname implies that a group of people have inherited, or think they have inherited, a common "endowment" from the very beginning. Thus, a person's natural endowment is both collective and individual. There are physical as well as spiritual aspects to such a gift, and the latter may be similar to what we call "character." In ancient times, however, it was attributed to nature.

All human societies create communities, because the ability to dominate others is due to the ability to cooperate and combine to form a superior force. The way groups form begins with the natural reproductive unit—in other words, the couple, the parents and children, the family—as the basic unit, which then expands into the clan, or the regional community. However, in the case of Chinese society—probably due to the long history of farming, attachment to the land and reluctance to move—the expansion of the family into a lineage or a clan became the basic way to concentrate people in one place. As mentioned above, members of such a group would see themselves as having a shared "endowment," which would also be their basic shared identity. Thus, their collective life is realized through social ethics, and is also manifested in the union of gods and ancestors.

Archaeological data from the Shang dynasty, including tombs and ruins of settlements, as well as documentary data from oracle bones, provide us with a clear understanding of notions of ancestral spirits during this period (1600–1046 BCE, approximately). At the center of Shang royal tombs were the coffins of the kings, surrounded by those of his consorts and servants, as well as fully armed guards. The tomb is surrounded by an orderly arrangement of armed troops, and the entire tomb is shaped like the pattern of a palace or tent where the deceased had lived. The tomb complex contains several burial sites, organized according to seniority, and represents a continuity between life and death. In the questions inscribed on oracle bones, the living would often request the former kings and dukes to enlighten them about their difficulties and doubts, and would solicit their blessings and support. On the oracle bones, we also often find references to an imperial sacrifice, and while we still do not fully understand the specific meaning of the sacrifice, it appears to have involved building a bonfire (a ritual of honoring the deceased kings) to sacrifice to the heavens. If this is a reasonable interpretation, then perhaps the deceased kings were asking Di, the ruler of heaven, for assistance for their descendants through the medium of the sacrifice. Gods and ancestors are, after all, both objects of worship.

In the ethics of the human world, the extension of a group is the kinship system of fathers, children, and grandchildren. Since the time of the *Book of Poetry*, the intimate relationship between parents and children in China has been based on the emotional components of early childhood, as we see from the following passage of the *Book of Poetry*:

Fatherless, who is there to rely on?
Motherless, who is there to depend on?
When I go abroad, I carry my grief with me;
When I come home, I have no one to go to.
O my father, who begat me!
O my mother, who nourished me!
Ye indulged me, ye fed me,

Ye held me up, ye supported me,
Ye looked after me, ye never left me,
Out and in ye bore me in your arms.
If I would return your kindness,
It is like great Heaven, illimitable.[1]

The above lines describe the hard work of parents in raising and caring for their children. How do you transfer this feeling to the hierarchical ethics of the father-son relationship? The Confucian philosopher Mencius's 孟子 (372–289 BCE) efforts in this regard are worth mentioning. Mencius referred to the "four beginnings" in arguing that people are naturally good, and gave two examples. One was that of the son who, after the death of his parents, could not bear to see their bodies exposed and decaying. Another was that of someone who saw a toddler playing near a well and carried the toddler to a safe place, not because of any prior relationship with the child, but because they could not bear the thought of the child falling in. According to Mencius, this kind of compassionate impulse is the beginning of benevolence. The same compassion then extends to a sense of shame, to a willingness to yield, and to a sense of right and wrong, and ultimately becomes the source of benevolence, righteousness, propriety, and wisdom. From a psychological perspective, the basic principle of social coexistence, which involves the capacity of putting oneself in someone else's place, is constructed on the basis on the biological parent-child relationship.

Chinese rituals are also psychological projections of emotions. In the "Meaning of Sacrifices" (*Jiyi* 祭儀) section of the *Book of Rites*, for example, the scene of a proper sacrifice is described as follows: even though one's parents are no longer with us, one must think of the voice and appearance of the deceased, as if one could hear the sound of their footsteps, the sound of their breathing and coughing, and so on. This is the basic attitude one must adopt when making offerings and paying respects

---

1 James Legge, trans., "Liao E," Chinese Text Project, https://ctext.org/book-of-poetry/liao-e.

to one's loved ones. You make offerings to your family as if they were there, and you sacrifice to the gods as if they were there. You put yourself in someone else's place. There is nothing rational about it; it is simply an emotional projection.

At the age of 16, a woman could get married and a man could start to work. In ancient China, this moment in life was marked by the discreet rituals of the capping ceremony (for the young man) and the hair-pinning ceremony (for the young woman), which marked a change in the way in which the young people dressed and presented themselves. The ceremony was a way of telling them that this was the beginning of a new stage in their lives and that henceforth they would take up their individual responsibilities as members of the community and society, just as their parents and grandparents had done. The rules and restrictions of the coming of age ceremony will also remind them not to disappoint their parents' love, hopes and expectations for them, and not to tarnish the family's reputation. This kind of admonition is still commonly used by parents in Chinese families today to counsel their children to be 3good. The basic idea of these rituals is to remind parents and children, through the physical continuity of their relationship, of the components of parenthood that extend their responsibilities to society, both in the present and in the future.

In old age, the body weakens, personal involvement in society diminishes, and responsibilities are handed over to the children. Using farm work as a metaphor, the man works the field (the Chinese character for "man" [*nan* 男] is made up of the two compounds for "field" [*tian* 田] and "strength" [*li* 力]) and the woman keeps the household peaceful (the Chinese character for "peace" [*an* 安] is made up of the two compounds for "roof" [宀] and "woman" [*nü* 女], the woman situated under the roof), and this is the basic way in which an adult couple forms a family. In the prime of a man's life, he pushes the plough, just as his father once did. But, later, the elderly father leads the oxen, and his son follows behind, doing the heavy labor of pushing the plough. When the man's own children are old enough, the boy will take over the job of leading the oxen from his grandfather. And a few years later, the young man leading the oxen and the father pushing the plow swap places. This goes on generation after generation, as young and old exchange the tasks of production. In rural communities, the experience of the elderly is invaluable. They know the weather and what it takes to grow crops, and this experience has been passed down from fathers and grandfathers to sons and grandsons. Older people have more leisure time to care for their grandchildren, which includes not only nurturing and caring, but also teaching and imparting knowledge.

Thus, the extension of the community and the continuation of society can be practiced under the system of family ethics. All of the above illustrates that the construction of a stable society is the result of religious feelings experienced directly in life and then transformed into rituals and expressed as family ethics. This process began in ancient times, and has continued in China for at least 2,000 years. A peaceful, settled society with a steadily growing population came to form the largest human population in the world. It is because of these arrangements that the Chinese people have been able to continue to grow and prosper.

In terms of spirituality, the ancients believed that in addition to the flesh and blood life of the individual, there also exists a soul, which is related to spirit. In ancient times, the word "soul" was used in different ways. For one kind of soul, known as *po* 魄, the vitality must remain in the body, while for another kind of soul, the spirit, known as *hun* 魂, represents the invisible self. Generally speaking, the soul comes to life with the physical body and follows it through aging and death, at which point it disappears. When the spirit and the body cannot coexist simultaneously—in other words, when the body disappears but the soul remains—this homeless soul can become a ghost. And even if body and soul march to the same rhythm, with the death of the physical body, the soul has to go somewhere—which is where the burial system comes in.

The Zuo Tradition contains a story that explains how wandering souls become ghosts. At one time, there were two groups of nobles in the state of Zheng engaged in a fierce struggle for power, and one of the groups organized a raid to kill Bo You, a Zheng minister, who was asleep after having got drunk. A few days later, people in the capital city of Zheng saw Bo You dressed in armor. crying that one of these days he would kill his enemies, which frightened the residents. The minister of Jin asked Zichan, the most learned man in Zheng, for an explanation, and Zichan replied that when souls had nowhere to go, they became ghosts. Moreover, Bo You's family had been in power for three generations and was a prosperous and numerous clan. In other words, they were prosperous and dominant in both spiritual and physical terms, and then Bo You was suddenly killed. His richly endowed spiritual essence did not disappear easily with his physical body, but rather became a ghost in the world of humans. This explanation, often quoted in studies of Chinese religious history, illustrates the relationship between the soul and the body. On the one hand, a group's endowments are not solely innate, but can also be acquired later in life, with variations in strength and weakness. The one who obtains more resources and power will be strong in soul and body; on the other hand, those without access to adequate resources are generally spiritually and physically weaker. How to properly handle the soul after the death of a human body is an important question in life.

Let's start with the ancient treatment of death and observe their concept of the soul. The chapters on the "funeral rites" in the Book of Ritual (Yili 儀禮) and that on "sacrifices" in the Book of Rites contain detailed descriptions of how to deal with the death of a person. When a person stops breathing, the first step is for the mourner to climb up on to the roof of the house, bringing the clothes of the person who just died, and then call his name and ask him to return. If, after calling three times, the person has not returned, the next step is to put the clothes back on the bed of the deceased, to give the soul somewhere to go. At the same time, the mourner immediately calls for a pair of banners with the name of the deceased on them to be inserted into a small bowl of porridge (in later years this became a bowl of rice) to provide sustenance for the soul. Later on, a wooden tablet is prepared with the name of the deceased written on it; this tablet then represents the soul of the deceased, so that the deceased will have something on which to "perch." In this process, the word "perch" is often used as a verb to describe the attachment of the soul, just like birds who have to perch to rest after flying.

In modern times, Chinese funerals also include a ritual known as "strike through the god and dot the king" (*chuanshen dianzhu* 穿神點主) in which the descendants of the deceased prick their fingers to draw blood, with which they draw a line through the character *shen* 神 (god) and add a dot on the top of the character *wang* 王 (king), transforming it into the character for "master" (*zhu* 主); the meaning of the rite is that the blood of the descendants represents the life of the deceased.

When I was young, I attended my grandmother's funeral. The seventh day after the funeral is called the "return of the spirit," and it is said that the spirit will return in the form of a bird. The Daoist priest will look at the ash which has previously been scattered on the ground and point out the marks of bird's claws. This ritual only concerns the image of the soul in Chinese folk beliefs, and the analogy to a flying bird shows that the soul has a concrete image, and is not merely an abstract existence.

The Chinese refer to burial after death as "being laid to rest in the earth," and according to what we read in the ancient texts, "the *hun* returns to the sky and the *po* returns to the earth," which suggests that the *po* remains with the corpse. In Han dynasty tombs, written documents accompanying the burial are often found, which are called tomb scrolls, or tomb-quelling texts, sometimes engraved on lead plates, ceramic tablets, or written on wood or bamboo fragments. There are various forms of text in this category, but the general content is fairly consistent, and tomb scrolls record from whom the land for the grave was purchased, who witnessed the purchase, and the price of the land. More importantly, it states that the graveyard is for the exclusive use of the deceased who had purchased the land. If there were other corpses buried here earlier (who had not purchased the land), they would be enslaved and become the servants of the newcomers. A more complex tomb scroll might make broader claims concerning the rights involved in this purchase and burial, announcing it to the spirit officials of heavenly court on high and of the netherworld below. The document might also mention various local officials who sent such a verified transaction to their counterpart, i.e. officials of the underworld, thus declaring the sovereignty of the deceased over the land. Even more complicated is the question of burial items, which are left in the tomb to care for the daily needs of the deceased. In the documents found in the tombs, the contents are even more complex: they might mention soybean seeds and other items buried with the dead, to provide expenses or pocket money for the deceased in the other world.

Many funerary wares have been unearthed from Han tombs. The most common of these are small models of houses, but more complex examples include complete courtyards, with pigsties, fields, and ponds, all of which were necessary for the deceased to live in the netherworld. Of course, the tombs of the imperial family and the aristocracy were even better equipped. For example, in the mausoleum of the First Emperor of Qin, not only was the shrine on the top of the tomb facing the east—symbolizing that he was still the ruler of all of China—there also were thousands of terracotta warriors, officials, and generals underground, as if ready to conquer the world for their master. The tombs of the later emperors were fancy or simple, depending on the funds available, but all basically had a hall in front and a sleeping chamber behind, and there were stone statues of civil and military officials standing along the tomb passage, symbolizing the authority of the emperor and his comfortable life after death.

All these arrangements indicate that, before the arrival of Buddhism, in the Chinese people's minds, human life continued from generation to generation, and each generation was an extension of the world of the living into the world of the dead.

Generally speaking, Christians believe in a final return to God and heaven; for Muslims, heaven is a place where people fulfill their worldly dreams of wine, meat, fresh flowers, and beautiful women. There are also popular Buddhist beliefs that there will be a seven-story pagoda and flying fairies in heaven. According to Chinese folklore, heaven is a place for the gods and heavenly officials to work, not a resting place for ordinary people. "Resting in the ground" simply means those who lived before are still living the same life underground, resting forever.

There is also archaeological evidence illustrating the boundaries between heaven, humans, and earth in ancient China. A silk painting from a Han tomb in Mawangdui, Hunan province, depicts a tree with 10 golden crows on top, representing the heavenly realm. The roots of this great tree penetrate through the world of humans to reach the underworld. Just below ground level, we find the image of the tomb occupant and her housemaids; at the next level down, we find the roots of the tree, growing out of the Yellow Springs, below which there are a few strong men holding up the universe.

At the Sanxingdui site in Sichuan province, a large bronze tree with many big-billed birds has also been unearthed, but we know nothing about the arrangement of its roots. In Mircia Eliad's interpretation, this would be the tree of life, which, like the symbol of a towering mountain, constitutes a link between the upper world, the heavens, and the under-world. In Chinese folklore, there is a peach tree that links heaven and earth, and its roots open into the underground world. Likewise, Mount Tai has been a sacred mountain in Chinese folklore from ancient times to the present, and in the Han dynasty it governed both life and death. During that period, the so-called "Governor of Mount Tai" was in charge. In later Daoist beliefs, Mount Tai was the seat of the Jade Emperor, and was part of the heavenly realm. In the tomb texts of the Han dynasty, it is common to find texts mentioning a "return to Mount Tai," with the phrase "the *hun* go to Liangfu and the *po* to Gaoli." The *hun* waited on Mount Tai to be dispatched to the human world by the heavenly realm, while the *po* remained peacefully in the netherworld.

Eternal rest in the underground world is the wish of all Chinese people. Two poems from *The Songs of Chu*, which contains texts from the Warring States period to the Han dynasty, called "The Great Summons" (*Dazhao* 大招) and "Summons of the Soul" (*Zhaohun* 招魂), both warned the dead, in the form of calling back the souls, that the east, south, west, and north were not to be visited, because in those regions there were all kinds of spirits and strange creatures that devoured the souls. The poems call the souls back to their native land, where they will be provided with pavilions, food and wine, and servants to make their lives comfortable. This kind of advice shows that the Chinese see the world after death as an eternal extension of life on earth, a status that will never change.

At the time that Buddhism was introduced into China, the concept of life and death was already changing to some degree. The *Scriptures of the Great Peace* (*Taipingjing* 太平經, a Han-dynasty religious text) represents early Daoist religious thought, and in this text we already find the notion that "it will be difficult to avoid judgment on the merits and demerits of one's life." Even if people manage to escape the judgment of the government during their life, after death, they cannot avoid the judgment of the gods and the underworld, and there will be retribution for both the good and evil deeds committed during their life. In the latter years of the Eastern Han dynasty, Buddhism had clearly already entered China, and the idea of a judgment after death, which was not prominent in Buddhist texts, nonetheless inspired the Chinese belief that such judgment was necessary.

The sect of the Heavenly Masters (*Tianshidao* 天師道) of the Bashu (Sichuan) region, early practitioners of what would become the Daoist religion, believed that the dead were responsible for their conduct in life—whether they took this from the *Taipingjing* or were influenced by Buddhism is not known—and further argued that punishment after death is stricter than that dealt out by the authorities in the living world, and that there is no escape. We find several tomb writings from the late Eastern Han period that state that the deceased's behavior should not implicate the living. The idea of "inherited burden" (*chengfu* 承負), which argues that the living are affected by the past behavior of their dead ancestors, differs somewhat from the ideal of the Spring and Autumn and Warring States periods, where the blessings and calamities of the living and the dead were always linked. Such a notion was changed in later days: The faults of the deceased should be borne by the deceased themselves, and the living should not be made to take on responsibility for them.

As mentioned above, the religious concepts of the Neolithic period included the fear of nature and the concept of ancestral spirits, which are two separate traditions, gods on the one hand and ancestral spirits on the other. By the time of the Shang dynasty, it is clear that faith in ancestral spirits was stronger than the faith in nature. When did the change begin? Historical documents do not provide clear evidence.

In the "Discourses of Chu" (*Chuyu* 楚語), part of the longer work *Discourses of the States*, we find:

> Then came the decadence of Shaohao, when the Nine Li disrupted government; people and gods commingled, and things no longer stayed true to category. Everyone made sacrifice, there were shamans (*wu*) and scribes (*shi*) in every family, and there was no sincerity. Although people exhausted themselves in sacrifice, they had no wellbeing. Sacrifices were not measured, and gods and people occupied the same positions. People recklessly made sworn alliances that were utterly without authority. The gods imitated the people and had no measure in their behavior. Good things did not descend, and there was nothing to offer in sacrifice. Catastrophes multiplied, and no one lived out his life. When Zhuanxu received the Mandate, he ordered the southern rector Zhong to take charge of heaven in order to organize the gods, and he ordered the northern rector Li to take charge of earth in order to organize the people. He made all return to the ancient norm, when there was no mutual intrusion. This is what is meant by breaking off communication between earth and heaven.[2]

In this passage, the mention of "breaking off communication between earth and heaven" is like dividing the human world and the heavenly court into two spheres. The heavenly court is an extension of the shamanic tradition of worshipping and fearing nature, while the worship of the ancestral spirits has been the focus of this chapter. The counsel to pay careful attention to one's parents' funerary rites with proper sacrifices suggests that the main concern is to continue communities of blood relatives. To speak to the ancestors, one does not need to go through a shaman because the descendants themselves have a blood bond with the ancestors, and their

---

2   Translation taken from Lin Fu-Shih, "The Image and Status of Shamans in Ancient China," in *Early Chinese Religion, Part One: Shang through Han, Vol. 1*, ed. John Lagerwey and Marc Kalinowski (Leiden: Brill, 2008), 402.

communication can be facilitated by feelings of kinship, so the ancestors can ask for protection from the gods on behalf of the descendants in the human world. At the same time, the religious feelings concerning the worship of the gods has not disappeared, but the relationship between gods and humans is mediated by ancestral spirits. In the next chapter, when discussing Chinese traditions or religions, the relationship between the gods and humans will be described more clearly.

In the Han tomb-quelling texts and scrolls, gods of all levels appear, as if they had authority over the dead. This phenomenon is probably related to the development of the bureaucratic system from the Qin-Han period onward, in which the government established its domain over all its subjects. Theoretically, everyone, no matter how noble or lowly, is responsible for his or her own conduct. Therefore, even those lucky enough to escape punishment in life will be judged and punished for his or her actions in the underground world, or by the underground government in the other world. It is interesting to note that in one of the tomb-quelling texts, apparently to deal with the responsibility of "the inherited burden," a few ginseng plants were among the burial items, which were meant to take the place of the deceased and bear his or her punishment (because the character for "person" [*ren* 人] is part of the two-character compound meaning "ginseng" [*renshen* 人參]). This arrangement once again shows that the Chinese see the underground world as an extension and continuation of the world of the living. There is an obvious difference between this concept of life and death and the Judeo-Christian idea that after death one rests in God's world awaiting the final judgment.

In Buddhism, there is the idea of karma and reincarnation. For example, if one commits a murder in one's lifetime, one may be murdered in the next life, as karmic retribution is involved in the process of rebirth. In ancient China, there was the notion that calamities and blessings are shared within families, as we see in expressions such as "the retribution suffered by the sons and the grandsons" or the retribution suffered by future generations, which functioned in parallel with retribution meted out in this life. The idea of retribution to be meted out in future generations was clearly influenced by Buddhism, while the idea behind "present life retribution" is that one has to take responsibility for one's own actions prior to death. Should this not occur, recompense for good behavior and suffering or punishment for bad behavior will be deferred to one's children and grandchildren. The saying the "the family that accumulates goodness will have much to celebrate" makes clear that this is the common responsibility of the family and the realization of family unity.

On questions of life and death, the Chinese tradition is like that of other peoples in that they inevitably entertained the dream of eternal life. *The Classic of Mountains and Seas (Shanhaijing* 山海經), probably composed in the Warring States period or the Qin-Han era, with different parts being written at different times, is a book about a magical world outside of human experience. The book divides the world into concentric circles, and thus we find the "Classic of the Mountains," the "Classic of Regions Within the Seas," the "Classic of the Regions Beyond the Seas," and the "Classic of the Great Wilderness"; surrounding the middle mountains are four mountains, and beyond the mountains are four seas, and an even further circle is "beyond the sea," and the four directions are all given a specific orientation. In the *Shanhaijing*, the mountains and oceans teem with all kinds of mountain demons, water monsters, strange birds and beasts, as well as with various immortal gods, each with his own supernatural powers and particular jurisdictions. These gods, who are not organized into a court, seem to exercise their powers within their own areas of control. Shamans have certain abilities to intervene in the world of these gods, by channeling their spirits, or using magic tools or objects to influence these deities.

In the classic of the "Inner Western Sea" section of the *Shanhaijing*, we read: "East of the Openbright there are Shaman Robust, Shaman Pushaway, Shaman Sunny, Shaman Shoe, Shaman Every, and Shaman Aide. They are all on each side of the corpse of Notch Flaw and they hold the neverdie drug to ward off decay. "[3] These great shamans have the magic

---

3   Anne Birrell, trans., *The Classic of Mountains and Seas* (London: Penguin Books, 1999), 141.

power to protect themselves and others with the Elixir of Immortality. The names of these great shamans, some of which have appeared in other ancient books, may be references to famous shamans, out of which the authors of the *Shanhaijing* fashioned the shamans in their text. Concerning the ideal of immortality, which is also an important concept in Daoism, I will have more to say in the next chapter.

Another record of immortality is that of some of the gods in the *Shanhaijing*, such as Xingtian, a hero who challenges the gods of heaven. Although he was defeated and beheaded by the heavenly gods, he did not surrender, and using his breast as his eye and his navel as his mouth, he continued fighting the gods with his weapons. In the thirteenth stanza of his "Reading the *Shanhaijing*," the poet Tao Yuanming 陶淵明 (365?–427) writes: "Jingwei carries tiny pebble bits in her mouth with which to fill the vast sea; Xingtian wields his axe, his determination remains undiminished. Before their transformation, the two were without reluctance; after their transformation they are still without regrets." As noted, Xingtian had been "transformed" when the gods beheaded him. Jingwei was the spirit born of the death of the daughter of the Yan Emperor, a legendary sage-ruler. The poem celebrates the indomitable spirit of the two, who continued their struggles after their "transformations," which are the equivalent of death. The poem also honors the heroes of failure. In the history of China, this kind of sympathy for the losers is not uncommon. I will have more to say on this phenomenon in the next chapter.

Finally, the Confucian concept of the "Three Immortals" should be mentioned. *The Zuo Tradition* records a story in which Shusun Bao of the state of Lu visited the state of Jin, where he met a Jin general surnamed Fan. Fan asked Shusun about the ancient saying concerning "death without perishing," and when Shusun did not answer, Fan opined that his own family line, prominent now for many centuries, might be an example of what the ancients meant. Shusun disagreed, saying that Fan's family had achieved worldly fame, while true immortality was defined by one's ability to leave one's virtue, accomplishments, and teachings to the ages. These three "immortals"—virtue, speech, and merit—are the effects left by humans, not eternal immortality in a biological sense.

Confucianism sublimated immortal concepts into great human virtues, which were left for the world to commemorate. This religious-like sentiment, without any religious magical qualities, is the highest realm to which Confucianism can aspire in terms of human nature. In Taiwanese folk beliefs, people who inspire admiration are called "personalities" (*jîn-keh-tsiá* 人格者) in the Taiwanese Hokkien dialect, and people miss them when they die. The tutelary gods in many parts of China are, in many folk beliefs, a recently deceased "personality" who has been appointed as the local protector of the area. The temples of these gods have to redo their icons every now and again, and the remodeling is often based on a certain "personality." Confucius himself was known as the "Master Teacher of Ten Thousand Generations" in later times, and before the imperial examinations were abolished, Wenchang—the god of literature—was an object of worship for scholars. All of these represent the immortality of the word.

At the local level, officials who have benefited the local community are forever remembered and even regarded as gods. Li Bing 李冰 (3rd century BCE) and his sons, who built the Dujiangyan River water-control project in Sichuan, and Zhang Bo (known as "Emperor Zhang"), who created similar projects in Suzhou and Anhui, are both examples of meritorious individuals who have been regarded as gods by thousands of people throughout the ages.

Many of the phenomena mentioned above reflect the traditional views of Chinese society on life and death. What I saw in the first half of my life was not far from tradition. In recent decades, China has undergone tremendous changes, especially in mainland China where, after many revolutions, the traditional concepts of life and death have been completely transformed in terms of rituals and philosophies. However, in Taiwan and overseas Chinese societies, although some of the rituals that were practiced in the past have been simplified or modified, at an emotional level, the notion of being prudent, honoring one's ancestors, and worshipping virtue still exists. The ancient folk beliefs discussed here have been extended to the present day, and generally still exist, which is why in modern times funeral rituals and the burning of various kinds of paper objects still exist.

Among people of my generation, memorials for the anniversary of one's parents' deaths are still observed. In my hometown, ancestors are worshipped on New Year's Eve, New Year's Day, the Qingming Festival and Winter Solstice. My family has been living away from our home in China since the Sino-Japanese War. My father wrote the name of our direct ancestors on a scroll and hung it up as a memorial for New Year and at festival times. When my brother and I moved to the US, each family household had a scroll of our ancestor's names, and at least on New Year's Eve and New Year's Day we would bring them out to honor our ancestors. These customs, like the tomb items and underground palaces of the Han dynasty, are in fact consistent with the attitude of offering sacrifices to one's relatives as if they were present, and of treating them as if they were living.

Most people in Taiwan today are descendants of immigrants from mainland China and often have ancestral tablets in their homes. The names of the ancestors' hometowns are inscribed on the back of the tablets, and these are worshipped year after year to so that people do not forget their roots. In Taiwan, if there is a funeral in a town or village, the family concerned will have a street blocked off and set up a stall to receive their relatives in what is an important event. They also burn paper burial objects (including houses, cars, furniture, clothes, televisions, computers, and so forth) for the deceased's use in the afterlife. From what I have seen, the Chinese in the United States have no ancestral graves to visit, and no memories of their ancestral genealogies. However, in everyday life, the parent-child bond within the family still extends to three or four generations. Not only do family members care for each other, but Chinese friends in the same city also care for and support each other.

Overseas Chinese have been away from home for generations, but still miss their ancestors. At the Overseas Chinese Cemetery in Manila, in the Philippines, there are halls in front of and behind the graves that are similar to sanctuaries where ancestors or gods are worshipped, allowing relatives who have come to sweep the graves to rest and relax inside, and in front of the tomb is a "car" carved in stone or cast in concrete, for the personal use of the deceased. I once visited Malacca in Malaysia, where there are many Chinese graves that have been there for hundreds of years, and on special days such as New Year's Day, people pay homage to their ancestors by sweeping their graves. There is a building in the Chinese quarter of Malacca, on the top floor of which is a temple dedicated to Mazu, while on the lower floors are clansmen associations, each family occupying a room with a plaque dedicated to the ancestors. The Chinese community in Malacca is said to have existed for 800 years. When I visited the site more than a decade ago, I saw the carved couplets on the Ming and Qing period gates and the sculptures on the stone-paved streets; standing there I felt as if I were on a Chinese street at dusk. The impression of that time and space remains etched in my mind down to the present day.

As stated in the beginning of this chapter, the religious sentiments of the Chinese are not necessarily attached to the established religious system and the rituals of that system, but are integrated into and embedded in everyday life. This is true about questions concerning life and death, and extends to the memory of our ancestors, so that individuals come to be parts of clan groups. There are also intricate kinship ties between clans, which gives rise to the concept of "compatriots" in Chinese culture. To this day, the Chinese call themselves "the descendants of the Yan Emperor and the Yellow Emperor." For thousands of years, China's agriculture has been based on farming. Intensive farming requires mutual cooperation, making small villages the basic unit of a larger society. People with same surname often occupy the same village and there are marital relations between the neighboring villages. These are the elements that have made the societies encompassed by Chinese culture into one of the largest communities in the world. Some of the religious sentiments described in this chapter are what hold this vast community together.

VII. The Many Gods Who Protect the People

This chapter addresses another issue under the general topic of religious belief. As mentioned in Chapter VI, Professor C. K. Yang's study of Chinese religions argues that the beliefs of the Chinese people are not found only within the systems of institutionalized religions, but are better understood as rituals and concepts integrated into the fabric of everyday life. If we were to discuss the topic of institutionalized religions, this would require serious theological research on various themes. In the case of the two major institutionalized religions in China—Buddhism and Daoism—many great thinkers in the past have probed various theological theories, asking important and insightful philosophical questions. However, none of this seems to have had much impact on average believers. Today, if you talk to ordinary believers of Buddhism and Daoism, they neither understand nor particularly care about scriptures and theories. What they do care about, however, is which gods have what kind of influence in their own individual lives, and how they should think about the way they live their lives. These are the things that have affected the common people of China from generation to generation, and they are the basis of their spiritual life. In addition to these questions, this chapter will also touch slightly on institutional religions in the modern era.

The religious feelings of humanity basically come down to the two ideas of respect and fear. The former involves feelings of veneration, while the latter touches on uncertainty. Many scholars of primitive religions have probably tried to imagine how humans chose which objects to worship in these two categories. To sum up the beliefs of many ancient peoples, we can probably divide them into these two categories: One is reverence for the forces of nature, and the other is the worship of the dead, especially of the ancestors. In the latter category, we also note feelings of longing and affection. The first category, the worship of the natural forces, became the system of nature gods, and the second became the worship of the ancestral spirits. In the previous chapter, we mentioned the ancient Chinese concept of totem-like beliefs, which combined nature and ancestral worship into one, integrating objects or phenomena to be feared with the origins of one's own ancestors, resulting in explanations of the origin of life.

For example, we look up to the heavens with a kind of admiration and respect; we are in awe of the sun, the moon and the stars, and when we look at the earth, the source of life from which plants grow, we may think of the earth and the mother as sources of life. By the same token, mountains, oceans, storms, rain, and dew, all have a great influence on our lives, and we take them as objects of worship.

This makes me think of a personal experience. During the war, when I was about 11 years old, we were anticipating that Japanese troops would advance toward the region where we were living. My father had to stay with his unit on the front lines, and the rest of the family had to retreat to a safer area. Everyone was on foot, and only the luggage and provisions were carried by porters. I couldn't walk because of my disability, so they put me on a pile of luggage and carried me as well. There was a part of the trip where we had to cross part of Mount Daba in western Hubei province. We climbed up to the mountain pass from the plains, and it took more than a day to get to the top. Next to the mountain top, there was a small stone structure. There were probably five or six litters, and more than ten porters, who arrived at the pass one after the other. The head porter called out, "Let's go worship at the mountain temple." This was the little structure, a simple temple made of stone slabs forming a platform at the peak of the mountain. The size of the platform was no more than 10 feet in circumference; the wind was blowing, and the trees around it were no more than two feet high.

Looking around from the summit, you could see the towering Mount Daba to the west, while the peaks to the east, south and north bowed their heads. Looking up at the boundless sky, the only thing that broke the silence was the sound of the howling wind. The porters knelt down at the mountain temple to offer their respects, while I sat on top of a pile of luggage and looked around, bewildered. None of the 10 men spoke. The porters were all squatting on the ground in a circle, facing south, distracted as I was by the sight of the boundless sky. We sat in silence for more than 10 minutes before getting up silently and starting down the south slope. After a short walk, we suddenly found ourselves on a path where the oleander was in full bloom. At the end of the flowered path, there was a little terrace and a village of some 10 families, with children running around and laughing, adults working, a few dogs barking at us—an oasis of peace in the middle of a war.

These two scenes occurred within an hour of each other. I was young at the time and didn't understand religion. Later on, however, when I took courses in social anthropology, ethnology and religious studies, the feeling of awe that I had experienced at the mountain temple resurfaced as a vivid memory. It is precisely because of our insignificance in the face of nature that we imagine a great power, and personify this power as the gods that represent the various forces of nature, such as the gods of heaven, earth, mountains, and water.

In the category of ancestral spirits, as mentioned in the previous chapter, the most important feeling is the love and longing for the parents who gave birth to us and raised us, and the hope that their lives will never come to an end. For those who die before their time, we always feel like a part of their life is still with us, resulting in the phenomenon of what we called "ghosts" in the previous chapter. These various feelings account for the psychological conditions behind the worship of the spirits of ancestors.

In the era of primitive religion, there were some people, due to their particular sensitivity, who were seen by others as uniquely capable of communicating with the gods. Such people eventually became "spirit mediums" who constructed a set of interpretations and rituals that they thought would help them to communicate with the spirits. In a primitive community, spirit mediums often become leaders. Different religions have different names for these people; some are called priests and others are called shamans. In the previous chapter, I quoted a passage from the "Chuyu" section of the *Discourses of the States*, in which Guan Yifu 觀射父 discussed shamanism. His remarks make clear that before there was an institutional religious system, almost anyone could be a medium. It was only during the reign of Zhuanxu 顓頊, one of the mythological Five Emperors, that a system of political leadership evolved, and the realms of heaven and humans were divided into separate systems. Rituals to the heavens were henceforth performed by mediums, and the management of the human world was the responsibility of the human kings. Under Zhuanxu's reign, we see the emergence of possibly the earliest calendar in China, a periodization organized according to agricultural production. This calendar represents the union between people and heaven, rather than an order of events dictated by priests and mediums. In the passage from the *Discourses of the States* mentioned above, this is referred to as "cutting off the communication between heaven and earth," establishing separate orders to replace the prior confusion.

In the pre-Qin era, China was a patriarchal society that combined ancestor worship and "feudalism." Theoretically, the king of the human realm represented the point of union between humankind and their ancestors. All the prayers and wishes of humankind were to be presented to the ancestors by the ruler, who was the leader of this patriarchy, and the ancestors would then give their blessings. The ancestors, on behalf of their children and grandchildren, prayed to the divine court of natural forces for providence and blessings. Such a belief system does not have an independent, separate church. Japan's historical theocracy is an example: the Japanese belief in the emperor and in Shinto is such a belief system. The priests found in Shinto shrines in Japan are simply workers who serve the gods, while the link between gods and humans is the emperor (the first emperor, "Emperor Jimmu," was actually the great shaman of that time, Himiko).

The two main religious systems in Chinese culture are Buddhism and Daoism. The former was not introduced into China until the Han dynasty, and the gradual organization of the latter took place at the same time as the introduction of Buddhism. Before the Han dynasty, Chinese religious beliefs were in fact a combination of the gods, deities, and ancestral spirits that I have been discussing. Prior to the Qin-Han unification, each region of China had its own local beliefs, and there was no single belief system encompassing all of China. As they were developing, neither Buddhism nor Daoism remained fixed in theological terms. In the process there were many changes, as for example when a local belief grew to become an important part of a certain Buddhist or Daoist sect.

It would be an extremely difficult task to arrange the divine court according to the objects of worship of the various Buddhist and Daoist sects existing today. For example, popular beliefs concerning the celestial court are based on the story of Jiang Ziya's deification in a Ming-dynasty novel called *The Investiture of the Gods* (*Fengshen yanyi* 封神演義),[1] which contains a detailed discussion of the ranks and duties of the officers of the

---

1   This novel, attributed to Xu Zhonglin 許仲琳 (d. 1560) and Lu Xixing 陸西星 (1520–1606), tells the story of the decline of the Shang dynasty and the rise of the Zhou dynasty, and the characters include historical-mythological figures as well as various gods and demons who participate in the battles and plots. See Chapter X for more on this. —Trans.

celestial court. Mainstream Buddhism and Daoism reject this, but this is how the common people saw it.

We can actually uncover some principles behind the process of the evolution of the people's ideas about the celestial court. Something that happens frequently is the personification of a nature god, as when the majestic God of Heaven is personified as a father figure. Mount Tai is the main sacred mountain in eastern China and appears to be especially lofty because it is a towering mountain in the relatively flat land of Shandong province. The god of this mountain, Great Emperor Dongyue, is often identified with the emperor of the celestial court, because high mountains reach up to the heavens. On the other hand, earth gods are linked to productivity, and are personified as mother figures; images of the mother goddess, in turn, focus on the mother quality's as a caregiver, and on the forgiving nature of maternal love. Thus, the supreme goddess is often the image of a compassionate, forgiving, redeeming mother. The same principle explains why mountain gods represent great masculine power, while water gods represent soft, feminine power.

Ancient farmers revered the productivity of the land because they depended on it. According to the "Fangji" 坊記 section of the *Book of Rites*, farmers worshipped Xiannong 先農, the god of agriculture, and Xianse 先嗇, his wife, during the planting and harvesting seasons, as well as the channels and dikes of the irrigation system, and even the tigers that drove away wild boars and the cats that drove away rats. In the mind of the ancient farmers, such gods might seem trivial, but they nonetheless possessed important divine powers that had to be revered and worshipped in order to secure needed blessings.

Another principle is to commemorate a real person whose special contributions are remembered after his death; on the one hand it is a gesture of thanks, and at the same time it marks the hope that his or her achievements will endure. This principle is what the Chinese call "merit makes people virtuous," which means that the intelligent and the upright can become gods. Guan Yu 關羽 (also known as Guandi 關帝 or Guangong 關公, d. 220) is a very important god in Chinese folklore for the following reasons: Guangong was a man of gallantry and righteousness in his life. He died to keep his promise to his blood-brother Liu Bei 劉備 (161–223), a famous military figure, and thus became the object of public commemoration. Because of his bravery, he is seen as the protector of the vulnerable common people.

In the original Buddhist system, Guanyin 觀音 was a bodhisattva, not a buddha and not a woman. However, in Chinese folklore, Guanyin became the main Chinese Buddhist deity because of the forgiving and redeeming power of the mother figure, so she is portrayed as a goddess worshipped by everyone to save them from suffering and distress. The goddess Mazu, who is revered by sailors and fishermen in the coastal areas of southern China, is also known as the "Holy Heavenly Mother," and was a Song-dynasty woman named Lin Moniang 林默娘. The story is that she rescued a shipwrecked crew in her dreams, becoming the protector of seafarers and fishermen, and later a mother god who blessed and redeemed the people.

Everywhere in China there are "city gods" and "tutelary gods," which are, respectively, the protectors of individual counties and neighborhoods. Their positions are projections of both the governmental administrative system and the functions of the elders in community life. Stories about the city gods are often similar: after the death of a certain magistrate, who was a great benefactor of the region, he was invited to serve as a city god. In a local community, if an elderly person is generally respected and constantly committed to the local community, once he dies, someone will say that he has now taken on the responsibilities of the local protector. The people will then remake the image of this deity, more or less modeling it on the respected elder.

In this section, I will take my hometown of Wuxi, and Taiwan, where I have lived for a long time, as examples to illustrate the differences and similarities between the gods worshipped by the common people in these two places. I'll start with Wuxi.

Wuxi is a medium-sized city in the Jiangnan region[2], which has a history of more than 2,000 years. Transportation is convenient, the area is rich, and all kinds of religions are very active. Solely in terms of institutionalized religions, Wuxi has ancient and important temples and shrines. For example, both the Chongan and Nanchan Buddhist temples were already flourishing during the Southern dynasties in the fifth and sixth centuries. In modern times, during the period of the Sino-Japanese War, activities in these large temples were limited to routine ceremonies, and large ritual events with scripture readings virtually disappeared. Chongan Temple has been in ruins since the Taiping rebellion in the mid-nineteenth century. On its original site, there used to be a humble Daoist shrine, the Leizhen (Thunder) Temple. Chongan Temple is quite famous and is a well-known food hall.

As for Daoist temples, there are Dongyue Temple and Doumu Pavillion, among others, whose functions seem to be limited to everyday worship, divination, and praying for good fortune. Wuxi Daoism is mostly an offshoot of the Maoshan 茅山 sect, which specializes in managing ghosts and spirits. I was once fortunate enough to be able to hear Daoist music. After the end of the Sino-Japanese War, Daoist groups from all over Jiangnan organized a performance of traditional music in Wuxi, where troupes played many important pieces of music that were famous in the past. Beyond performances like these, the common people seldom ran across anyone preaching religion to them in their daily lives. A more common occurrence is the custom of placing the name of a newborn baby boy under the throne of a god in order to be protected with his blessing.

---

2   Jiangnan 江南, literally "South of the River," is a geographic area referring to lands immediately to the south of the lower reaches of the Yangtze River, and encompasses the city of Shanghai, the southern part of Jiangsu province, the southeastern part of Anhui province, the northern part of Jiangxi province and the northern part of Zhejiang province. —Ed.

In addition to these groups connected with institutionalized religions, there are some temples that are more involved in daily life. It is said that there are more than 100 ancestral shrines in Huishan, in the western part of Wuxi, but a large percentage of them are family shrines and ancestral halls, which are private in nature. When large lineage groups discuss the distribution of clan resources, this often occurs at a family temple.

I would like now to introduce some special figures of folk worship in Wuxi: some are already recognized as gods in popular customs, while others are local historical figures who are commemorated by the people and worshipped in Daoist temples and monasteries. The most famous of the first group is the main figure of worship at Dongyue Temple, the Great Emperor Dongyue, the god of Taishan. Another is Lord Nandou (*Nandouxing jun* 南斗星君), the God of the Big Dipper, who is in charge of the human life span and is worshipped at Yanshouci Temple. When my family was in Chongqing, we lived for a time in the Wuxi Community Hall, a kind of club for blacksmiths from Wuxi who were working in Chongqing. According to them, the meeting place for the blacksmiths in their hometown was in the Yangshouci Temple.

The most famous example of the second type is the Great Emperor Cishan (*Cishan dadi* 祠山大帝, whose real name was Zhang Bo), venerated at Zhang Yuan Temple. Zhang Bo was a Han-dynasty magistrate who is said to have drained a swamp to construct a useful canal in the Guangde region in Anhui, channeling various rivers and marshes into the Yangzi and Qiantang river systems. Temples to him can be found all over Jiangnan, where he is revered as the "Great Emperor." Another example is the figure of veneration at the Immortal of the Southern Waters Temple (*Nanshuixian miao* 南水仙廟), Wang Qiqin 王其勤 (1531–?), who was a county magistrate who served in Wuxi at the end of the Ming dynasty. He was credited with organizing local fishermen into a militia to fight against the Japanese pirates. Because of his contribution to keeping Wuxi safe, he was worshipped in the southern part of the city after his death and was called the "Immortal of the Southern Waters."

This shrine is close to Huangbudun, where ceramic vats were made, so the kiln workers used the Immortal of the Southern Waters Temple as their meeting place. The same place also became the meeting place for local fishermen, thus combining the cult of the local magistrate with that of the water god worshipped by the fishermen. Another example is the Ming-dynasty county magistrate, Liu Wuxu 劉五續, for whom the Immortal of the Western Waters Temple (*Xishuixian miao* 西水仙廟) was built. During his tenure, Liu devoted himself to the management of rivers and lakes, to opening new waterways, and to the development of tidal land. After being accused of corruption by a political foe, he was removed from office and was punished. The people sympathized with his misfortune and were grateful for his contributions, so this temple was dedicated to him. It was built at the junction of the Grand Canal and Lake Tai, and became a meeting place for boatmen and fishermen who worked on the water and on the canal.

There are also some real historical figures in Huishan whose contributions and deeds are remembered by the people. During the An Lushan rebellion in the mid-eighth century, Zhang Xun 張巡 (708–757) and Xu Yuan 許遠 (709–757) held Suiyang and thus safeguarded regions of both the Yangtze and Huai rivers, and the people of Jiangnan built a temple called the Zhang Zhongzheng Temple to commemorate them. Another example is Shaobao Temple, built for Yu Qian 于謙 (1398–1457), who fought against a Mongol invasion in the Ming dynasty. Xia Yunyi 夏允彝 (1596–1645) and his son, Xia Wanchun 夏完淳 (1631–1647), who fought against the Qing dynasty on Lake Tai at the end of the Ming dynasty, are also worshipped at Shaobao Temple.

Every year in the third lunar month, eight ancestral temples celebrate the birthday of Emperor Dongyue at the Wuxi Temple Fair. The temples mentioned above—including Yanshouci Temple, the Dongxiuxian, the Immortal of the Western Waters Temple, as well as Yansheng Temple (which commemorates the third-century hero Zhou Chu 周處 (236–297), who removed the three scourges[3] during the Jin dynasty)—together with the city gods of Wuxi and Jingui counties, all gather at the Zhongchung ancestral temple, where they are received by the administrators of the hall, i.e. the temple masters, and in different groups make their way to the Zhang Bo Temple, and finally to the temple of the Great Emperor Dongyue.

This annual temple fair attracts tens of thousands of visitors from around Jiangnan; Wuxi is packed with people, every family has relatives and friends staying with them, and the event is well known throughout China as a famous temple fair. In the course of this fair, various professional guilds, such as those of boatmen, fishermen, blacksmiths, kiln workers, etc., gather at the temple where they usually meet and serve as basic elements of the temple fair procession. Each temple has local sponsors that visit frequently, supplying the banners for the processions and following along. The cultural and martial arts troupes of each temple perform continuously on the way: for the cultural processions, young girls standing on a bamboo platform act out a piece of theater; for the martial arts processions, younger practitioners from all walks of life, with a parade of guides and escorts, perform martial arts along the way.

Part of the hustle and bustle of these processions is quite meaningful. Among the procession, some are dressed as jailed convicts, bound in shackles, and others are dressed as *yamen* runners[4] and jailers who drive the convicts forward: among these "criminals," some have dozens of needles sticking out of their wrists, and lanterns and gongs hanging from

---

3   The scourges included a tiger, a dragon, and ironically, Zhou himself. He had been a local bully and realized to what extent he was resented by the people after killing the tiger and the dragon. He subsequently changed his ways and became a beloved general. —Trans.

4   The officials' offices in traditional China were generally referred to as *yamen*; *yamen* runners were the personnel attached to these officers, particularly the low-level personnel. —Trans.

their bodies. Behind them are numerous carts, or litters, carrying letter boxes full of written notes—either notes composed by believers as they read the sutras, or the daily ledger of an individual's merits and demerits,[5] as is encouraged in Confucianism—all of which reveal the prayers and remorse of believers in the city. The "jailed convicts" in the procession are volunteers, standing in to be punished on behalf of the "sinners" of the world; and the papers in the letter boxes represent the daily reflections of the common people, a means of redeeming the offenders from their sins (more on this in the next section). The "convicts" cannot change into their regular clothes until after they have had an audience with the Great Emperor Dongyue, as a sign that they have been cleansed of their sins.

The above is an overview of temple fairs in Wuxi. The following section is about folk beliefs and temple fairs in Taiwan, after which I will compare the similarities and differences between the folk beliefs of the two different communities.

Taiwan is the place where I settled when I left mainland China. I grew up there, and my career began in Taiwan, and although I later worked overseas, my heart stayed in Taiwan. I also know a little bit about Taiwan's folk beliefs. Moreover, I am fortunate to know Mr. Lin Hengdao and several Taiwanese folklorists, and through their explanations, I have a clearer understanding of certain details concerning Taiwan's folklore beliefs.

The main temples in Taiwan's cities and towns include the following: the Temple to the God of Literature (Confucius Temple), the Martial Temple (Guandi Temple), the City God Temple, the Wenchang Temple

---

5   The idea behind a "ledger of merit and demerit," which was a physical volume, was to note one's good and bad acts every day in the hopes of understanding the evolution of one's moral life. —Trans.

(where the god of literature is also worshipped), the Dragon King Temple, the Mazu Temple, the Fire God Temple, the Altar to the God of Agriculture, and shrines to women who died defending their honor or chastity. Taiwan's principle deities include Shennong the Great (God of Agriculture), Taiziye (the Marshal of the Central Altar), the Monkey King, Lu Dongbin, the Living Buddha, Master Tiger, Monkey General, and others. There are also Lord Big Tree, the Lord Who Responds, Lady Ten Thousand Surnames, Lord Great Tomb, Lord Ten Thousand Surnames, Lord Flowing Water, Lord Universal Salvation, the Eighteen Lords and gods connected to militia and feuding, and so on.

Most of the Taiwanese gods are actually the same as those on the mainland: there are gods with specialized functions, such as Guandi and the City God; there are also some whose deeds and stories are extracted from folklore and enshrined as gods, such as Taiziye, the Monkey King, Lu Dongbin, and so on. Cults devoted to tigers, monkeys, big trees, etc., are a form of reverence for certain animals and plants that are long-lived or magical. As for those who have died with no heirs, such as the Lord Who Responds, the Lady of Ten Thousand surnames, and those connected with Taiwan's history of inter-factional feuds who died fighting, they are worshipped by the people so that they will not become powerful spirits haunting the world.

There are also some "royal lords," such as Wen Fu, Chi Fu, and the 36 royal lords, all of whom died unjustly. Some stories say that they were 36 scholars who were on their way to study for the exams and were shipwrecked; others think they died in an epidemic that killed all the people on board. But from the perspective of the ritual on Taiwan, performed during the Hungry Ghost Festival, in which the royal lord boat is set afire and then pushed out to sea, the point appears to be to send the plague god abroad in ships belonging to the lords. Hence the "royal lords" may in fact be plague gods, particularly given the similarity between the Chinese characters for "plague" (*wen* 瘟) and that for the surname "Wen" 溫.

Other gods were brought to Taiwan by the immigrants who opened Taiwan up in the 17th and 18th centuries, protective gods that they brought from their hometowns, and which served as a symbol of unity for people from the same hometown to rally around. For this reason, people in Quanzhou worship Master Chingshui, Venerable King Guangze, Venerable King Lingan, Doctor Baosheng (a famous doctor named Wu Ben 吳本), and Venerable King Boyi. Zhangzhou people worship the Sage King Kaizhang (Chen Yuanfang 陳元放, who opened up the Zhangzhou region in the Tang dynasty), General Fu Xin (Ma Gongye 馬公爺), and Great Emperor Detian (commonly known as Lin Fang 林放, one of the 72 disciples of Confucius, who is revered as an ancestor by all Lin families).

The Hakka[6] worship the King of the Three Mountains, referring to the three mountains outside Chaozhou, which represents the memory of their hometown in Guangdong. This kind of nostalgia for the homeland is found not only in Taiwan, but also among the overseas Chinese who migrated to Southeast Asia and settled there hundreds of years ago, and who took the protective gods of their homeland overseas to worship forever. This nostalgia is also motivated by a desire to remember the source of one's life and not to forget one's roots. More importantly, having arrived in their new destination, pioneers from the same place can gather in groups and cooperate with each other. In the history of Taiwan, armed conflicts between ethnic groups of immigrants were common, such as those between Quanzhou and Zhangzhou people and between those coming from Fujian and Guangdong (the Hakka). Those who died in these feuds were also worshipped for their courage and righteousness. There are many sad memories associated with the history of Taiwan, and the worship of the gods that protect these communities remains in our hearts.

---

6   The Hakka (客家, literally "guess families") are Han Chinese people whose ancestral homes are chiefly in areas around Guangdong and other southern provinces. They form closely-knit communities and speak their own Hakka language. —Ed.

⌒∽⌒

The way people worship in Taiwan is quite different from how they do it in my hometown of Wuxi, in mainland China. In Wuxi, Buddhism is Buddhism and Daoism is Daoism, and the people celebrated in the area each have their own temple according to their nature and deeds. In Taiwan, however, everything is all mixed up, and almost every temple is a shared place of worship for many different gods. Let's take the Wanhua Longshan Temple in Taipei as an example.

Many gods are worshipped at the Wanhua Longshan Temple, including important deities of Buddhism, Daoism, and Confucianism. According to the temple guide, the temple is divided into the front hall, the main hall, and the rear hall, which can be further sub-divided into many altars with over 100 statues of deities. The temple also has seven incense burners dedicated to Guanyin, the Lord of Heaven, Mazu, the Venerable King Shuixian (The King of Water), Zhusheng Niangniang (The Protector of Pregnancy), Wenchang (The Lord of Letters), and Guandi, to which believers offer incense to seek their blessings.

The highest incense burner near the main hall is dedicated to the Lord of Heaven; the largest one near the front hall in the atrium is for Guanyin. In the rear hall of the temple, worshippers begin their worship in the middle of the hall, and then make offerings on both sides, first to the dragon side, and then to the tiger side. The front hall is dedicated to the Three Jewels (the Buddha, the teachings, and the spiritual teachers), so those who follow Buddhist rituals start here before proceeding to the rest of the temple.

The main hall, also known as the Yuantongbao Hall, is dedicated to Guanyin (the name Yuantong is taken from a chapter on the Guanyin bodhisattva in a Buddhist scripture). Guanyin is the bodhisattva of great compassion, and is associated with Amidha (Amitabha) Buddha. Wenshu (Manjushri) Bodhisattva symbolizes great wisdom, and Puxian (Samantabhadra) Bodhisattva symbolizes great deeds, and both are associated with Shakyamuni Buddha. Weituo Bodhisattva, Qielan Bodhisattva, and the Four Heavenly Kings are the guardians of Buddhism. It is said that Master Zhiyi 智者大師 (538–579), founder of Tiantai Buddhism, once saved the soul of Guan Yu, who became a Buddhist protector. There are also statues of the 18 *luohan* (arhats) surrounding the temple in all directions.

The rear hall of the temple is dedicated to deities of different natures: the Hall of the Heavenly Sacred Mother is dedicated to Mazu, with the Hall of Wenchang (for the civil deity) on the left and the Hall of Guandi (for the military deity) on the right. Mazu is a folk deity, whose real name was Lin Moniang, and she is also known as Tianhou (Heavenly Queen). This is the most important goddess in Taiwan folk religion. This story is that Lin, whose seafaring family lived in Meizhou, in Fujian province, was born mute, hence her name Moniang, which means "silent girl." Her father and brother were both sailors. Once, their ship capsized, and it is said that Moniang's spirit left her body and went to rescue her father and brother at sea, and she led the shipwrecked crew back to land with a red lantern that she held in her hand.

Along the coast of Fujian Province, everyone is either a sailor or a fisherman, and all earn their living from the sea; Lin Moniang became their protector goddess. Though she was just a young girl when she became deified, her icon depicts a stately queen. Early images of her had a black face, but later evolved to depict a white-faced noblewoman. From being a protector of seafarers, her status continued to rise and she finally became a mother figure to all human beings, a role very similar to that of Guanyin. Her assistants of the left and right are called Thousand-Mile Eyes and Wind-Accompanying Ears, two special abilities needed to navigate the ocean: sharp vision helps protect sailors at night, in the fog and during other inclement weather, and sharp hearing helps sailors distinguish favorable winds from coming storms. However, over time, her assistant Thousand-Mile Eyes came to be able to see disasters everywhere in the world for Mazu, just as Wind-Accompanying Ears could hear all suffering. In this world, if we are poor, we call out to the gods, and if we are in pain, we call out to our mothers. Just like a mother, Mazu has become the focus for people seeking protection and comfort.

In the left wing of the Hall of the Heavenly Sacred Mother, the Venerable King Shuixian is worshipped as Yu, the emperor of the Xia dynasty who controlled the great flood, and who is also known as the King of the Sea or the sea god. Also worshipped here are Wu Zixu 伍子胥 (526–484 BCE), Qu Yuan, Li Bai and Wang Bo 王勃 (649–676), four famous historical figures popularly identified with water. We also find the icon of the City God, the administrative god of the underworld, responsible for rewarding good and punishing evil. There is also Fude Zhengshen, the god of the land, who protects agriculture and commerce. There is also the Dragon God, the God of Rain and the God of the Sea. These are the typical functional gods of the Daoist system. We also find these gods in the popular beliefs of the people of Wuxi.

In the right wing of the Hall of the Heavenly Sacred Mother, the main object of worship is Zhusheng Niangniang, but there is a secondary altar dedicated to Lady Chitou, said to have been a pregnant woman who was killed by Zhangzhou migrants during a feud between Zhangzhou and Quanzhou people when she tried to wake up the Quanzhou fighters. There is also a shrine to the Twelve Old Ladies, protectors of women in labor. The descriptions here are self-explanatory: childbirth in traditional Chinese society posed many risks and going into labor was tantamount to walking through the gates of hell. It is only natural that there be gods and goddesses next to Mazu offering special protection for women.

The Hall of Wenchang is dedicated to Wenchang emperors. In most temples, five Wenchang emperors are worshipped (Wenchang Xingjun, Wenkui Xingjun, Ziyang Fuzi, Guansheng Dijun, and Fuyou Dijun), while three are worshipped in the Longshan Temple—Wenchang Dijun, Dacheng Kuixing, and Ziyang Fuzi. The traditional Chinese scholar regarded passing the imperial examination as the proper path for entering the government. Therefore, the worship of Wenchang also serves the needs of the scholars because it is only with his blessing that scholars have the opportunity to advance. It goes without saying that the Huatuo hall is dedicated to Master Huatuo 華佗 (145–208), a famous Han-period physician known as the god of healing. Huatuo is for everyone since everyone needs health care. But many of the crises faced in daily life require specific gods who will help the believers to avoid disaster and obtain good fortune.

The Emperor Guansheng hall is dedicated to Guan Yu, with secondary shrines devoted to Guan Ping (Guan Yu's son) and Zhou Cang (a fictional character in the novel *The Romance of the Three Kingdoms*). Lord Guan is worshipped everywhere in China, in some places because of his righteousness, and in others because his martial arts abilities allow him to drive away evil spirits. In Taiwan and southern China, Lord Guan also doubles as the god of wealth. I have consulted folklorists as to how this came to be, but no one really knows. Some say it comes out of the episode in *The Romance of the Three Kingdoms* where Cao Cao offered Lord Guan gold and silver every day in an attempt to keep him on Cao's side, although Guan took none of the money when he finally left, taking only a robe. But this seems a bit far-fetched to me, and perhaps the functions are confusing only because he's so powerful that there is nothing beyond his concern.

The Three Great Emperor-Officials (*Sanguan dadi* 三官大帝) are the Heavenly Official, the Earthly Official and the Water Official, of which only the Water Official is worshipped at the Longshan temple. The Dizang Bodhisattva (Ksitigarbha), a symbol of the great Buddhist vow to save all sentient beings, is worshipped as the redeemer of the souls of the dead from hell. Yue Lao, the Old Man under the Moon (*yuexia laoren* 月下老人), is worshipped in the hall of the same name. He is in charge of marriages, so many believers often pray to him for the success of their love life. Further down the corridor is the shrine to the White Tiger, one of the four symbols of Chinese mythology on the outer wall of the hall to the Old Man under the Moon.

Thus you can see that there are many gods worshipped in the Longshan temple, with complex and multiple functions, and that the Buddhist and Daoist gods, as well as gods from the folk tradition, are all worshipped in one place. This is a reflection of the fact that the custom in Taiwanese folk beliefs is to serve all the gods that need to be worshipped. None can be ignored in one sacred space so that every one of these deities—once they are asked for protection—must respond, a practice that also enables believers to avoid offending some force they might have inadvertently overlooked.

Professor C. K. Yang pointed out that Chinese folk beliefs are very specific and utilitarian, and aim to bring to bear mysterious divine power in every aspect of life. Taiwan is an immigrant society opened up in the 17th and 18th centuries. When people crossed the deep waters from Fujian and Guangdong to arrive in Taiwan, entering a completely unknown world, they faced plagues, typhoons, and earthquakes, as well as man-made disasters such as inter-ethnic feuds. Life was extremely unsafe, the future hard to predict. There is a Taiwanese proverb that says, "two die, three stay, and five turn back," which speaks to the difficulty of migrating to Taiwan. In such circumstances, fear and hope were inseparable. Therefore, in terms of religion, believers would rather be all-inclusive in the worship of the gods, be they Daoist, Buddhist, or anything else worthy of worship, and they prefer that the gods fill the temple from front to back, so that they can show respect to the gods and pray for their assistance anywhere and at any moment. Of course, in real life one indeed would need certain places to pray for specific needs, such as the altars of the gods of fertility, marriage, and peacekeeping.

Although there are many gods and goddesses worshipped in Taiwan, and Guandi, the plague gods, and native deities are worshipped in a variety of ways, the cult of Mazu remains the most important. Here I will use the Mazu pilgrimages and incense offering as an example to illustrate the relationship between folk beliefs and local communities. There are more than 2,000 Mazu temples in Taiwan, at least one in almost every town. People continue to argue over which Mazu temple was established first. In Taiwan, the custom is for a new Mazu temple to be viewed as an offshoot of a main temple, which is accomplished by bringing some ashes from the main temple's incense burner, a process known as "dividing the incense." This system also establishes the relationship of "seniority" between the temples, and the Mazu temples in different locations are numbered one, two, three, etc. In other words, the sequence of "dividing incense" creates worship circles centered on main temples. Of course, if we take all of the Mazu worship circles in Taiwan together, this constitutes the Mazu belief community. This belief circle may well cover all Taiwanese people, with the exception of Christians and Muslims, who reject folk beliefs, and those who neither accept them nor reject them, meaning that some 75% of Taiwanese people belong to the Mazu belief community.

Looking now at individual Mazu communities throughout the island, the two whose processions are the most wide-ranging are those of Nanyao Temple in Zhanghua and Zhenlan Temple in Dajia, Taizhong, both of which claim to have taken their incense directly from the original main Mazu temple in Meizhou, on the mainland. The Nanyao network covers an area stretching from Zhanghua to Jiayi, with 200 to 300 towns and villages, each of which has a Mazu temple belonging to the Nanyao community. The Zhenlan network covers the area from Xinzhu to Taizhong, crossing the Dajia River, where there are more than 50 Mazu temples of considerable size, all of which took their incense ashes from the Zhenlan temple. These two temples carry out their processions at different times. For every procession, believers must welcome Mazu's holy palanquin, follow the procession as it travels through the network's territory, and then follow it back to the main temple. The itinerary lasts seven to eight days and the number of participants is over 100,000, which is considerable number.

During the Koxinga[7] (1624–1662) era, Taiwan mainly consisted of the southern areas of Tainan, Gaoxiong, and Pingdong, and the area to the north of Taizhong was little developed. Once the Kangxi Emperor conquered Taiwan in 1683 and Taiwan became part of China's territory, government

---

7 Koxinga is the Dutch-Romanized version of Zheng Chenggong, who wound up occupying Taiwan as part of his resistance to the Qing conquest of China in the mid-17th century, defeating the Dutch, who had outposts on Taiwan (then known as Formosa), and establishing a dynasty on the island that lasted from 1661 to 1683. —Trans.

offices were gradually established. From the Koxinga era to the cession of Taiwan to Japan in the Sino-Japanese War in 1895, the development of Taiwan continued for 300 years, yet no matter which regime was in power, the scope and the efficiency of their governance remained limited. Most immigrants came from Quanzhou and Zhangzhou in Fujian, and the Hakka communities of northeastern Guangdong, and there was both competition and collaboration among them, with Mazu temples serving as a base for both. Another level of protection were the temples to native-place deities brought over by each community—for example, the Kaizhang Shengwang cult, which was the center of the Zhangzhou community only. Since Mazu is the main protector of the southern maritime border and of the life of Chinese seafarers, she naturally became a common focus, bringing together immigrants from different native places, thus creating a ritual community that transcended the native-place gods. Hakka immigrants sometimes joined this community, but more often they clung to the cults of the King of the Three Mountains and Guandi, though they would not ignore Mazu. Here we will take the two largest temple processions as an example, because they are the most influential and cover a vast area.

Mazu territorial processions generally include a number of other icons in addition to that of the main temple. The faithful carry the goddess's palanquin, preceded and followed by others, and on arrival at the various temples where the incense is divided, local processions will join in, carrying their own palanquin and other auxiliary deities. The most indispensable of these gods are Thousand-Mile Eyes and Wind-Accompanying Ears, the two secondary gods required for seafaring activities. In addition, among the group leading the main palanquin are judges and other "administrative personnel," and leading these "personnel" are Master Seven, Master Eight, and the two generals, Xie and Fan[8]; one is tall and

---

8 Their full names, which are taboo, are plays on words: Fan Bizui can mean "crimes must be punished" and Xie You'en can mean "give thanks for forgiveness."

black, and the other is short and white. The names of these two generals indicate that Mazu is also a goddess who punishes evil and rewards good. However, as we can see from the rituals in our daily life, there is always a specific purpose to burning incense in the temple: that is, to pray for the blessings of Mazu or other gods and goddesses, in order to avoid disaster and obtain good fortune. It does not seem that prayer involves reflection on one's personal behavior. If the prayers are answered, you return to the temple and make an offering of thanks for the grace received. In other words, in this kind of folk belief, praying for happiness and avoiding disaster is a functional exchange; first you state what you want, and then the gods act on that statement. In the process of opening up Taiwan, there were so many unknown disasters, and any harvest could be at risk, so we cannot condemn such an attitude.

What's more, if the believer's wish is not granted, some believers may not return to the temple of the god who failed them and may even seek blessings from other gods. In addition, there is an "ungrateful" custom in Taiwan in which a devotee may welcome a small god into his or her house in order to accomplish a specific goal. For example, at a time when lotteries and playing the stock market were popular in Taiwan, devotees would ask a god to show them a "clear sign." If they won the lottery or their stocks gained value, they would of course give thanks to the god; if they didn't, the day after the lottery, you would see the body parts of smashed icons next to the river! From this angle, "faith" seems to be rather pragmatic. On the first and fifteenth day of the lunar calendar, many shops will burn incense on the ground in front of the entrance, or in front of the Guandi shrine inside the shop. If business is particularly prosperous that month, they will increase their offerings. From these details, we can understand the practicality of folk beliefs. This is concrete proof of what C. K. Yang meant when he talked about sacredness being masked by secular elements.

If we compare the phenomenon of Wuxi's folk beliefs with the situation in Taiwan, I think the first thing to note is that Wuxi represents a tradition of hundreds or even more than a thousand years; local resources are fully developed and have been stable for a long period of time. An affluent region must pay attention to the links between state power and civil society. The relationship between the gods may be said to reflect these links: Dongyue represents central power, while figures like Guandi, Zhang Xun, and Yu Qian represent heroes who defended the nation, and Emperor Zhang, the Immortal of the Southern Waters and the Immortal of the Western Waters represent development and stability at the local level. As mentioned before, every temple is a meeting place for a particular trade, and the god of that temple is the protector of that trade, and is closely related to the economic development of the locality. Wuxi was the starting point of the Grand Canal that brought grain from south China to the capital in the north. The rice collected in the south was first brought to Wuxi and then transported by ship to northern China.

Wuxi is the land of fish and rice and the center of the silk industry, so shipwrights and textile workers also constitute an important part of the local economy. Each temple is related to a certain group of gentry for several generations. The gentry families fully participate in the grand temple fair and the functions of the temple in the local community. The activities of these temples, especially the annual great temple fair, bring together the various local elites and socio-economic participants, facilitating the unity of their community. As described in Chapter I, the welfare work in Wuxi is led by the elite of the community, who organize businessman and industrialists to take care of the poor, the unrepresented, the widowed and the widowers, the orphaned, and the lonely—in short, the ordinary people. This is a mature society where few unexpected things happen, but it is a society that always needs to maintain the established order and make it work properly.

As mentioned above, Taiwan is a society of pioneers. Although Taiwan has been developing for 400 years, the first 300 years were cut short by the Japanese occupation. After 1949, a large number of immigrants once again entered Taiwan. All of this means that for 400 years, Taiwan has been an unstable society in the process of development. Due to 400 years of repeatedly changing political regimes, Taiwan never managed consistently to produce a cultural elite to manage the society. Any mechanism for imposing order or dealing with the unknown thus became a source of fear and anxiety for the people. On the one hand, the people of Taiwan had to make use of the conditions at hand to bring people together, as through the cults of the native-place gods, in order to maintain the unity of the people of the same origin. Another example is that the gods were the only source of relief and comfort for people to pray to to prevent accidents and for the mourning of those who died in accidents. On the other hand, immigrants often came to Taiwan alone, with no real family or community to rely on. In times of difficulty, burning incense was all they could count on. The objects of their prayers were often quite specific: when they were sick they prayed to the medicine god, when pregnant they prayed to the goddess of childbirth, when looking to marry they prayed to the marriage god, and so forth.

What the activities at Longshan Temple show us is that every believer has a specific goal that leads him or her to enter the temple and seek the gods' help. Inside the temple, there are various functions to choose from, so that they can pray to the god of their choice. And while they are there, they might as well roam around through the rest of the temple, to be sure to not miss a possible source of assistance. For this reason, Longshan Temple has a great variety of gods and goddesses, and there is almost nothing you cannot do once you enter the temple. In addition to prayers and offerings, worshippers also engage in fortune telling and divination, and seek help from the temple officials to answer their questions, so that they can achieve good fortune and avoid misfortune. All of this reflects the fact that Taiwan is not a completely stable society, and that all kinds of changes are taking place in the process of development, which pose challenges at the collective and the individual level; thus, Taiwan's uncertainty is indeed very different from the collective identity of the small community in Wuxi.

In the Mazu processions mentioned above, a number of smaller groups from towns and villages coalesce to become the larger circle enveloped by the main temple, and the circles defined by the main temples coalesce to form an island-wide belief community. This expansion of groups into neighborhoods, and neighborhoods into territories, is characteristic of a frontier society: a necessary expansion leads to integration, only after which a fully functioning society is possible. The examples of the Nanyao and Zhenlan temples above show that a large belief community transcends the administrative units of the state: village, town, country, and region.

From the perspective of location theory, the areas covered by these two major belief communities have a complementary division of labor within each region. There are seaports, railway transit centers, road networks, cities, towns, villages, and hamlets. Within these circles, the resources of industry, agriculture, commerce, and fisheries are exchanged, which can satisfy almost all daily needs. The law and order of this large worship community is based on believers in the temples, with the core management staff of the temples and, of course, the local leaders of various trades and industries as the backbone—this three-tiered structure is capable of achieving the consolidation of the region. Much welfare work can also be accomplished by gathering the labor and resources of all within this community.

My point is illustrated by the existence of the Taiwan hospital called the En Chu Kong Hospital 恩主公醫院, which grew out of the Guandi cult on the island. In times of disaster and hardship, Mazu temples and other temples can often pool their strength to provide assistance. They are also collectively involved in local public works. Since the democratization of Taiwan, these large and small belief circles have become an important network for political figures seeking grassroots support. For example, the manager (now known as the "chairman of the board") of Zhenlan Temple is an important figure in the local community. If he so desired, he could almost certainly be elected as a member of the Legislative Council. Other temple officers are also often elected as local county and city commissioners.

From such perspectives, we can understand that while Taiwan's urbanization has gradually transcended the limitations of a single city, and the subway and high-speed rail have bound all of Taiwan together, these worship communities are in fact the real substance of people's lives, defining the ambit of their regular activities, in which they put their trust. At a time when urbanization in Taiwan has not yet reached the scale and extent of that in the United States, this kind of local society defined by faith communities may be one of the few social phenomena in the Chinese cultural milieu that is still functioning. In US society, local boundaries have been blurred; the average citizen is basically a fragmented individual with little to rely on, lonely and isolated, and has no one to turn to for support. Looking at the world that still exists in Taiwan, we can only enjoy the infinite sunset as we await the approaching dusk.

The above comparison between the societies of Wuxi and Taiwan mostly concerns the past. There is a danger that China's urbanization, now being promoted by the government, will succeed only too well. Taiwan's urbanization was a natural process that followed the island's industrial and commercial development. In both cases, the ultimate result will probably be to push Chinese culture and society toward an American-style urban setting. This makes me wonder: Before the local Chinese community fades into history, how can we transform ourselves so that Chinese people will still have a small area in which to live peacefully, even while we flock to megacities like those of Europe and America? A place where kids can play in the street without fear? A place where neighbors and townspeople can help and comfort each other? I think it is worthwhile for all of us to think about these issues and plan for them together.

To conclude this chapter, if we want to separate the sacred from the secular, in the Chinese folk belief system we might say that the sacred is secondary to the secular. The system of the functions of gods resembles a system of government and administration, with the same principle of division of labor. The idea of transcendence found in most religions is subsumed in the patterns of daily behavior inscribed in Chinese folk beliefs. Even the concepts of retribution, reincarnation, and so on may only be subtexts in folk beliefs, not core concerns. Communication between humans and gods remains essentially the same as transactions between people. There is a request and a reply; there is a prayer, and there is an answer. Therefore the transcendence that marks most religions is not obvious in folk beliefs. In this chapter, we have seen that these belief systems are closely related to the integration and creation of community, as illustrated by the comparative examples of temples and processions in Wuxi and Taiwan. And the communal life within the neighborhood serves many purposes. In a normal institutional religion, belief is more concerned with life than with a temple fair. The phenomenon of the small community, as encompassed by folk beliefs, may be compared to the pre-modern European and American Christian and Catholic churches, with the unifying power of the small community as a center. In modern Chinese Buddhism and Daoism, it is difficult to combine the profound and extensive ritual circles and the specific secular nature of the folk temples in Taiwan and Wuxi. In the next chapter, we will discuss institutional religion in China, and there are some echoes of that chapter in this one.

VIII. Secular Religion

In his discussion of Chinese religion, C. K. Yang put institutional religion to the side. In our earlier discussion of folk beliefs, we followed the same principle and did not touch on the traditional Chinese religions of Buddhism and Daoism. In fact, on this topic, something of note that happened over the course of the past century was the secularization of institutional religions. When we seek a solution to the pain and suffering of this world, either we imagine a world of peace, in which human misery is no more, or we engage in introspection, temper ourselves through severe trials, and find peace on our own terms. The first involves looking outward, the second looking inward. Confucianism pays more attention to the latter, but it also hopes to build a more decent world through self-cultivation and bringing equanimity to society. Confucians engage with the world to make it a better place, and in the final analysis it is a philosophy. Other choices within Chinese culture include the various schools of Buddhism and Daoism.

In the pre-Qin period, there actually were groups that resembled institutional religions in China. One example is the doctrine of Mohism preached by the philosopher Mozi 墨子 (468–376 BCE), who was born slightly after Confucius died and whose ideas were more popular than those of Confucius at the time. The moral philosophy of the Mohists of the Warring States period might be seen as belonging partly to the genealogy of Confucianism. However, Mohists had their unique perspectives on "heaven" (that heaven's will was that all people love one another equally, which is quite different from the Confucian emphasis on family), their own notions concerning "ghosts and spirits" (that fearing and placating them was beneficial to the social order) and their own religious leaders (*juzi* 鉅子, literally "chisels"—Mozi was also a talented carpenter) who governed and imposed discipline on the Mohist community. When Mohists talked about "illuminating ghosts," they were not concerned only with the souls of the dead, but with all kinds of mythical forces, although they did not develop their ideas on this topic much further. It seems unclear if these have to do with retribution or instead are the threats of an evil spirit. In the academic classification of Mozi in the Han dynasty, scholars grouped Mohism with the Daoist tradition. As a result, although Mozi gradually disappeared over the course of the Han dynasty, Mohist classics were rediscovered in later times in the Daoist canon. The emergence and disappearance of Mohism can be understood as the case of an indigenous Chinese institutional religion that came to a premature end before it could take shape.

In the Chinese cultural world, which includes China, Japan, Korea, and Vietnam, Confucianism was always the mainstream ideological system, so no matter how prosperous Buddhism and Daoism became, the mainstay position of Confucianism remained unchallenged. Confucianism is not a religion per se, but it draws on deep religious feelings: the ideas of "taking care in the burial rites of parents and subsequent sacrifices to them,"[1] and "honoring the virtuous and rewarding the meritorious"[2] are expressions of emotion.

---

1   *Shen zhong zhui yuan* 慎終追遠, from the *Analects*. The philosopher Zeng said, "Let there be a careful attention to perform the funeral rites to parents, and let them be followed when long gone with the ceremonies of sacrifice —then the virtue of the people will resume its proper excellence." James Legge, trans., *The Analects*, Chinese Text Project, https://ctext.org/analects/xue-er.

2   *Chongde baogong* 崇德報功, from the *Shangshu*. James Legge, trans., *Shangshu*, Chinese Text Project, https://ctext.org/shang-shu/successful-completion-of-the-war.

Let us take Wen Tianxiang's "Song of the Spirit of Righteousness" as an example. Wen regarded those exemplary figures in history as having achieved righteousness: "In the world there is the spirit of righteousness, taking many forms, bestowed on the everchanging things. Below they are the rivers and mountains; above they are the sun and stars."[3] The righteous are those identified as having been loyal, righteous and virtuous. They defined their lives in terms of righteousness, and in order to cling to righteousness, they were willing to sacrifice their lives. This is a religious sentiment. There are visible things in the universe, and mountains and human bodies are only vehicles; only the spirit of the universe, represented by righteousness, is eternal and true. In this light, even if we do not call Confucianism a "religion," its essence is nonetheless religious. Consequently, the relationship between Confucianism, Daoism and Buddhism is a question one often encounters in Chinese culture.

The Scripture on Great Peace (*Taipingjing* 太平經), an Eastern Han text, was undoubtedly one of the sources of Daoist doctrine. One of the most prominent features in the *Taipingjing* is the concept of equality, and the text argues that wealth, status, fame, etc., all jeopardize the equality that human society deserves. Another emphasis in the text is on the cultivation and improvement of the individual character to achieve a certain level of moral development. Taken together, these suggest that Daoists were seeking a harmonious world, while at the same time trying to perfect their own character in this harmonious world.

What is the origin of the *Taipingjing*? It is not altogether clear. In my view, Han Confucians had their own view of a world of great peace and unity, as described in the "Li Yun" chapter of the *Book of Rites*[4], and before arriving at this final stage of great harmony, the world would pass through

---

3   Feng Xin-ming, trans., "The Song of the Spirit of Righteousness" (2008), http://tsoidug. org/Literary/Spirit_Righteousness_Comp.pdf.

4   James Legge, trans., "Li Yun," Chinese Text Project, https://ctext.org/liji/li-yun.

another stage known as that of "moderate peace and prosperity." When we add the present day to these future eras, it means that Han Confucians saw the world as progressing through three stages. However, the world as described in the *Book of Rites* is based on the world of the ancient kings, and is not seen as a new world to come in the future. At the same time, Han Confucianism also believed that the universe functioned through the interaction between heaven and humans, which connects transcendent divine power and our own actions into a system of reciprocal response. The most basic philosophy of Confucianism, of course, originated in the time of Confucius himself, and was particularly marked by its insistence that people develop their character through introspection and self-cultivation. These features are quite consistent with some of the concepts put forward in the *Taipingjing*. The question is how one makes the transition from the transcendent Confucian system, with its complementary worship of nature and ancestral spirits, to an institutional religion. Can it occur gradually without external stimulus? There is no way to know.

It is generally believed that Buddhism entered China in the Eastern Han dynasty, in the first or second century CE, but all we can see in the documents is information concerning Buddhist scriptures and teachers being brought into China. Confucianism and texts like the *Taipingjing* had already prepared a propitious platform for the various scriptures the early Buddhists brought in, and Buddhism was able to develop gradually into a large institutional religion in China, which has continued with considerable vitality for two millennia.

When Buddhism first arrived, the miscellaneous sutras were cobbled together into what was called the *Forty-Two Chapters Sutra* (*Sishier zhangjing* 四十二章經), which in fact lacked major texts and was not a systematic presentation of Buddhist doctrine. The early teachers were mostly from Central Asia, where Buddhism had already undergone the stimulus of revelation (discussed more fully below) and transformed into

Mahayana Buddhism, which was already quite different from the original native Buddhism of India. Buddhist terms were originally conveyed in Sanskrit, which is an Indo-European language, quite different from the Sino-Tibetan Chinese language. As a result, many terms and sentences, when translated into Chinese, were borrowed from what were originally Confucian and Daoist terms in Chinese, which are known as "interpretations" (*geyi* 格義), many of which inevitably missed the mark. This problem was not corrected until a large number of Buddhist texts entered China in the Tang dynasty. During the long interregnum between the fall of the Han in the late 2nd century and the Sui-Tang unification in the late 6th century, some of the non-Chinese rulers on China's western periphery believed that the Buddhism practiced in Central Asia was more closely related to their own ethnic origins, and therefore they became the self-appointed guardians of Buddhism. Among these rulers, the Later Qin Kingdom supported the famous Kucha Buddhist monk Kumarajiva's (344–413) translation of some important scriptures, many of which are still used in Buddhism today.

In the Tang Dynasty, the Chinese Buddhist monk Xuanzang 玄奘 (602–644) traveled westward to India in search of the scriptures and brought back a large number of texts. He devoted his life to translating the Buddhist scriptures and teaching his disciples at the White Horse Temple in Chang'an. The Sanskrit Buddhist scriptures he brought back were translated directly into Chinese, which was quite different from the early scriptures translated by Kumarajiva and others. Xuanzang's translations of Indian texts, in fact, included many philosophical, aesthetic, and even literary works of Indian culture, not all of which are Buddhist religious literature. These texts were of great significance in introducing Indian culture to China. (Unfortunately, Chinese scholars made little effort to explore Indian culture outside of Buddhism due to the obscurity of Buddhist texts.) Many texts were translated during the Tang dynasty, but because they came from different periods, the Chinese came to accord different meanings and emphases in their interpretation of original Buddhism. When monks constructed a set of interpretations of Indian Buddhism based on certain texts, this became a sect or a school of Buddhism. At the height of Buddhism between the Tang and Song dynasties, there were more than a dozen major schools. The proliferation of these schools certainly reflected the popularity of Buddhism; on the other hand, it also inevitably gave Buddhism a profoundly academic character, which was not helpful in teaching the content of these doctrines to the broad mass of believers.

The schools of Buddhism at the time included: the Lüzong (school of Monastic Discipline, or Vinaya; *zong* means "school"), the Chengshizong (the "Tattvasiddhi school" of scholastic exegesis), the Jushezong (better known by its Japanese name Kusha), the Sanlunzong (the Three Treatise school) the Niepanzong (the Nirvana school), the Dilunzong (based on the Daśabhūmikā sutra), the Chanzong (better known by its Japanese name Zen), the Shelunzong (the Mahayana Saṃgrāha school), the Tiantaizong (based on the Lotus Sutra), the Jingtuzong (the Pure Land school), the Weishizong (the Mind-Only, or Yogacara, school), the Huayanzong (Huayan or Flower Garland school), and Mizong (Tantra). Among these 13 schools, the Nirvana school is part of Tiantai, the Dilunzong is part of Huayan, and the Shelunzhong is part of the Yogacara school. Only 10 schools of Buddhism still exist today. Among these 10, the Jushezong and Chengshizhong were later judged to belong to the Hinayana tradition.

Therefore, among the Chinese Mahayana schools, the eight that remain influential and popular today are: Sanlunzong, Tiantai, Huayan, Mind-Only, Lüzong, Zen, Pure Land, and Tantra. The characteristics of each of the major schools are customarily described as follows (two simple rhyming sentences in Chinese): "The secret Tantric path requires wealth (for making extensive ritual offerings), while Chan is rooted in poverty (you don't need anything special, best carried out in simple retreat settings), and Pure Land practice is convenient (just recite the name of Amitabha, anyone can do that). For the Mind-Only school, you need to endure vexation (because the intellectual demands are considerable), and the Sanlun tradition focuses on emptiness. Huayan hands down the entirety (of Buddhist teachings), while the Vinaya tradition is characterized by self-cultivation (the practice of identifying faults and correcting them, in accordance with monastic regulations); for system-atized principles, Tiantai's the thing."

Among the eight Mahayana schools in China, the Mind-Only school constructs an idealistic view of the universe; the Sanlunzong engages in philosophical argumentation. Huayan and Tiantai can both be seen as aesthetic philosophies, and the Tantric school is close to this as well. The Lüzong focuses on precepts and rules, the foundation of any institutional religion. It is logical to imagine that all religions have teachings and rules. Chan, by contrast, focuses on personal enlightenment and direct observation of the essence of the *dharma*. Master Taixu 太虚 (1890–1947), the famous monk who sought to modernize Buddhism during the Republican period, once said: "The essence of Chinese Buddhism is Chan." All schools of Buddhism share this basic spirit.

From the late Tang dynasty onwards, the Pure Land school attracted large numbers of believers, and the other sects gradually became more scholastic, and difficult for ordinary believers to understand. Although it is often said that Chan entered China in the Eastern Jin dynasty, the characteristics of Chan suggest that it is more likely that this school developed in China; I suspect that it was influenced by Mengzi's idea of "enlightenment." Chan stresses ignoring the scriptures and going straight to the "true thusness." This way of thinking is very different from the Indo-European textual dialectic. In the middle of the Tang dynasty, Chan Buddhism came to be divided into northern and southern branches, with the northern school being more concerned with textual explanations and discussions, while the southern school, under the Fifth Patriarch Huineng 慧能 (638–713), began to emphasize that even illiterate people could understand the Buddhist teachings. Since then, the Pure Land and Chan schools have remained the mainstream of Chinese folk Buddhism. The development of Buddhism in modern China is discussed below.

The conditions for the emergence of institutional religions were already present among the Chinese people and popular culture: there were religious sects, worship rituals, professional priests, and regular bodies of believers. The spread of Buddhism in China stimulated the development of Daoism. From archaeological clues, we can see that one of the routes through which Buddhism entered China was via the Gansu corridor in China's northwest, following the Silk Road; another was from India, via what is called the "southwest Silk Road," following the rivers and valleys of that region. In the Lianyun area of Jiangsu, Buddhist ruins on Mount Kongwang indicate that a sea route to China may have been a third channel for the introduction of Buddhism.

We find many traces of Daoism's own development in Sichuan as well, most notably the popular movement known as the "Way of the Five Pecks of Rice" in the Hanzhong region on the borders of today's Sichuan and Gansu, which was clearly an important source of the Celestial Masters school of Daoism. In the period following the fall of the Han dynasty, we find many people connected to Daoism, which may be due to the fact that indigenous groups in southwest China had a well-developed tradition of shamanism, which provided the local conditions for the development of the religion.

In the rise of the Yellow Turbans in the waning years of the Eastern Han dynasty, the region around Qingzhou and Xuzhou in what is now southern Shandong and northern Jiangsu was the key area. In the first century, the younger brother of Emperor Ming of the Han dynasty (r. 59–78), Prince Liu Ying 劉英 (d. 71) of Chu, also in northern Jiangsu, was a follower of Buddhism; such beliefs, together with his association with magicians, led to the production of scriptures full of prophecies designed to support a rebellion, and Liu was subsequently demoted and ultimately committed suicide. During the Three Kingdoms period, Ze Rong 笮融 (d. 196) from Danyang was one of the subordinates of Tao Qian 陶謙 (132–194), the governor of Xuzhou, and Ze was stationed in the nearby city of Xiapi. He built Buddhist temples that could accommodate more than 3,000 people, and when performing the rituals of bathing the statues of Buddha, he offered wine and food in an effort to attract believers. After Cao Cao captured Xuzhou in 194, Ze Rong led tens of thousands of men and women and 3,000 horses to flee south to Guangling, in present-day central

Jiangsu. These two stories of Buddhist patrons are a century apart, but they suggest that the expansion of Buddhism in the Qingzhou and Xuzhou area was extensive and rapid. The Yellow Turban movement is intimately connected to the Daoist Celestial Masters. The development of Buddhism just discussed should thus be related to the growth of Daoism.

In short, these clues lead us to believe that the two major regions of Daoist development, the southwest and the east coast, coincide to a considerable extent with the two routes by which Buddhism was introduced. Of course, all this is speculation and quite difficult to prove. Perhaps someday the archaeological data will provide some useful evidence, but for now, my suspicion is that the development of Buddhism and Daoism in China was almost like the growth of twin brothers.

In the beginnings of Daoism we find the movement known as the "Way of the Five Pecks of Rice," which set up an earthly paradise of its own imagining, a local community of mutual aid which included economic sharing and a common public treasury to help the poor, as well as local medical facilities and organizations to help the sick. The teachings of the Yellow Turbans in the east may have been derived from the egalitarianism of the *Taipingjing* and the "Three Great Sacred Officials" beliefs (the Heavenly Official, the Earthly Official, and the Water Official, now understood to be important Daoist gods, immediate subordinates to the Jade Emperor). The two can go hand in hand to create a utopian faith.

As stated earlier, the original religious impulse of humankind aspired to an organization of equality and mutual aid. As Daoism evolved into a religion, it naturally gave priority to Daoist philosophy as the core of this new theology. However, in terms of techniques, it drew instead on the mysteries of shamanistic beliefs and nature worship, which gave rise, among other things, to the widespread Daoist use of talismans, a kind of magic writing used to dispel disasters and seek good fortune, and to command the gods and spirits.

Beginning from the Six Dynasties period—the centuries-long interregnum between the Han and the Tang—folk healing was combined with cultivation practices such as breathing exercises and massage to form the

"Cinnabar and Crucible" (*dan ding* 丹鼎) school of Daoism, a kind of alchemical practice that cooked up medicines and elixirs for the practice of "outer alchemy" while developing complex internal cultivation practices known as "inner alchemy." The talismans and alchemical practices eventually became the chief characteristics of Daoist ritual and technique.

The surname of the royal family in the Tang dynasty was Li—the same as that of Laozi, the supposed founder of Daoism—and Daoism became the state religion. In the Song dynasty, especially in the second half of the Northern Song dynasty, Daoism was the religion of the emperors, and the study of alchemy and talismans became extremely popular. The talismanic tradition thrived, and Ming emperors believed talismans could grant them longevity. In the south, the Zhengyi school of Daoism (which later became known as the Heavenly Master School of Daoism) at Longhu Mountain in Jiangxi province, has long been the mainstream of Daoism due to the support it received from the central government, which considered it the hereditary head of the Daoist religion founded by the Celestial Masters.

During the periods of Jurchen and subsequently the Mongol domination of north China, the Han people were no longer ruled by Han rulers. Yet new Daoist teachings spread among the people in Hebei and Shandong in the form of the Quanzhen and Zhenda sects, which established a considerable degree of autonomy at the local level, maintained law and order on the ground, and established a relationship of mutual respect with the foreign rulers.

Qiu Chuji 丘處機 (Master Changchun, 1148–1227) of the Quanzhen sect was once summoned by the Mongol imperial court to travel to the far west, finally meeting with Genghis Khan in Central Asia. Qiu Chuji counseled the Khan to stop the killing. Many Chinese readers today know the names of Qiu and his Quanzhen sect from the Hong Kong writer Jin Yong's martial arts novels, and think of it only as a martial arts-based school. I have visited various sites around Zhending, in Hebei province, accompanied by archaeologists. In this area, we saw many remains, monasteries, and inscriptions of these new Daoist religions just described. These records show the activities of the Quanzhen priests at that time, their achievements in education, medicine, health, irrigation, and roads, as well as their efforts to maintain law and order, and to find compromise and reconcile the relationship between the government and the people, so that the people could have a rather peaceful and stable life. They did their best to try to build something close to an ideal society on earth.

Since the Han dynasty, Confucianism, Buddhism and Daoism have been the three major faiths of the Chinese people. In addition, Chinese culture has been subject to other external influences. The most important of these were the beliefs prevalent in the Middle East and Central Asia. In my view, both Orthodox Christianity, known as "Nestorian Christianity" in China— a religion that prevailed in the Middle East before the rise of Islam—as well as Mahayana Buddhism—found in Central Asia as well as in Pakistan in northern India—both trace their earliest roots to the Persian cultural system of Zoroastrianism and its derivative, Manichaeism.

At that time in Central and Western Asia, there was a widespread religion, inherited from the ancient Persian Zoroastrian religion, which preached that a savior would reveal a new heaven and earth after the world had experienced a calamity. In ancient Persia, the universe was divided into lightness and dark, and further subdivided into three stages: beginning in obscurity, the second stage was the struggle between darkness and light, and in the third stage, light prevails and a new world is born. In this new world, humankind is forever happy. The concept of the "promise" of divine grace radiated out from Persia and influenced Judaism, Christianity, and later Islam, all of which entertained the hope of eternal life in a new world. This ideal may have combined with Indian Buddhism and perhaps explains the evolution of original Buddhism's "salvation of self" toward the impulse to "save others," which led humanity to hope for a life that will be forever free from suffering.

From the 2nd century BCE through the 6th century CE, there were many such revealed religions in Central and Western Asia. The name of the first god of Zoroastrianism is Mazda Ashura, and the savior at the end of the tribulation is named Mithra. Mithra's name is spelled differently by different sects of the religion, but the pronunciation is similar, and it appears to be the same god. Thus, according to the eminent Chinese historian Ji Xianlin 季羨林 (1911–2009), the Buddhist deities Amitabha and Maitreya are also "Mithra." It was only after Zoroastrianism had spread to India that we see in Indian Buddhism the parallel development of the Western Pure Land Buddha (Amitabha) and the Future Buddha (Maitreya), who would save the world after the three cataclysms.

At the grassroots level in China, the authority of Confucianism is relatively weak, and the promise of redemption provides something for everyday people to rely on. The *Taipingjing* and the beliefs of the Yellow Turbans evolved, on the one hand into Daoism, through the vehicle of the Celestial Masters; on the other hand, it combined with Persian Manichaeism to develop into a local secret religion associated with the rebel Fang La 方臘 (d. 1121) in the Song dynasty, and finally into the White Lotus Teachings, which emerged in the Yuan dynasty or later. This set of beliefs, which is rooted in popular culture, has continued down to the present day, appearing under different names at different times.

Although these grassroots groups are based on the belief in salvation and hope for a new heaven and earth, in many places they also adopt some of the teachings of Buddhism or Daoism, and thus might be thought of as pluralistic folk sects. As part of Buddhist beliefs, faith in Maitreya was originally a product of the combination of Buddhism and Central Asian ideas of redemption; as the future Buddha, Maitreya comes after Shakyamuni, who will save the entire world and usher in everlasting peace after holding three "Dragon Flower Assemblies," where the gods will send Maitreya to the world. Those practicing the Maitreya teachings or following the White Lotus Teachings often revolted against the government during the Song and Ming dynasties.

These folk groups, whose beliefs are quite syncretic, also incorporate elements from folklore and even from literature, and are practiced widely among the people. At the end of the Yuan dynasty, the White Lotus movement evolved into a kind of Manicheism, which inspired the first Ming emperor, Zhu Yuanzhang 朱元璋 (1328–1398), to expel the Mongols and found the Ming dynasty (the word for Manicheism contains this same character *ming* 明).

In the Qing dynasty, during the late eighteenth and early nineteenth centuries, the activities of the White Lotus Teachings spread throughout north and central China. At the end of the Qing dynasty, they appeared again in the name of the Boxer Rebellion, causing great confusion. All these folk religions can be said to be a mixture of the Buddhist and Daoist concepts of redemption and the foreign salvationist religions that came to China from Central Asia.

Faith in Amitabha, which appears to be similar but is in fact different from belief in Maitreya, does not place the ideal world in the future, but in another world after death. This faith is based on the theory that Amitabha, who came before Shakyamuni Buddha, helps and protects people while they are alive and guides their souls to the Western Pure Land after death. Here, a peaceful and tranquil Pure Land is an alternative universe to the filth of this world. In this realm, souls who believe in Buddhism and are free from evil deeds do not have to go through the cycle of rebirth (*samsara*). Therefore, there will be no more suffering and, of course, no need to wait for the final world that the Maitreya faith says will come after the three apocalypses.

Belief in Amitabha also evolved into belief in Guanyin. Guanyin was originally a bodhisattva and Amitabha's main assistant. In Indian scriptures, Guanyin was a male bodhisattva, but after entering China, Guanyin's function as a compassionate savior gradually evolved into a mother figure, and thus a female bodhisattva. In the Indian scriptures, Guanyin has 33 bodies, i.e., a variety of different images, including, indeed, several images of women. In China, the belief in Guanyin takes the form of a mother who comforts and saves the souls of those in distress and suffering. In a third wave of development there appears the Dizang (Ksitigarbha) bodhisattva, also attached to Amitabha Buddha. The meaning of the characters *dizang* 地藏 was originally "as vast as the earth" (*di* 地), and "as deep as a depository" (*zang* 藏). But taken together, the compound in Chinese Buddhism means the savior of the underworld, the redeemer of hell.

The Dizang bodhisattva once made a vow, saying "until hell is empty, I will not become a Buddha." By definition, a bodhisattva is a deity capable of achieving enlightenment and becoming a Buddha, but who refuses and stays in the world to help others; Guanyin is also a bodhisattva. The three stages in the Amitabha, Dizang and Guanyin faiths, in contrast to the Maitreya faith, are at the level of the individual and do not seek a new world at the level of the group. This choice to remain within the world made the Guanyin and Dizang cults the most popular among the people, replacing belief in Maitreya.

The ideal world of Daoism is in a distant heaven, but it is within this human world; Daoist alchemical cultivation is also practiced at the level of the individual. Outer alchemy uses substances that seek to prolong the life of mind and body, i.e. eternal life. This school originally evolved out of alchemy to convert metals into gold, but later on combined with cultivation theories of Chinese medicine, becoming a set of methods that use medicines and drugs to prolong life and maintain health. The school of inner alchemy, by contrast, attempts to reunite the *yin* and *yang* factors within the human body into a spiritual body, a body that is not subject to the limits of physical metabolism or even the death of the physical body. When the "primordial spirit," as the new body is called, is fulfilled, it can exist forever without its unsustainable physical body, meaning that it has reached the realm of eternal life.

In Daoism, "earthbound immortality" (*dixingxian* 地行仙) and "daytime ascension" (*bairi feisheng* 白日飛升) are both descriptions of the "primordial spirit," finally shedding the body and becoming the immortal self. In Daoism, the fabled "Eight Immortals" were gods who claimed to be able to live forever. Among these eight figures are men and women, noble and base, people from different walks of life and different identities, and are in fact meant to show that anyone in the world can attain immortality.

The ideal world of Daoism became the 36 cave-heavens and 72 blessed places listed in the Daoist scriptures, most of which are Daoist belvederes or places where Daoism originally developed. These sites are often deep in the mountains, or imagined to be in the sea, at some unknown place. Some scholars believe that the poet Tao Yuanming's "Peach Blossom Spring" is in fact a Daoist ideal of a blessed land, where one has to pass through a cave to reach a peaceful and quiet society free from outside interference. In the history of Daoism, the Celestial Masters organized a society of mutual aid where the benefits were distributed equally.

As mentioned above, many of the Daoist monasteries were located deep in the mountains, and Mount Qingcheng, Mount Wudang and Mount Longhu are still famous as Daoist holy places. Daoist priests are allowed to marry and have families, just like ordinary people. A Daoist temple is often a collection of several families, and a mountain Daoist temple is a small self-help community where people share the good times and the bad. I've seen this myself. The White Cloud Temple (*Baiyunguan* 白雲觀) in Beijing is being restored, with the men and women of all ages involved in almost every aspect of the restoration task. In the homes in the rear of the temple complex, young boys and girls are being taught by their mothers, sisters, and brothers to read and write.

During the Sino-Japanese War, I lived in Hubei, and in many towns of the region there were branches of the Wudang Mountain Daoist community. These temples were the center of community life, and during the Japanese invasion of Hubei, village militia groups helped the Nationalist Army resist the Japanese invaders. Within these militia groups, the most common figures were the Wudang Daoists. They taught martial arts and assumed command in the battles, and were unsung heroes during the war. In this respect, the Daoist choice of an ideal world is the human world, which means that the Confucian concept of worldliness is in fact quite consistent with Daoist ideals.

Thus, we see attempts, both at the grassroots and elite levels, to integrate these different beliefs into one system. Fujian's Lin Zhaoen 林兆恩 (1517–1598) founded the Three-in-One (*Sanjiao heyi* 三教合一) religion, which advocated the unity of the three faiths: Confucianism, Daoism and Buddhism. The Three-in-One school was short-lived and quite regional, but similar movements that developed later almost all bear the imprint of Lin's experiment. The concept of the unity of the three religions would have been familiar to well-read scholars at that time. This means that accomplished scholars were completely capable of accepting the Buddhist and Daoist beliefs of other family members.

In the Republican period, there was an attempt to organize a "Confucian church," which was not successful. However, what was known as the "Red Swastika Society" was a sort of three-in-one religion. This group was based in Jinan, Shandong and was started by a group of people, men and women of faith, who participated equally in the development and management of the group. In the early years of the Republican period, prior to the Sino-Japanese War, the Red Swastika Society developed rapidly. By then Manchuria had fallen to the Japanese, and the Red Swastika flourished under the Manchukuo regime as well. In my hometown of Wuxi, the Red Swastika Society held many Buddhist prayer meetings and also had what were called "vegetarian halls." The former was where many housewives, especially elderly women, would meet regularly, and the latter was where elderly believers, with no one to turn to, could organize themselves to live together.

In these organizations, the chanting drew on Pure Land traditions of repeating the Buddha's name, and the sitting meditation was no different from the Chan or Daoist meditation practices. The Red Swastika Society had no clergy, their worship of the gods was carried out at Daoist or Buddhist temples, and their ancestor worship was in individual homes or ancestral temples. My grandmother was a very active member of the Wuxi Red Swastika Society. Behind her bedroom, in a small courtyard, was her Buddhist temple, which contained the main statues of Confucianism, Daoism and Buddhism: Confucius, Guanyin, and Laozi. The main text they preached at the Buddhist prayer meetings was the *Ultimate Treatise on the Response to Behavior* (*Taishang ganying pian* 太上感應篇), which preached the idea that actions have consequences. This group of elderly ladies was the backbone of local charities, providing relief to the poor, widows, orphans, and so on.

The Luo Teachings represent an even more grassroots example. It was founded by a Ming-dynasty soldier and first developed along the Grand Canal among boatmen, migrant workers, and military guards, and later spread widely on the Yellow River, Yangtze River, Huai River, and the southeast coast. The founder of the religion was called "Patriarch Luo" (Luo Menghong 羅夢鴻, 1443–1527) and there were many "Patriarch Luo huts" scattered along the water and the docks, where elderly people with no home could stay for the rest of their lives.

The Luo Teachings combined many of the doctrines and traditions of Chan (Zen) Buddhism and Daoism. From Chan, Patriarch Luo absorbed the concept that "the mind creates everything," believing that suffering is caused by human desires, and thus Luo practitioners seek to achieve an elevated inner state by residing in non-action and renouncing desires. From the very beginning, Luo practitioners saw themselves as a branch of Chan. They also absorbed certain Daoist mysteries to explain the formation of the world. They believed that the world evolved out of a "home in the true emptiness" which ultimately became the world and everything in it. Therefore, in the Luo Teachings, the external world is not a projection of the mind, as in Chan, but exists in reality.

As for the eight schools of Buddhism mentioned above, only Pure Land and Chan have flourished in modern times. As already noted, the other schools are somewhat more scholarly. A follower of the Pure Land emphasizes the sincerity of his or her faith in the Buddha chiefly through reciting the name of the Buddha. By contrast, the process of enlightenment in Chan began by "pointing to the truth," the idea being to focus on one thing at a time to gain instant spiritual enlightenment and awaken to the Buddha's teachings; Chan places less emphasis on the study and interpretation of the scriptures. For the average believer, the Chan path is also a convenient path.

In Chinese Buddhism from the late Tang dynasty onwards, Chan was the most popular school, and Chan and Pure Land eventually became one. In the modern era, there have been many outstanding Buddhist figures: Jichan 寄禪 (1851–1912) and Xuyun 虛雲 (1840?–1949) from the Chan school, Yinguang 印光 (1862–1949) from the Pure Land school, Hongyi 弘一 (1880–1942) from the Lüzong school, Dixian 諦閑 (1858–1932) from the Tiantai school, Danxia 丹霞 from the Huayan school, and Ouyang Jingwu 歐陽競無 (1871–1948) from the Mind-Only school. Some Confucian scholars in modern times have drawn on Buddhist thought to organize their philosophical systems. For example, Xiong Shili 熊十力 (1885–1968) brought Buddhism into Confucianism via the Buddhist text *Weishilun* 唯識論 (Treatise on the Mind-Only Doctrine), which subsequently became a part of New Confucianism; Thomé H. Fong 方東美 (1899–1977) combined the Huayan cosmology with certain aesthetic theories, creating an idealistic philosophy that is highly valued in modern Chinese philosophy. All of this was largely due to the arrival of modern culture from the West, which stimulated the traditional elite to revisit and renew its own traditions.

In sum, since Buddhism entered China, Buddhism and Daoism have been moving in parallel, stimulating and supplementing each other, forming two major belief systems. Before the Tang dynasty, both were in a period of system-building, starting from nothing, increasing in sophistication, and by the Tang and Song dynasties, these two religious systems had become the two mainstream examples of Chinese institutional religions. Both Buddhism and Daoism have split into many schools, each of which began with a doctrinal difference that led to the development of its own particular emphasis: for example, the Buddhist Mind-Only school and Huayan both grew out of profound doctrinal discussions. The same is true of Daoism, with its internal and external cultivation, its alchemy, and its talismans. After the Tang and Song dynasties—and especially after the Song dynasty—Buddhism was dominated by Pure Land and Chan, while Daoism was dominated by the Quanzhen school, one of the new Daoist religions in the north, and the Longhu Mountain school in the south.

At this point, both Buddhist and Daoist sects gradually tended to become more absorbed into folk religion and oriented toward personal conviction, with most grassroots people believing that faith was more important than doctrinal understanding. This development gradually led the established religions to become more integrated into popular religious practice.

In the mid-20ᵗʰ century, China was divided with the founding of the People's Republic, and on the mainland, the government suppressed all kinds of religious activities because they were seen as superstitions. In particular, under Mao Zedong, there was a violent suppression of "counter-revolutionary sects and secret societies" in the early 1950s, so that popular religious activities were almost completely wiped out. As for the established religions of Buddhism and Daoism, all that are left are the major temples and schools that have been incorporated into the government-managed system. I am not familiar with trends in the development of underground religious activities in the Mainland, so I will say nothing about them. My observations concerning the development of religion in modern China will be mainly based on the situation in Taiwan.

In the late Qing-early Republican period, Master Xuyun, witnessing the decline of Buddhism, and having himself cultivated the five principle Chan schools, combined them in such a way as to carry forward the past and point the way toward the future, hence becoming the patriarch of modern Chan. His contributions have been instrumental in inspiring Buddhism in post-war Taiwan. Even more important is that in Taiwan, Buddhism became a humanistic Buddhism, with an emphasis on life as lived in the here and now.

As mentioned above, this trend began in the early years of the Republic with Master Taixu's concept of "Buddhism of the human realm." In post-war Taiwan, Master Yinshun 印順 (1906–2005) interpreted Master Taixu's "Buddhism of the human realm" as having taken aim at the traditional Chinese Buddhism that focused on the importance of ghosts and death, and hence, the concepts of reincarnation and karma, and reoriented it toward a concern with reality as lived in today's society. He quoted the Āgama sutra to the effect that "All Buddhas appear among humans, and do not become Buddhas in heaven." Yinshun firmly believed that a human-based Buddhism's attempts to create a pure land (i.e., paradise) meant swearing a vow to create such a paradise, and this is what it means to be a human being. You must go together with the Buddha and the bodhisattvas into the human world and create a new pure land, and not seek to be "reborn" somewhere else, which is simply avoiding the ills and evils of the world in which we live.

There have been at least four major Buddhist movements in Taiwan over the past six decades. One is that of Master Wei Chueh 惟覺 (1928–2016), whose monastery is Chung Tai Chan Monastery in Taichung. His idea was that "doctrine is the means of fixing knowledge, merit is the means of acquiring resources, and meditation is the means of understanding the nature of the mind," in order to achieve the great task of "attaining the supreme path of internal enlightenment and propagating the Dharma to benefit the living." His training of monks was based on the requirements of the Lüzong school: "The Four Exhortations of Chung Tai: be respectful to those above you, be kind to those below you, treat people in peace, and manage the world in truth." The administration of the monks and nuns at Chung Tai Chan Monastery is in strict accordance with the Chan tradition of "Baizhang's Rules of Purity" (*Baizhang qinggui* 百丈清規)[5]: "A day without work is a day without food." All monks and nuns spend about half a day at work, either tending crops in the vegetable garden or vineyard, or baking cakes in the bakery, or sewing clothes in the sewing room. These products are not only for the use of the temple, but also for the daily meals of the primary and secondary school students at the schools organized by Chung Tai Chan Monastery.

---

5   Baizhang (720–814) was a Tang-dynasty Chan master. —Trans.

The main building of the monastery was designed by the famous Taiwanese architect Li Zuyuan 李祖原 (b. 1938) and is magnificent. What is praiseworthy is that as you mount from the ground floor to the fifth, highest floor of the Buddha Hall, the decor becomes increasingly simple, and on the top floor there is only a white jade statue of Buddha. This symbolizes a return to the basics of the Buddha's teachings, ascending step by step from the mundane to the ultimate, pure Dharma.

Another example is the Dharma Drum Mountain Nung Chan Monastery (*Fagushan nongchansi* 法鼓山農禪寺) in Jinshan, Taipei, which was founded by Master Shengyen 聖嚴法師 (1931–2009). Shengyen was not a direct disciple of Yinshun but was deeply influenced by him: his own thesis in Buddhist studies in Japan was a translation of Yinshun's history of Chinese Chan Buddhism into Japanese. The name of Nung Chan Monastery clearly reflects the fact that the temple is Chan-based. The six ethics endorsed by Shengyen are family, life, school, nature, work, and community. He believed that everyone should uphold the concepts of responsibility, dedication, respect, and care for others in order to create a harmonious and happy society when dealing with their roles in the complex world described by the six principles. From this, we can see that his six ethics are in fact a set of principles derived from the Confucian concept of loyalty and forgiveness. It looks as if there is more "worldly" Confucianism here than "otherworldly" Buddhism. Although Nung Chan Monastery claims to be a Chan temple, it actually trains its monks and students in a way that emphasizes both Pure Land and Chan teachings, with the students choosing the direction they want to focus on.

Dharma Drum Mountain also founded a university, about half of which is a college for training monks, while the other half offers a general university education—although at the moment, its university component is not fully developed, with few courses and limited numbers of students. The clerical college is the focus of their work.

The campus of Dharma Drum Mountain was designed by the architect Yao Renxi 姚仁喜 (Kris Yao, b. 1951). Its most striking feature is the large square pond in front of a rather plain wooden building, surrounded by fields. The meaning of the square pond is like the symbolism of the image of a flower in a mirror, or of the moon on the water—that is, all the phenomena of the world are in fact only illusory shadows. Around the main building of Nung Chan Monastery, we see engravings of sayings from a Vajrayana sutra, such as "develop a mind which does not abide in anything." There are also famous sayings from the Heart Sutra such as "all of the five Skandhas[6] are equally empty" and "This Body itself is Emptiness, and Emptiness itself is this Body."[7] These classical sayings, of course, are part of the Pure Land tradition and part of the Buddha's birthright.

One of Yinshun's own disciples was Master Cheng Yen 證嚴 (b. 1937), who founded the organization known as the Tzu Chi Foundation. Cheng Yen did not really study with Master Yinshun, but Yinshun accepted her into the faith and shaved her head, and then sent her to another Chan monastery where she was ordained. When Cheng Yen vowed to devote herself to the work of giving, she was truly following Yinshun's direction. The Tzu Chi organization has a university that is only partially devoted to training nuns; most of it is open to the community for general university education. Tzu Chi has seven or eight hospitals, located all over Taiwan. Cheng Yen also regularly raises money for relief funds to help the poor and needy in various places. The organization is very much like an enterprise, with a centralized division and various administrative and executive branches.

---

6   The Sanskrit word *skandha* is usually translated as "aggregate" (the five elements of the human body and mind in Buddhism). —Ed.

7   Translation taken from Thich Nhat Hanh, *The Other Shore: A New Translation of the Heart Sutra with Commentaries* (Berkeley: Parallax Press, 2017), 23.

The general idea is for practitioners to organize their own fundraising activities, in small local groups or branches; some members contribute regularly to the Tzu Chi activity fund after joining the organization. It is said that eight million people around the world have joined this organization, so if everyone makes a regular donation to Tzu Chi, no matter how large or small, the sum will be considerable. The example of Tzu Chi is a reflection, through giving, of Yinshun's ideal of a socially engaged Buddhism of the human world. As for Tzu Chi's efforts in terms of Buddhist instruction and teachings, there are Cheng Yen's "words of contemplation," which are maxim-like phrases whose contents, when examined, resemble advice and encouragement found in other Chinese cultural traditions, and are not exclusively Buddhist.

Another important Buddhist movement is that of Master Hsing Yun 星雲 (b. 1927), a monk who organized the Fo Guang Shan Buddhist Group, the largest Buddhist organization in Taiwan. Fo Guang Shan has two bases in Taiwan, in Kaohsiung and Yilan, and several worship centers in Taipei City, and has developed overseas bases in the US, Australia, and Malaysia. Hsing Yun also worked with Zhao Puchu 趙樸初 (1907–2000), the mainland Chinese Buddhist leader, to erect a large Buddha at Mashan in my hometown of Wuxi, beneath which is found a massive Buddhist temple which is the headquarters of the World Buddhist Organization (WBO).

Fo Guang Shan has an institution for training monks in Yilan, established in conjunction with the University of South China, and a similar school in Kaohsiung. There are young monks and nuns in all of Fo Guang Shan's worship centers, studying and working at the same time. Master Hsing Yun's aim is to educate and spread Buddhism. His motto is simple: "Be a good person, have a good heart, and say good words." His engagement with the human world is easy to see. His demands of his disciples are those of general Chan training, teaching them to recite sutras and sit in meditation, but more importantly, to experience the spirit of service to others in real life. In his worship centers, the general atmosphere is lively and peaceful, free and easy, but not unruly. The atmosphere of Fo Guang Shan is completely different from that of Chung Tai Chan Monastery.

In addition to these four Buddhist institutions, there are also two Buddhist universities, Huafan University (*Huafan daxue* 華梵大學) and Hsuan Chuang University (*Xuanzang daxue* 玄奘大學), both of which cater to monastic training and general university education. Neither is very large, and their influence is relatively limited. When it comes to doctrinal affiliation, they make no distinction between Chan and Pure Land. These six Buddhist groups have a total of approximately two to three million followers, making up at least one-tenth of Taiwan's population, without counting Tzu Chi's eight million donors. Their influence can be seen everywhere, especially in health care and education, and although the universities do not stand out in terms of academics, they are nonetheless well-known institutions.

These humanistic Buddhist groups can be said to have a considerable influence on the general atmosphere of life in Taiwan. In the absence of their activities, religion in Taiwan would be confined to the folk beliefs mentioned in the previous chapter, limited to pragmatic and specific offerings and prayers. The Buddhist groups integrate Confucian ethics into the Buddhist teachings, becoming a sort of cultural education for the people.

The development of Daoism in Taiwan is relatively limited. One reason is that, because of the suppression of Daoism during the Qing dynasty, Daoism did not have the good fortune to produce leaders like those we find in modern Buddhism; in addition, the Daoism that migrated to Taiwan from mainland China was the Lingbao branch of Daoism found in South China, Fujian and Guangdong, and was not one of the major schools in mainland China. In Taiwan, the ancient shamanistic traditions of the south already occupied an important place in the temples of Taiwan's folk religion, in the form of spirit mediums. This meant that it was difficult for orthodox Daoist religion to get its foot in the door. Despite these difficulties, some important changes have occurred in Taiwanese Daoism. For example, in the Xingtian Temple in Taipei, where Guangong is worshipped, they have done away with the rituals of burning incense and paper, and are using the donations of the faithful to open medical clinics and free hospitals, as well as some secondary schools or vocational schools, which are also free. Guangong and Lü Dongbin are the main gods found in Taiwan's Daoist temples, and spirit writing is used to help the faithful answer their questions. Such engagements with believers display a strong spirit of secularism.

Not many Taiwanese Daoists are scholars. However, there were some scholars who became Daoist priests after studying Daoism, such as Lee Fong-mao 李豐楙 (a researcher at the Academia Sinica, b. 1947) and Kristofer Schipper (a Dutch sinologist who resided in Taiwan for several decades to study Daoism, 1934–2021). This phenomenon can also be seen as another side of the secularization of Daoism.

It is important to recognize that Daoism is different from Buddhism in that its fundamental spirit is positive. In the *Yinfujing* 陰符經 (The Classic of the Hidden Agreement), we find the statement "The universe is in your hand, and all changes are born in the body," and in the *Zhenqi huanyuan ming* 真氣還元銘 (The Inscription of True Qi Returning to its Origin) the statement, "Heaven is like me, and I am like heaven," both of which stress the concept of the basic commonality between heaven and humans. It is possible for a person to cultivate to the point that they are as immortal as heaven and earth, so that they need not die. It is possible to open a cave-heaven or a blessed spot on earth, and thus avoid awaiting the arrival of the new world that is to come after the apocalypse. Thus, Daoist gods and goddesses—such as the "Eight Immortals"—can be used to redeem those in the world who are destined for redemption. If sages can save people and the world, then of course they can also teach the world by meditating, breathing, or qigong, or by using medicine or nutrition to gradually improve their health, in the hopes of cultivating their primordial spirit. Why not heal the sick and save the needy, to redeem them from ordinary misery?

During the anti-Japanese war, I once met a Daoist priest from Mount Qingcheng who was revered as a "medicine master" by the locals. He spent seven to eight months of the year living in the mountains with a cane and a handy shovel, collecting herbs during the day, and spending the rest of the year touring remote villages, practicing medicine and helping people. This act is a kind of cultivation. The spirit of the Daoist temples in Taiwan is certainly secular in its promotion of the way of cultivation through medicines, but is it not also a concrete implementation of the original Daoist philosophy?

The last popular religion to be discussed is Yiguandao (The Unity Way), which is quite widespread in Taiwan. This is a modern branch of the three-in-one tradition, which, according to Yiguandao literature, has its origins in the above-mentioned Luo Teachings. The Luo Teachings spread throughout the country and intermixed with other popular religions. By the late Qing, during the early Republican period, Yiguandao was already quite developed, with branches in Sichuan, Manchuria, and Hebei. In 1948, on the eve of China's division, an Yiguandao branch from Tianjin spread to Taiwan, following the wife of a sect leader. In the early period of the group's stay in Taiwan, the government suppressed the religion. However, the religion continued to grow in popularity, and after Taiwan's democratization, the religion was finally legalized in the 1980s and became a group with many members. At present, there are millions of Yiguandao practitioners. They are divided among 50 or 60 "branches" that have developed independently of one other, seemingly without a unified headquarters. Each branch chooses the particular focus of its worship, so that practitioners in different branches have different levels of knowledge, doctrinal emphasis and even read different scriptures. This flexibility may be the reason for their rapid growth.

Yiguandao practitioners support and care for each other. The elderly, the sick, and those who live alone are visited by someone who will ask after them. If an elderly person is lonely, he or she can also donate money to the temple and live out their remaining years there. When a practitioner dies, there will be a full team of volunteers to take care of the funeral and burial. This happened to a relative of mine, so I have direct knowledge of Yiguandao practices.

Yiguandao claims to preach the unity of the five religions: Confucianism, Daoism, Buddhism, Islam, and Christianity. The real practice remains a synthesis of Confucianism, Buddhism and Daoism. The Yiguandao text *Renli guizhen* 認理歸真 (Understanding Principle and Returning to Truth) sums up this unity as follows: "Confucianism sees an individual's basic nature in terms of conscience. Buddhism sees this basic nature in terms of *vajra* (a ritual weapon) or *bodhicitta* (the 'enlightenment mind'). Daoism sees it as the gateway to immortality. In sum, it is all Buddha-nature."

Although Yiguandao is called the unity of the five religions, it is based on three religions: practicing the rituals of Confucianism, using the inner self-control of Daoism, and keeping the precepts of Buddhism. However, they dispense with Buddhist and Daoist rituals of beating the drum and gong, chanting scriptures, composing talismans, and saying magic spells, and instead follow traditional ancestor worship rituals, with their formal dress, silent prayer, and bowing instead of kowtowing.

The Buddhist precepts are as follows: "Do not kill, do not steal, do not engage in improper sexual behavior, do not eat meat or drink wine, and do not engage in wrong speech (lying)."

Yiguandao practitioners are vegetarians, a concept that we can trace to Buddhism, but it is not impossible that it is a continuation of the Song-dynasty tradition of the Manichaeans, who were also vegetarians. There are many vegetarian restaurants in Taiwan, and in the early morning before work, or after work when things quiet down, these "places of worship" become meeting places for Yiguandao practitioners, where they can hear the scriptures and worship. Yiguandao, as a mixture of various religions, combines the teachings of other religions in a process that sometimes distorts their meaning. This is particularly true in the case of Christianity and Islam. Elsewhere in the world we find similarly syncretic religions: for example, the Bahai faith, which developed in the Middle East, is not immune to the same problem of distortion.

Yiguandao teaches that before the beginning of the universe, there was no life in an empty world, but "The Unborn Mother in the native land of true emptiness" had many "original children of the Buddha," who ultimately descended to the human world. The supreme god of the universe is called the "the Emperor Light-Shining" (another name for the Unborn Mother), who uses the sun and moon as his symbols and is not only a great god who rules the universe, but also has the power to judge each individual's actions. After coming to inhabit the earth, human beings—under the influence of their passions and desires—gradually lost their true nature, and the Unborn Mother divided the history of the universe from the beginning into two large bodies of time, each of which was made up of 12 "occasions," each lasting 10,800 years. Another scheme divides time into the three phases of the Green Sun, the Red Sun and the White Sun, each phase with its own length, the transition from one phase to another being marked by a great calamity. Because of their behavior, people must be cleansed by the calamity before being able to forego it and await their arrival in the final resting place.

Nonetheless, some Yiguandao believers now believe that the third phase, or White Sun, is the time for Confucianism to reign, which means that the people's hearts will be saved by practicing Confucian self-cultivation, which will move everyone toward great harmony. Others have predicted the return of Maitreya, which means that practicing Buddhism is the way to achieve salvation as they await Maitreya's coming. Still other believers see the apocalypse as an inner spiritual calamity, which means that the path to liberation lies in the cultivation of "pure words, a pure body, and a pure mind," opening new realms through the revelation of faith.

All of this would suggest that this group, because of the flexibility of its doctrine, does not have one single leadership figure. The various branches of the group, because of the composition of its members, have their own texts that they have chosen to read, as well as their own interpretations of the doctrine. There are no priests in Yiguandao, and no one has the authority to remove karma on behalf of the gods. Every individual in the congregation is responsible for their own misfortunes. It is only when one takes full responsibility for one's own actions that one can ride out the storm, that is, by using one's "heart" to achieve control oneself. Since each branch has its own interpretation, the understanding one "branch" in a university campus or in one neighborhood may differ greatly from that of another lesser educated congregation. In my view, it is precisely because Yiguandao is still in the process of development, because there is much room for improvement and change, that its future is boundless.

To sum up, the religious beliefs of the Chinese people, be they Buddhist, Daoist or a mixture of these, have all shown a tendency towards what C. K. Yang called "secularization" over the centuries. The direction is moving away from theoretical explanations and toward devotion and practice, away from seeking liberation from the world and toward engagement with the world, offering help and assistance. Such a trend may, on the one hand, grow out of the Confucian tradition of self-cultivation and bringing peace to the people. At the same time, it is also similar to the development of Christianity in modern times—for example, the movement away from a focus on theological theories and toward a focus on piety. This shift from the "sacred" to the "mundane" may be a general trend everywhere.

As for the current situation in Taiwan, several religious systems interact and learn from each other, mostly by going out into the world and engaging with society. On the whole, this has had a good effect on Taiwan's customs. Social work performed by religious groups can also complement and enhance the work of the state and other groups. Moreover, as can probably be seen from the above discussion, there is a tendency for these religions to become somewhat more humane, generally diminishing the superstitious elements of many of the past religious beliefs. The process of urbanization has gradually weakened the functions of communities and small areas that used to bring individuals together. With the existence of these religions, individuals are less likely to get lost in uncaring crowds, and society is less likely to run the risk of anomie.

IX. The Human Networks that Bind Us

Human beings are animals that live in groups, and they form collective organizations because individual human beings do not have the claws or teeth of a tiger or a leopard, the speed of a horse or a goat, or the size of an elephant or a rhinoceros. People cannot fly like a bird or swim like a fish, and in physical terms are incapable of competing with other creatures. It is precisely because humans can cooperate that they have finally achieved mastery over the planet and domination over other creatures.

We find collective organizations throughout human history; at the outset there were villages and tribes, while in modern times, it has become peoples and nations. These larger groups are not as adept as smaller communities in terms of their capacity to bring individuals together. In China, for thousands of years, groups of individuals have coalesced in what are commonly thought of as kinship groups and extensions of kinship groups. Compared to people of Indo-Iranian origin (the majority of Caucasians), the cohesive force of Chinese kinship organizations has been far more durable and resilient than the military groups formed by Indo-Iranian civilizations. Moreover, the fundamental principles of kinship organization, while beginning in families, ultimately expanded into non-kinship groups that imitated these principles, lending these organizations a (pseudo)-biological character that makes the demands of living together seem more natural.

The core of the kinship group is, of course, the nuclear family made up of the couple and their children. In many parts of human society, this nuclear family is the most basic organization. Yet if a certain number of nuclear families expands over the generations, adding grandfathers and great-grandfathers (or grandmothers and great-great-grandmothers) to the newly formed individual nuclear families, they will combine to form a larger group. Tribes or villages are made up of large groups of related people, living together in a common community. This in itself is nothing rare in ethnographic research. However, China's history of kinship organization, and the expansion of this organization to form the basis for other communities, is extremely ancient. And when we add to this the use of Confucian ethics as the basis of the kinship system's legitimacy, the Chinese concept of the family becomes almost unique in the history of the world in ethnographic and sociological terms.

In his study of rural social organization in Southeast China, Fei Xiaotong referred to the interpersonal relationships displayed in this type of large community as the "differential mode of association."[1] Looking back to the more distant historical past, it is possible that the Neolithic

---

1 In the words of Gary Hamilton, the translator of Fei's *From the Soil*, Fei argues that "in Western societies, individuals form organizations, whereby each organization has its own boundaries defining who is part of the organization and who is not, and the relation of each individual to the organization is the same. All members in an organization are equivalent. He calls this an 'organizational mode of association' (*tuanti geju*). In China, on the contrary, each individual is claimed to be surrounded by a series of concentric circles, produced by one's own social influence. Each web of social relations has a self as its center. Each circle spreading out from the center becomes more distant and at the same time more insignificant. Everyone's circles are interrelated, and one touches different circles at different times and places. On different occasions, one's own social network encounters someone else's. He calls this mode of organization a 'differential mode of association' (*chaxu geju*)." See Fei Xiaotong, *From the Soil: The Foundations of Chinese Society*, trans. Gary Hamilton (Berkeley: California University Press, 1992), 60. —Trans.

societies in pre-Shang China were organized on the basis of kinship. However, we do not have sufficient data to reconstruct the characteristics of such organizations. The ruling group of the Shang dynasty shared the surname "Zi 子" which encompassed the royal family. Clearly, there were a number of separate groups who had been given fiefs by the royal family in return for pledges to defend the capital city; however, we lack details concerning such organizations. With the fall of the Shang, the Western Zhou unified the Central Plains and set up their own feudal vassals to protect the Zhou regime. This feudal order was also centered on the royal family, and each sub-unit was either a descendant of the royal family or a relative of the royal family by marriage. The ruling group was made up of the Ji 姬 clan (the family name of the Zhou regime) together with its old ally, the Jiang 姜, the two of which ruled the kingdom. In the huge feudal network of the Zhou, the feudal lords were either surnamed Ji, or were relatives of Ji.

In *Western Chou Civilization* (1988), I explained that rulership and clanship were inseparable: the upper-level rulers (the king and the royal family) constituted the major clan, and the lower-level rulers (the "feudal lords") were the lesser clan, a sub-unit of the major clan. The major clan had the right to offer sacrifices to the ancestors, while the lesser clans could only obtain the blessings of the ancestors through the sacrifices of the former. Thus, the distribution of political power was a pyramid, in which many small pyramids made up a larger pyramid, layer upon layer, and their closeness to or distance from one other determined how much power they had. From the Western Zhou to the Spring and Autumn period, the pattern remained roughly the same. Of course, the Spring and Autumn period saw the gradual disintegration of this pyramid; in the Warring States period, the pyramid of power was already decoupled from the pyramid of kinship.

I have mentioned the surnames Zi, Ji, and Jiang. The original meaning of "surname" was that those bearing the surname originated from the same ancestral group. In anthropology, what we are calling "ancestors" here may be what some scholars call "totems," which means that they are not necessarily "people," but could also be special creatures or deities. Of course, all of them are based on a fictional legend that combines many different small groups of relatives to build a larger group, affording them the power to compete and co-exist with neighboring groups. In the Western Zhou dynasty, we find the concept of *shi* 氏, which is a sub-branch of the "surname."

For example, the Zhou royal family with the surname Ji had distributed a number of kingdoms to princes of the Zhou royal family, calling these kingdoms Lu 魯, Jin 晉, Wei 衛, etc.; here, the Ji were the surname and Lu, Jin, and Wei the sub-units. The sons of the Duke of Lu, such as Meng, Shu, and Ji, were another *shi* at a lower level within the kingdom of Lu. The establishment of a *shi* required three generations before it could be officially treated as a "unit." The first two generations—those of the sons and grandsons—were still part of the original *shi*. The distinction between surname and *shi* began to blur during the Warring States period, and by the Qin-Han period, they meant the same thing.

Together with this system of clan and surname relations, Western Zhou society practiced marriage exogamy. This meant that people of the same surname did not marry, and wives were chosen outside the surname group. Within this arrangement, marriage relations allowed for the exchange of females between groups, in which certain surnames established alliances. The two surnames Ji and Jiang intermarried for generations and were two important parts of the ruling class from the beginning of the dynasty. Of course, there were also marriages to other surnames. Thus, the vertical link is lineage, and the horizontal link is marriage. The feudal network of the Zhou dynasty connected all the feudal rulers of China through the two links of clan and marriage. In this large network, there were close and distant relatives, and as the generations got further apart, so did the relationships. This was especially true of in-laws, because if intermarriage was not continued over the generations, the intimacy between the relatives would fade. This is what Fei Xiaotong meant by the term "differential mode of association."

In my view, we can explain this mode of association through the idea of concentric circles. We can see each individual as the center of a larger network of people of varying degrees of closeness, their relationship with the central individual being defined by how close the two are. In a kinship relation, the individual expects the protection of the group; as the saying has it, there is strength in numbers, and living in a group is better than fighting alone. On the other hand, an individual who enjoys the protection of a kinship community must also have certain responsibilities towards that community. Rights and responsibilities are determined by the "distance of social relations." The obligations of close relatives to help each other are more concrete than those of distant relatives, and it is more natural for close relatives to help one another. This means that Chinese people view the rights and duties that regulate interpersonal relationships as relative. In today's Western world, the logic of individualism tells us that all relationships are equal, which is not the same as interpersonal relationships in China. The two represent completely different ways of thinking.

In clan sacrificial rituals, this distinction between close and distant relatives is reflected in the order and height of the individual's cemetery tablets. In Chinese cemeteries, the graves are arranged in the shape of a fan, and the location of the individual tomb is chosen in relationship with the other tombs. An even clearer manifestation of this is the funeral service, where the mourning clothes differ according to the closeness with the deceased. For those who are closest, such as filial children mourning the loss of a parent, mourning clothes are made of the coarsest linen with no stitching and no hem. The more distant the relationship, by contrast, the finer the mourning clothes, and very distant relatives wear something closer to regular clothes. These differences in mourning garments reflect their relationship with the deceased, as well as their rights and obligations.

I remember when I was young, obituary notices of the deaths of friends and relatives had to be sent to at least six categories of relations: relatives (those sharing the same surname), in-laws (relatives by marriage), old friends (family friends of more than two generations), colleagues (work-related), fellow graduates (people who passed the civil examination in the same year), and fellow students (classmates). Relations with neighbors were often quite close, and they went into the "old friends" category in the absence of anything else. This creates a vast network of relationships, and if the deceased is well known, it may come to hundreds or even thousands of people, often far from where he or she lived and died.

The differential mode of association also exists outside of family relationships, in relationships that look like family. In China, the schools of Buddhism and Daoism imitate Confucian concepts of kinship, teachers and disciples call one another "father and son," and when one takes a master he will be a father for life. The relationship between fellow disciples is similar to that of brothers and sisters in a family; by extension, the followers of the same disciples of a master are also called cousins, and respect the older generation as uncles. Likewise, apprentices in shops or who are learning folk crafts treated their "master" as if he were their own father. In addition, many groups in society, such as the famous "Caobang,"[2] a society founded by workers on the Grand Canal, adopt many of these principles, and new members had to have a "master" (the word for "master" in Chinese, *shifu* 師父, includes the word for father, *fu* 父) to join, and the relations between members were like family relationships. In the Chinese underworld, there were all kinds of grassroots religious and professional organizations, almost all of which were modeled on kinship relations.

In the past, scholars who studied in the same school, even private schools and colleges, quite naturally also imitated family relations. By extension, under the imperial examination system, the students who

---

2   The Caobang ("Water Transport League") was a self-help organization founded in the 18th century by those who worked on the Grand Canal, hauling tribute grain from South China to the imperial court in the north. It later evolved in a variety of directions, and is vaguely linked with secret societies and even criminal gangs like the Green Gang, which played an important role in the Republican period. —Trans.

passed the imperial civil examination in the same year recognized those who graded and administered the exams as "masters," and saw one another as brothers. In official circles, those who passed the imperial examination in the same year made up an important support network on which to build groups such as "fraternities" and power factions. This instance is, of course, a case of mutual benefit, not necessarily a case of true affection, and calling these "kinship" relations can at times be far-fetched.

Thus, the differential mode of association forms the basis for networks of relations found everywhere. The distinguishing feature of this mode is that each network constitutes a family in relation to the external world, while internally there are distinctively intimate groups of members. As mentioned above, these distinctions determine in a concrete manner the rights and obligations of individuals within the relationship. Aside from mourning practices, in the actual practices of social relations, differences in behavior defined by degrees of closeness are often addressed under the rubric of "ethics." What we call the "five cardinal ethical principles" are all relative: in public, the ruler is benevolent and the servant is loyal (the ruler-servant relationship is the first ethical principle); in private, the father is benevolent and the son is filial, the husband and the wife are loving, and brothers are mutually respectful—all of these kinship relationships are relative. Friends and neighbors are fair to each other, and friends rank each other in an order similar to that of brothers in terms of age and qualifications. Such relationships, with their different demands and levels of intimacy, invariably dictate the tone of interpersonal relationships and the kind of help one expects to give and receive.

One can see all of Chinese society as enveloped in such a huge, dense network. There are certain pre-determined relationships between people which do not require laws and have their own rules that must be followed. On the positive side, an individual living within such a network is never completely alone and there is always someone to lend a helping hand in times of hardship. Chinese people fully understand their position in the network, and do not feel lonely.

The downside of such a system is that the behavior of individuals is always and forever under public scrutiny, and the rules applied to interpersonal relationships can be stricter than the law. In this traditional social network, people are constrained and supervised by one another, which can create a feeling that there is no escape. The individual freedom of Western society is difficult for traditional Chinese to understand. Chinese "cultivation" includes a clear understanding of one's place in the network, which cannot be overstepped. A person must know his or her place among the multitude and know how to endure strict rules within the confines of the differential mode of association. In the early Tang dynasty, nine generations of the Zhang family lived together in the Yun Prefecture of Shandong. Emperor Tang Gaozong 唐高宗 (628–683) asked the elder of this family, "How have you been able live together for nine generations without dividing up the family and the property?" The patriarch of the family wrote the character for "forbearance" on a piece of paper, hence the name of the family's ancestral hall, "Hall of One Hundred Forebearances."

From the perspective of a lived community, the differential mode of association means bringing together a group of related or quasi-related people in a kind of profound cooperative organization in which they share life and death, honor, and shame. In the Ming dynasty, the Zheng Clan from Zhejiang lived together for over a century and were known as the "the most virtuous family in the world." The story has it that at mealtimes, no one would eat until all members were present; even the dogs of the Zheng clan waited until all the other dogs arrived before being fed. In the New Territories of Hong Kong, I once visited the Zheng village of Tai Wai, a large village of over a thousand families, all of whom lived within the village walls in ordered dwellings of no more than three rooms each. The whole clan owned in common newly opened land in Haipu, which was cultivated according to the labor power of each family. There is also the Wen clan in the New Territories, which functions in the same manner: the clan as a whole owns newly opened land, which is divided up every year for cultivation according to the laboring population of each family. This "mini-communism" does not require a Marxist ideal, but merely a living community organized according to China's differential mode of association.

From the Eastern Han dynasty through the Tang dynasty, great clans like the Zheng and the Wen could be found throughout north China—tens of thousands of people—and built forts to defend themselves against the northern nomadic people ("barbarians"). Migrants who moved to south China from the north also organized themselves as lineages and worked in groups to open up the land. From the Song dynasty onwards, local kinship groups became the most common form of organization. This type of community has continued into modern times and is known as a clan or lineage organization.

For almost a millennium, these groups have shouldered the task of collective welfare at the local level. In any given county, the number of people belonging to lineages like these was two or three hundred, or at most, five or six hundred. They had a nucleus, usually in the form of an "ancestral home," either inside or outside the city, enclosed inside a compound. This property does not belong to any particular individual, but rather to the entire community. There may be more than a hundred rooms in the property, but they are not allocated to any branch or sub-branch. The entire clan uses the space according to its needs. Usually the most developed branch's members will live in the main inner courtyard, while others occupy more peripheral rooms, or members may live in various branches and sub-branches, depending on the needs of the lineage. Each branch or sub-branch spends its days separately; even when living together, they never share their property. Only during festivals and ancestral rituals would they have meals together as a clan.

A clan usually owns some ancestral property, perhaps land or a shop. The income from the rental of these properties is the common property of the clan. The old, the weak, and the poor among the lineage members usually rely on the income from this ancestral property. The same is obviously true for widows and orphans. The clan generally will have a school and use the ancestral property to hire teachers, perhaps elderly scholars who are also clan members, to teach the children. When the families of promising children—in the past they tried their luck with the examination system, in modern times they have to go to school—are unable to provide the support they need, the shortfall will be provided from the common lineage property. The same thing happens in the event of a marriage too expensive for the individual family to handle. This kind of clan-based "small communism" has saved a significant portion of China's population from starvation for almost a thousand years, and has given them the opportunity to grow and prosper.

I will offer my personal experience as an example. In Wuxi county, as far as I know, there were 50–60 clans, and each clan owned various amounts of ancestral property, which provided the basic security for clan members. Our family's ancestral home was in the eastern part of the city of Wuxi, with a five- or six-*mu* compound and a mulberry orchard; outside the city there were dozens of *mu* of good land to rent to tenants; inside the city we also owned some rental houses, the rent of which also counted as part of lineage property. The expenses of subsidizing the old, the weak, the poor, and the needy, of maintaining schools, etc., mentioned in the previous section, were paid from this ancestral fund. One of the more special things I remember is the mulberry garden with its hundreds of mulberry trees. In the spring, my grandmother, the matriarch of the main branch, led the women of the whole clan to pick mulberries and raise silkworms, whose cocoons were collected by the silk shops. The income earned from these activities became the pocket money of all the women in the clan, as well as extra subsidies for the widows, the cost of clothing for the girls who went to school, the cost of dowries for the daughters' marriages, etc. Students often used the stray threads of silk from discarded cocoons to line their calligraphy boxes.

During the late 18th and early 19th century, my family had a large population. There were hundreds of people solely in the big compound, including clansmen and servants. During the Taiping Rebellion (1850–1864), the southeast region suffered greatly, and every family mourned its losses. My family—the Hsu family—lost 38 men and women, and two of their four branches died out. The clan was scattered all over, and some never returned to Wuxi. The ancestral home was occupied by one of Taiping generals as his headquarters and residence, and part of the courtyard was turned into an arsenal for the Taiping army. After the Taiping Rebellion, the family had to deal with the deaths of 38 clan members, but only four male members remained, and the responsibility fell to women of the clan who had married out. They too had suffered greatly, but they did their utmost to return to their birth homes and take care of the funerals.

This is kinship, defined by both blood relations and marriage, supporting each other in times of trouble. In the period between the defeat of the Taiping and the beginning of the Sino-Japanese war, my great-grandfather, grandfather, and father—through three generations of hard work—restored the ancestral home and the ancestral property, so that the compound remained a place where the whole clan "sang, wept, and gathered." As far as I can remember, there were at least 20–30 large families in Wuxi city and in the suburbs, all of which had deep, "old" ties with our family. Without this kind of kinship-based community, many of the great clans would not have been able to survive such difficult times.

In fact, the internal organization of all sorts of social groups imitated these kinship organizations. This is true of religious groups, as seen in the organization of Buddhist and Daoist temples, and in other religions. It is also true in folk organizations, such as gangs and other underground or semi-underground groups. These organizations also use the language of "father and son," "uncle and nephew," and "brother" to define their interpersonal relationships, which we may call "fictive kinship organizations." Monasteries and temples are also like family structures; therefore, their members have a certain obligation to help and support each other.

As mentioned above, the Caobang was a large union-like organization of those who worked on China's Grand Canal. The members of the group were organized into large fraternal groups, who offered assistance when necessary in matters of livelihood, old age, sickness, death, etc. Most notably, there was a Luo Teachings temple at each important dock, where old, retired, or sick brothers could stay. Other groups included shipbuilders, ironmongers, and carpenters, all of whom had their own guilds, where they would worship the Southern Water God, the Fire and Star God (*Huode xingjun* 火德星君), or Lu Ban (the carpenters' god), and where they would be responsible for caring for and helping each other.

The combination of many different kinship or quasi-kinship networks, together with the idea of "native place," created a huge complex of local organizations, which is another way to understand traditional China, as these local organizations were an important link in the power structure. Although China claimed to be a unified empire, the power of the central government has been limited since ancient times, and where the power resided has varied across time. Leaving aside the question of ancient times, from the Song through the Qing dynasty, the county level was the real unit of governance. The society of a county was a more or less autonomous community. In the Qing dynasty, the county magistrate was basically on his own, with only three or four secretaries, together with a small number of subordinates and assistants; the entire personnel of a county government amounted to only 20–30 people. A county usually had a population of between 100,000 and 600,000 people; however, the real day-to-day affairs were not handled by the county government, but by the people through their own initiative.

Let's take my hometown of Wuxi as an example once again. Beginning from the early 19th century, the Jiangnan region became stable, and the Manchu government no longer worried about rebellion in the south. At the same time, the gentry groups in Jiangnan had been taking shape since the Ming dynasty. It was a handful of the most respected members of these gentry who actually carried out the local administration; in each generation there were some 20–30 of them, working in rotation and representing some 30–50 families, who participated in local administration. Such participation was not based on their wealth, nor were the gentry part of the official administrative structure. There was no clear-cut election system, and in general, the people's support was based on each individual's personal character and personality. Each gentry member who took part in the management represented at least two or three major clans, and there were countless marriages and friendships between the major clans, and they all knew that they could trust each other.

In addition to the gentry, there were of course also many businesses and workshops in Wuxi county. In modern times, Wuxi has always been known as the Little Shanghai, and many entrepreneurs from Jiangnan set up factories in Wuxi and elsewhere to produce daily necessities, as local resources in Wuxi were indeed plentiful. In the past, there were no special names for the gentry, but in modern times, they have been connected with the Chamber of Commerce, in which they played a leading role. After the Northern Expedition in 1927, which unified most of China under the rule of the Guomindang, the gentry leaders of Wuxi were Yang Hanxi 楊翰西 (1877–1954), followed by Qian Sunqing 錢孫卿 (1887–1975), neither of whom ran businesses, but were respected for their prestige of being learned and capable, and thus asked to run things. During the Warlord era, in order to prevent warlord troops crossing the border and harassing the local population, local leaders negotiated with the army and paid a fee to keep them out of the city. Local welfare programs in Wuxi included occasional bridge repair and road construction, as well as the annual provision of a certain amount of relief money for refugees fleeing the north for the south to escape the spring famine. Regular relief efforts also included a nursery (orphanage), a home for the elderly, and a place for beggars, all three of which probably began in the 18th century and lasted until 1949—more than two centuries. These expenses were routinely paid by donations from the corporate sector and the business community to the gentry, and were overseen and managed by reliable staff.

The ladies of the gentry family were not idle either. My grandmother was the vice president of the local Buddhist Sutra-Chanting Association; the president and the two vice presidents were all well known elderly ladies from the area. They used the Sutra-Chanting Association to raise funds for the poor, giving winter clothes and collecting food in times of need. They also oversaw the "vegetarian halls," where widows without means could live out their old age; people like my grandmother also worked in these old folks homes and in the nurseries.

Every morning, the gentry managers would meet in a tea room in the New Park to discuss public affairs, while outside there would be a room full of people waiting to make their requests. There would also be leading men from all walks of life, ready to listen to what the gentry had to tell them about the work to be done and the money they had promised. It was only towards noon that the county commissioner would arrive at the teahouse to listen to the decisions of the gentry. All county affairs were basically the responsibility of the people themselves, and the government only did their bidding.

This type of organization was not unique to Wuxi, as the same type of social structure was found throughout Jiangnan, where local affairs were managed by local people. Outside of Jiangnan, I believe that similar social structures probably existed in the more affluent parts of China.

Things were slightly different in the war-torn and unstable northern regions, but local people still organized themselves for the purpose of self-defense. During the Sino-Japanese war, my family lived for a period in northwest Hubei, where my late father was working. In this region, there was a man named Bie Tingfang 别廷芳 (1883–1940) who organized a self-defense force to defend the five counties in the area, so that bandits dared not enter. He was a local mid-level landowner and had attended a private school and a teacher's college. When he saw that his home village was being damaged by bandits, he took the initiative to rally his friends and relatives to put together a militia group to defend their homeland and to mobilize the people to join this armed militia. They developed small-scale irrigation systems to boost local farming income and set up small-scale modern enterprises such as a hydroelectric power plant, an agricultural tool factory, a textile factory, a flour mill, and more. He reinstituted the traditional *baojia* 保甲 mutual security system, in which everyone is responsible for the malfeasance of any community member, meaning there was nowhere in the village for bad characters to hide. Under such severe governance, the local authorities could actually keep the roads and the village safe. The county administer appointed by the Henan Provincial Government was only a figurehead, with no real power.

In Bie Tingfang's autonomous local organization, the networks he deployed were old kinship ties, local lineage organizations, and religious groups. On the basis of these complex relationships, he constructed a close-knit network based on the differential mode of association, relying solely on personal relationships to compose a strong force without recourse to the law. They emphasized the importance of everyone doing their best for themselves and others in order to maintain the safety and prosperity of their home villages, to pursue private ends for public good, and to realize the ideal society of traditional China.

From the above discussion, we can see that the differential mode of association was extended from kinship relations to geographical relations; every individual has a place in this large network, relying on the network to solve his or her problems, while at the same time contributing his or her own strengths to the network. The starting point of the network is kinship in its most basic form: the intimate interdependence of parents and children. Human beings' biological nature aims to secure each individual's survival and the survival of their descendants through repro-duction. The intimacy between parent and child is natural: they gave birth to me, nurtured me, took care of me. Parents sacrifice everything for their children, and children will do anything for their parents. Mencius believed that the starting point of "benevolence" is compassion, and he described compassion as starting from the moment when a child sees his dead parent's body exposed and goes back to pick up a hoe to bury the parent, because he or she cannot bear the sight.

Mencius' description is indeed an illustration of the care and attach-ment that inevitably exists between a parent and child. Kinship is only an extension of the parent-child relationship, and of course, the sibling relationship comes from being born of the same mother. These are the foundations on which human ethics develops out of basic biology. Marriage is not only a biological need, but also a social bond. Love is a fundamental element of interpersonal relationships, and the kinship constructed by marriage is a cross-cutting link between the families of the spouses, and an extension of the kinship relationship. Thus, the differential mode of association in Chinese culture extends outward from the most basic and natural part of biological nature, from the closest flesh and blood, to the clan, the hometown, and fictive kinship groups.

The Confucian ideal is based on benevolence, which is defined by loyalty and forgiveness. The Chinese character for "loyalty" (*zhong* 忠) places the character for "center" (*zhong* 中) over the character for "heart" (*xin* 心), and the Chinese character for "forgiveness" (*shu* 恕) suggests that my "heart" (*xin* 心) is "the same as" (*ru* 如) yours. "Benevolence" (*ren* 仁)—made up of the characters for "people" (*ren* 人) and "two" (*er* 二)—is the way to be practiced if people are to be together. The basic concepts of Confucianism are the foundation of Confucian ethics. In Daoist literature of the Warring States period, we note the appearance of the term *hui* 惠 (kindness, benevolence), which has the same meaning as the Confucian term *ai* 愛 (love). When Buddhism entered China, the emphasis was on its universal benevolence and love. The integration of these three concepts into one is the basic concept mentioned above of "putting oneself in the place of others."

It was only through this principle that Confucianism developed the concept of "to establish oneself, one seeks to establish others." Thus, in the *Analects* Confucius speaks of "self-cultivation," which should refer to the individual's efforts to understand and practice ethics. After cultivating oneself, the next step is to "pacify the people," or "pacify all the people." "The people" means people in groups close to you, which could well be a definition for mutual aid in a village context. "All the people" means all humanity, a vast territory. Therefore, Confucius said that the ancient sage kings found it difficult to "pacify all the people." He did not say that it was impossible, but rather that the world was too big, while the sage kings were only the kings of China, and hence could not necessarily take care of humanity as a whole. Nonetheless, Confucius still embraced this goal, hoping that one day, everyone's attempt to "bring peace to the people" would intersect and overlap, and develop into a large network, so that all human beings could be properly cared for even as they cared for others. At the beginning of this book, I discussed Feng Youlan's *A New Treatise on the Nature of Man* and *A New Treatise on the Nature of Dao*, in which he suggested that human ethics should be in a constant state of progress. In this chapter, our discussion also points out that ethical relationships in China progress from biological to social, and from social to transcendent universal values; such progress might be seen as interchangeable with Feng's vision.

This idea represents a combination of individualism and collectivism. The individual part is to understand the basis of human nature through "self-cultivation," the idea that an individual cannot be—nor should be—isolated. The collective part, on the other hand, is to take what is close and extend it, to strive to put oneself in the place of others. Once you begin to make progress, you hasten to take care of relatives and friends in your immediate environment, and as you gradually build a vast network on the basis of the differential mode of association, you will envelop a larger world. Within the differential mode of association, the individual has both rights and responsibilities; a person is not isolated, but neither is he or she subject to the arrangements of the collective. The line tracing the extension from the individual to the collective is continuous, not broken. Following the logic of the differential mode of association, the individual must exercise self-restraint, understanding at all times that he/she is part of a collective. However, individuals also know that they are not under the control of the collective, and that their obligations to the collective and the protection they receive from the collective are mutually dependent on each other.

In contrast to the extreme individualism of Western civilization, the differential pattern of Chinese culture can help to alleviate the isolation of individualism and prevent the inevitable disintegration of society due to the excessive development of individualism. Moreover, this kind of community is not a contract based on interest or profit, but instead on human feelings. When profits are exhausted, the relationship cools, but the natural affection between human beings endures regardless. This is the transcendent value of Chinese culture, which can be extended to become the universal value of human society to compensate for the faults of modern civilization.

Of course, this type of interpersonal relationship is no longer found in China today. However, we can still think of this type of society as one in which a group of people—a large group of people, in the course of human history, with a single ideal—practices this type of interpersonal relationship and cooperates with each other for mutual benefit.

X. The World Revealed in Novels

As was mentioned in the preface, the contents of many novels are derived from folk tales or are transformed from rhyming opera songs into the vernacular language. In light of this, it would seem that there would be no need to discuss fiction in this book. Moreover, when a novelist writes a story from beginning to end, it is the work of one person, reflecting the author's own ideas and viewpoints, and may not necessarily represent the viewpoints of the common people. However, Chinese novels can be divided into two categories: one is for literati and scholars to read, and the other is historical "romance" novels, which provide the basic plot for the storyteller to elaborate on, and can hardly be separated from the folk tradition of storytelling. A novel may be an amplification or an embellishment of the storyteller's art, and parts of popular novels may be adapted by a storyteller and added to his or her repertoire. Thus, there is no easy separation between historical romance novels and the popular tradition of storytelling.

Moreover, the educational background and social status of the authors of historical romances place them somewhere between the common people and the elite. Therefore, the influence of the historical romances can in fact transcend these two strata, even as they can also penetrate the culture of the ordinary people and become an important part of it.

The first book we will discuss in this chapter is the full-length version of *Water Margin: The Outlaws of the Marsh* (*Shuihuzhuan* 水滸傳), by Shi Nai'an 施耐庵 (1296–1372), not the much later, 70-volume emended version of Jin Shengtan 金聖歎 (1608–1661). Today, all Chinese people know *Water Margin*, and its story has become the subject matter of many plays and historical romances, and the names of the characters in the book are often used in everyday conversation as metaphors for various things. *Water Margin* was written in the late Yuan-early Ming period by Shi Nai'an, an educated man who was not part of the scholarly elite. The story is set in the Northern Song dynasty, 200 years before Shi's time.

The origins of *Water Margin* may go back to the Song dynasty. In essays and legends from the Southern Song period, we find stories about Song Jiang and his group of 36 men, who roamed the area north of the Yellow River, were later arrested and then given amnesty by the general Zhang Shuye 張叔夜 (1065–1127). The names of some of the characters in *Water Margin*, such as Guan Sheng, Song Jiang, Yan Qing, Wu Song and others, are found in other storytelling scripts. By the Southern Song, the story of Song Jiang, which had already been told in the Northern Song, had developed into a more complex series of tales.

In *Water Margin*, many of the social phenomena the author describes remind us of the situation under the Song rulers, although there are also differences. For example, some of the dishes that had become part of the daily diet in the Song continued unchanged through the early Ming period. Another example is that there was no distilled liquor in the Song dynasty, and the alcoholic content of the wine consumed at the time was not high, which is why the heroes of *Water Margin*, such as Wu Song and Lu Zhishen ("Sagacious Lu"), could drink more than 10 or 20 "bowls" at a time.

The compounds described in *Water Margin* in which the heroes lived, such as the Zhu family village or the Hu family village, were local self-defense groups organized by the Chinese for self-protection during the Liao and Jin dynasties, when north China had already fallen to non-Han people from the northern peripheries. During both the Northern and Southern Song, the outlaws who occupied the mountain forests, including

Mount Liang itself, Song Jiang's mountain lair in *Water Margin*, also gave their groups names like the "Taihang Mountain Loyalty and Righteousness Society." Before the rise of the Ming dynasty, there actually were such mountain stockades in China under the Mongols. From this angle, what we find in the *Water Margin* may well reflect real elements of life in China north of the Yangzi River during the Song and Yuan periods.

Here is a synopsis of the story of *Water Margin*: the main character is Song Jiang, a minor official in Yuncheng county, Shandong. Song's social status was not high, but he had a wide range of rough and ready friends, including local officials known at the time as *baozheng* 保正 (the equivalent of today's village cadres in mainland China), and street gangs that would hang around the marketplace. His reputation spread throughout both the outlaw and the street gang worlds, and he was ordered into exile to serve as a "conscript" in Jiangzhou (today's Jiujiang, Jiangxi) for allegedly having committed a crime. In Jiangzhou, he was rescued by his friends while at the execution ground, after which they all took refuge in the fortress at Mount Liang. From this point forward, heroes from all over flocked to Mount Liang to join Song and his band, coming one after another, for different reasons. Ultimately, there were one 108 hardy men and women from the four corners of the earth, from all different backgrounds, who swore an oath of brotherhood, saying that while they had different birthdays, they would all die on the same day.

Song Jiang's fondest hope was that one day he would be amnestied and make a name for himself on the battlefield. Later, this indeed came to pass, and the men from Mount Liang were sent by the imperial court to defeat the "Four Rebels" in the north and the south. In the first three battles, Liang Shan's heroes emerged unscathed, but the fourth battle against the rebel Fang La was a disaster, with both sides suffering heavy losses. The 20-plus survivors returned to the capitol in triumph and were given official positions in various places throughout the country. Later on, however, enemies at the court sent poison wine to Song Jiang as part of an imperial edict, and Song, knowing that he could not escape, invited his friend Li Kui to drink the poison wine with him (to avoid Li's rising up to avenge Song) and they committed suicide together. Two of their closest friends, Wu Yong and Hua Rong, also hung themselves before the graves of Song and Li. Of the original 108 men, there remained only Lu Zhishen and Lin Chong, who were ordained as monks at a Buddhist temple in Hangzhou, and Wu Song, who stayed in Hangzhou to take care of them. The earliest leaders of Mount Liang, such as Li Jun, chose to wander the rivers and lakes, and ultimately organized a fleet of ships to seize Siam, thus becoming kings overseas. Others who were lucky enough to survive were killed during the Jin invasion, trying to protect the country.

Further details of the plot of *Water Margin* need not concern us here; the point of the story is to illustrate the hardships faced by people who find themselves at the bottom of the social ladder. Just getting by was not easy, and many people, in order to make a living, wound up doing things that crossed the line between good and evil. The culture of the elite and the behavior prized by those at the top of society were out of reach for those at the bottom. Since they found themselves on the border of legality and illegality, the state's demands in terms of loyalty, sincerity and ritual propriety made little sense to them. Loyalty, filial piety, ritual propriety, and righteousness were the cardinal virtues of Chinese society, but the first three speak to ethical behavior in a stable society, while "righteousness" instead describes mutual trust and assistance between people. There was no place for these poor and desperate people in the government or in mainstream society. Some people could not even afford to start a family, or perhaps had a family but were separated from it, so the ethics of filial piety, ritual propriety, or kinship were beyond their means. When they were young they relied on their parents, and when they left home they relied on their friends, not only to make a living, but for assistance in situations of life and death. The obligations of friendship might lead to trouble, but the virtue of friendship was very strong.

This was the life situation of the heroes on Mount Liang; they gathered on the mountain and befriended each other as brothers, which is also how they referred to one another. Their dream was that one day they would be able to give up these identities and start a new life: to be amnestied and recruited by the government, to achieve merit and have a career so that things would finally turn out well. However, the vast majority of people at the bottom of the hierarchy never had the chance to realize their dreams, and amnesty wound up being just that—a dream. In the end, the story of Mount Liang ended with the shattering of the dream—those who died, died, those who parted, parted, and all that was left to the few who remained was the "righteousness" of friends, in which the dregs of society must place their hopes.

Ever since the publication of *Water Margin*, the righteousness celebrated in the story, symbolized by the 108 heroes who pledged brotherhood and loyalty to one another, entered deeply into the folk culture of China and came a permanent model for people to emulate. In the oaths sworn by underground societies like the Triads or the Green Gang, the righteousness of Mount Liang is always cited as a precedent. Nor is this limited to underground groups: artisans' and merchants' guilds also celebrate the same virtues. The influence of such notions greatly exceeded the scope of fiction.

The story of Mount Liang emphasizes the hardships of the good men who were "forced to ascend Mount Liang," the idea that official cruelty left the people no choice but to rebel. In other words, many people who could have been good citizens had no choice but to rebel against the injustice of the government, the oppression of the powerful, and the exploitation of the wealthy, so they holed up in mountain fortresses to challenge the established social order. To rob the rich and give to the poor is another dream of the poor: they see the unfair distribution of wealth and feel that the rich should help the poor; if the rich are unwilling to do so, the heroes take into their hands the wealth of the rich on behalf of the poor and redistribute it to those in need.

These two slogans, or two demands, have always existed in all societies, and there have always been people who, when cornered, propose just such a protest or solution. Therefore, in the history of China, in times of poor government or social unrest, when the powerful oppress the weak and the rich exploit the poor, the result is large-scale rebellion. The leaders of the rebellions called on the poor to organize armies, often using the same demands and slogans as those of Mount Liang. There were historical examples of this that preceded the publication of *Water Margin*, and the government continued to "force the people to rebel" as late as in the Ming and Qing periods, after the publication of the novel, with all such rebellions manifesting the wishes of the people at the bottom of the society to put an end to social injustice by robbing the rich to help the poor. The ideas expressed in *Water Margin*—the importance of righteousness, the fact that government oppression forces the people to rebel, the dream of robbing the rich to give to the poor—perhaps sum up the experience of people in the past, and points the way forward for people of the future.

When we return to the actual contents of the novel, there are in fact not many instances where the officials forced the people to revolt. Lin Chong was persecuted by Gao Yanei, which led to the breakup of his family, and he was exiled and forced to join the army; without the protection of Lu Zhishen, his life would have been lost. He was the first hero to ascend Mount Liang, but he was not treated fairly there and had to take a meager position under several people less capable and competent. Therefore, in the life experience of some people depicted in the novel, unfair treatment was not limited to the outside world. The various difficulties encountered by Lin Chong were not addressed until after Song Jiang joined them on the mountain. The story of Lin Chong is actually a further recognition of the importance of the word "righteousness" in *Water Margin*.

As for robbing the rich to help the poor, in the entire story of *Water Margin*, we do not see the Mount Liang heroes taking the wealth and distributing it to poor people in general. Whenever the story has them descend the mountain to engage in raids, it is often clearly explained that the problem was a lack of food in the mountain fort, and counties and prefectures had to be plundered to feed the outlaws. Sometimes they attacked the estates of the wealthy, again in part to take the food and grain that these places had set aside. It is only while they were on the mountain that fairness reigned, both among the leaders and the ordinary heroes. Only in this context did the word "righteousness" again take on a specific meaning, as in the story of the distribution of gold in the "Hall of Righteousness," the main building on Mount Liang.

And indeed, many of those who ascended Mount Liang wound up there because of the scheme of the Mount Liang leaders, so it was not a case of the government forcing the people to rebel. For example, Zhu Tong, Yang Zhi, Qin Ming, and Hu Yanzhuo constantly tried to recruit Lu Junyi and Li Ying. These people fell into the trap of Mount Liang for no reason at all and had no choice but to join their "brothers" on the mountain.

The story of Mount Liang claimed that all the 108 brothers assembled were totally equal, but let's take a closer look. The 108 "stars of destiny" were divided into an "elite" of 36 Heavenly Spirits (upper rank) and the remaining 72 lower ranked Earthly Fiends. Some of the 36 Heavenly Spirits, as the leaders were called, were too powerful to be excluded from the list, so their inclusion makes sense. At the same time, some of Song Jiang's buddies from Jiangzhou, like the petty rascals Xie Zhen and Xie Bao, were also listed among the Heavenly Spirits, which was clearly not "fair." Among the 108 people assembled on Mount Liang, Gunsun Long and Wu Yong recruited Jin Dajian, who was good at stone carving, and carved the names and ranks of all 108, claiming that this was a stone tablet descended from heaven and representing heaven's will. This trick was obviously carried out so that Song Jiang could arrange his position as he wished, and he used the idea of "heavenly decree" to lock in the positions of his old and new brothers according to his personal wishes.

In fact, it is often clearly revealed in the novel that Song Jiang wanted to be the boss, but that he only pretended to be properly respectful of ritual, bowing his head and yielding to the worthy. Whenever such a situation arose, Li Kui, whom he had recruited in Jiangzhou, would make a huge fuss.

When Chao Kai was leader, Song Jiang did not allow him to lead his troops down the mountain to make a success of himself, lest he be robbed of his glory. The last—and only—time that Chao led the Mount Liang brothers to attack Zengtou city, he died from wounds he received in battle. His final testament, established just before he died, was that whoever could capture alive the enemy who had shot him, Shi Wengong, would succeed him as leader. Later on, Lu Junyi captured Shi, and if Chao's will had been followed, Lu would have become leader. Moreover, the brothers of Mount Liang wanted Lu Junyi to be leader because of his outlaw appeal. However, during the discussion on who should be the leader, Song Jiang's old buddies from Jiangzhou, and especially Li Kui, all agitated on behalf of Song Jiang. All of this proved that Song Jiang was a hypocrite.

These and other acts depicted in *Water Margin* illustrate to the reader that the rough and ready rebels of Mount Liang in fact did many things that were not in line with the slogans they constantly repeated—something we have observed from time immemorial in the behavior of the heroes that bring down one dynasty and found another, or among the leaders of revolutionary uprisings.

Anyone who has read *Water Margin* knows that the 70 volumes making up the first half of the book contain what are known as the 10 Song Jiang chapters and the 10 Wu Song chapters. The stories of the exploits of Lin Chong and Lu Zhishen make up another 10 chapters; it is difficult to separate out stories concerning Lu Zhishen and stories concerning Wu Song because the two are partners. In any event, the importance of these four characters is obvious, and among them, Lu Zhishen occupies a particularly prominent position. When he went to Wutai Mountain to be ordained as a monk, his master, Elder Wisdom, gave Lu a verse that said, "Take action in the forest. Prosper in the mountains. Flourish amid the waters, but halt at the river." Later on, when he was fighting the Four Rebels, Elder Wisdom gave him another verse: "Take Xia when you encounter him. Seize La when you meet. When you hear the tide, round out the circle. When you see the tide, in silence rest." These two stanzas foretold the story of Lu Zhishen's life.

In battling the Four Rebels, most of the forces of Mount Liang perished. Before he captured Fang La, Lu had entered a world outside the world, where an elderly monk revealed to him how to leave the dusty world of mortals behind. Thus, when the great army made its triumphant return, Lu decided to remain at Liuhe Temple in Hangzhou. On the fifteenth day of the eighth month, the water of the Qiantang River rose, and Lu thought it was the enemy troops advancing to attack, but the monks told him that it was the Old Faithful Tide. Lu suddenly understood that now it was time to rest in silence (i.e., to die). Hence, he took a bath and cleansed his body, and sat in meditation until he passed away. He also left a *gatha* (Sanskrit for a type of Buddhist verse): "In life I performed no virtuous deeds, preferring murder and arson. Suddenly my metal shackles opened, the jade box shattered. Hark! The Old Faithful Tide comes on the Qiantang River, and today I know myself at last."[1] This is one of the characters in the novel who obtains good karma.

As already mentioned, the fate of the Mount Liang characters was that those who died, died, and those who were wounded, were wounded. Although the remaining 27 generals were rewarded and became local officials, the leading characters, Lu Junyi and Song Jiang, were poisoned to death, and Song Jiang's trusted advisors, Li Kui, Wu Yong and Hua Rong, were also martyred. Wu Song waited on Lin Chong, who had a broken arm, and Lu Zhisheng died while meditating, after which Lin and Wu succumbed to illness. Yan Qing, a trusted friend of Lu Junyi, left without saying goodbye after the return of the victorious troops. According to the account in the novel, he met his old friend Xu Guanzhong in Shuanglin

---

1   Translations from Shi Nai'an, *Outlaws of the Marsh*, trans. Sidney Shapiro (Olympia Press, 2016), Kindle Edition.

Town, who was living in seclusion in the countryside, and then disappeared from the world after achieving enlightenment. Li Jun, Tong Wei, and Tong Meng were on the high seas looking for a better world. Lu Zhishen, Yan Qing, and Li Jun, and others, were all searching to find themselves outside the world of Mount Liang.

At Song Jiang's request, Elder Wisdom of Mount Wutai gave him a *gatha* in which he said: "Song Jiang advanced with an [incense] stick, bowed, and palms together, addressed the abbot: 'I have a question, I wonder if I dare ask? One's life on earth is limited, though suffering is without end. Man's body is weak. His greatest concern is life and death.'" The abbot answered with another *gatha*: "The six senses bound, by the four elements restricted, several times you've tumbled in the flames of battle. Alas, all living things afloat in this world howl in futility in mire and sand." The meaning of this *gatha* is that all human deeds are nothing but emptiness in the end.

Another Buddhist monk gave the following comment on Lu Zhishen's meditation: "All men have minds, and all minds have thoughts. Heaven and hell are all born in thoughts. That is why in the three realms there is only the mind, and in the ten thousand dharmas there is only wisdom. If thoughts are stifled, all six paths will be eliminated, and the cycle of reincarnation will cease." These instructions did not lead Song Jiang to enlightenment and he eventually suffered a great calamity, while Lu Zhishen and the others were enlightened and were able to transcend the mortal world and find their own place.

All the above was perhaps part of the life experience of Shi Nai'an, the author of the *Water Margin*, who lived during of the chaos of the Yuan-Ming transition, and had his own misfortunes. His understanding of things is that of the last verse in the previous paragraph. From this series of hidden clues, I hope readers will understand that Shi Nai'an's intention was not to praise the righteousness of the outlaw world, nor to dream that Mount Liang would return to righteousness. His goal was instead to point out that many things we do in this world, just like the world of Mount Liang, are full of hypocrisy, pain, and disappointment, and in the end, all is in vain.

The second novel to be discussed is *The Romance of the Three Kingdoms* by Luo Guanzhong. Luo Guanzhong and Shi Nai'an were good friends, and Luo Guanzhong, who was younger, assisted Shi Nai'an out of respect. There are quite a lot of similarities in their works, because they learned from each other, and even helped one other to finish their works. Luo Guanzhong once participated in Zhang Shicheng's 張士誠 (1321–1367) Red Turban rebellion at the end of the Yuan dynasty, but he later left Zhang to concentrate on his writing. He wrote many books, but *The Romance of the Three Kingdoms* is probably the most important one and is a masterpiece of the Chinese romance novel genre.

The Romance of the Three Kingdoms is a narrative of the period of the end of the Han dynasty, when the world was divided and the three kingdoms of Wei 魏, Shu 蜀, and Wu 吳 were fighting for the throne. Historical information about the period can be found in Chen Shou's 陳壽 (233–297) *Records of the Three Kingdoms* (*Sanguo zhi* 三國志), which is the most detailed, and other sources include Xi Zuochi's 習鑿齒 (d. 384) *Annals of Han and Jin* (*Han Jin chunqiu* 漢晉春秋), and Chang Qu's 常璩 (291–361) *Chronicles of Huayang* (*Huayang guozhi* 華陽國志), both of which contain considerable information about the Three Kingdoms period. The latter, in particular, is a local history of the Shu region (present-day Sichuan), with the most detailed description of the historical facts pertaining to the kingdom of Shu Han. There are also some similarities and differences between these books. Chen Shou supported the Wei and Jin dynasties, while Xi Zuochi first supported the Shu Han, before finally endorsing the Jin.

Luo Guanzhong's *The Romance of the Three Kingdoms* covers a wide range of historical events. He based his narrative chiefly on Chen Shou's work, which presented Shu Han as the orthodox line and severely rebuked Cao Wei, while treating the Kingdom of Wu, situated in the southeast, as a legitimate collateral branch of the ruling family. Because of this perspective, *The Romance of the Three Kingdoms* praises as positive characters the three members of Liu Bei's brotherhood, as well as Zhuge Liang, while

Cao Cao 曹操 (155–220) is described as a treacherous usurper. Because of this stance and the need to provide exciting plot lines, the story we read in Luo's *The Romance of the Three Kingdoms* is quite different from the real history recounted in Chen Shou's *Records of the Three Kingdoms*.

For example, the Battle of Red Cliff figures as a major event in Luo's story, but in real historical terms, Wu was the main force resisting Cao Cao's southward advance, and Liu Bei's forces provided only minor assistance. The famous "borrowing arrows with straw boats" story[2] was in fact a feat of Zhou Yu's 周瑜 (175–210), and had nothing to do with Zhuge Liang. The famous journey in which "Guan Yu crossed five passes and slayed six generals"[3] took a completely wrong route. The distance from Cao Cao's headquarters in Xuchang to Yechang, the headquarters of Yuan Shao (d. 202), the warlord protecting Liu Bei, was only about 200 *li* (some 65 miles), so there is no way that Guan Yu made such a wandering journey through so many passes....But our purpose here is not to discuss the historical veracity of *The Romance of the Three Kingdoms*, but to treat it as a work of fiction, so we need not dwell on these errors.

The main plot of *The Romance of the Three Kingdoms* chronicles the fall of the Han dynasty, which began with a struggle between imperial relatives and eunuchs, leading to the seizure of power by Dong Zhuo's 董卓 (138–192) army. Emperor Xian 漢獻帝 (r. 189–220) was ultimately held hostage by Cao Cao, who seized power as Grand Chancellor. After many years of civil war, the empire was finally divided into three parts:

---

2   The story is that Zhuge Liang agreed to a dare to produce 100,000 arrows in three days or face execution if he failed. To "produce" the arrows, he sent boats full of straw across the river to the enemy camp, feigning an attack. The enemy shot thousands of arrows at the boats, enabling Zhuge Liang to win the bet. —Trans.

3   The story is that Guan Gong decided to abandon Cao Cao, with whom he had made a tactical alliance, and rejoin Liu Bei, bringing Liu's wives and consorts with him. In the novel, the journey is portrayed as long and violent, requiring that Guan cross five passes and kill six generals. —Trans.

the Kingdom of Cao Wei, located in the central plains; the Kingdom of Eastern Wu, located in the eastern part of present-day Jiangsu; and the Shu Han Kingdom, founded by Liu Bei, in the southwest. It was only later that China was briefly unified by the Sima Jin dynasty (265–316), the successor of the Cao-Wei regime. The first period of civil war between the vassals was dominated by the rise of Cao-Wei, which seized the emperor to threaten the vassals. After the Battle of Red Cliff, the novel enters its second period, an intermediate period of struggle among the three major forces. At this stage, the main axis is clearly the relationship between Shu Han and Wu, with Cao-Wei in the north being given a secondary role. Finally, in the third stage of the novel, after the relationship between Eastern Wu and Shu Han breaks down and Liu Bei dies, Zhuge Liang stands alone in the grand scheme of things, and the plot line is how Zhuge Liang persists in the cause of Shu Han.

In my view, the point of the book is to distinguish between loyalty and treachery in order to establish the guilt of Cao and Sima, the founders of Wei-Jin. The thread that runs through the whole book is that of loyalty and righteousness: Liu Bei, Guan Yu, and Zhang Fei, because of their shared loyalty, become blood brothers for life. The story of the "Peach Garden," where the three took their oath, has become a symbol of loyalty in Chinese folk ethics. The three of them were born in the wilderness, and decided to work together as a team, but ultimately found themselves separated by their hardships. Yet they never forgot their original vow, and even when Guan Yu and Zhang Fei secured their own safety, they never forgot to seek out Liu Bei. Guan Yu had to pledge allegiance to Cao Cao, even as he upheld the principle of surrendering to Han, but not to Cao Cao.

In the face of the courtesy with which Cao Cao treated him, Guan Yu remained unmoved, and as soon as he found out where Liu Bei was, he set aside his gold and abandoned his official position, and accompanied Liu Bei's two wives through the five passes and the killing of the six generals, ultimately taking up his place beside Liu Bei once again. The final test was the episode where Guan Yu failed to hold Jingzhou and died in the battle. When Liu and Zhang learned the bad news, Zhang, eager to avenge Guan Yu's death, blamed his own subordinates for not acting quickly enough and was then stabbed to death by them. At this point, Liu Bei had already occupied Sichuan, and his main strategy should have been to unite Shu and Wu to resist Cao Cao. However, because of Guan Yu's death at the hands of Wu, he was so furious that he mobilized his entire army to attack them. His anger also explained the carelessness behind his defeat. The three of them loved each other for the sake of righteousness, a value higher than life, throne, and career, and for righteousness, they sacrificed everything.

Another example of loyalty and righteousness is found in the relationship between Zhuge Liang and Liu Bei. Zhuge Liang was a man of extraordinary talent who barely managed to survive in a world of chaos and did not seek fame or position from the warlords. However, after Liu Bei visited his thatched hut and asked for his help three times, he was so grateful for Liu's acknowledgement of his skills that he was absolutely determined to help Liu Bei. Liu Bei's major strategy was the work of Zhuge Liang: the idea was to hold Shu, to unite with Wu and to fight against Cao Cao, and to await the proper moment to act. In the end, Liu Bei, Guan, and Zhang were killed and the strategy became impossible. Zhuge Liang accepted Liu Bei's last order before death to take care of his only son and did his best to maintain the base of Shu. During Zhuge Liang's reign, he stabilized Shu, conquered Yizhou to the south, and fought against Cao Wei in the north. Afterwards he launched his "six campaigns from Qishan,"[4] and found himself on the front lines in Gansu for a long period, with little

---

4   These were military campaigns launched and led by Zhuge Liang in an attempt to fulfill Liu Bei's strategic vision. There were in fact only five, and only two were launched from Qishan. The campaigns were unsuccessful but highly dramatic. —Trans.

to eat and much to do, and he finally died at the age of 54. He was ready to lay down his life for Liu Bei, just for the word "righteousness."

Righteousness also figures in the relationship between the rulers and officials in the Kingdom of Wu. General Sun Jian 孫堅 (155–191) died prematurely before achieving what he set out to do, but his sons Sun Ce 孫策 (175–200) and Sun Quan 孫權 (182–252) inherited their father's ambition and befriended the heroes of Jiangdong to gain control of the southeast. The elderly officials of the Eastern Wu remained completely loyal to the two brothers due to promises they had made to Sun Jian. Sun Ce and Zhou Yu knew one another when they were young, and were both outstanding figures, and they treated each other with the utmost respect. Zhou Yu shed blood and tears for this friendship and passed away while still in his prime for having given too much of himself.

General Lu Su 魯肅 (172–217) was also a good friend of the Sun brothers, and when he first met Zhou Yu, he gave him half of his family's savings to help him start his business. After Zhou Yu's death, Lu Su was the main stabilizing force in Wu, and he spared no effort to assist Sun Quan. The friendship between these four men was also a matter of righteousness. Fire was a major weapon in the Battle of Red Cliff, and the elderly general Huang Gai was willing to pretend to be tortured to make Cao Cao believe that he surrendered out of anger. However, Huang Gai himself led a fleet of fire ships across the river and set fire to Cao Cao's navy.[5] Huang Gai thus volunteered to risk his life in order to repay three generations of Sun for their recognition of his talent.

---

5   The basic elements of the complicated ruse were as follows: Huang Gai was serving under Zhou Yu, and both were against Cao Cao. Huang wanted to find a way to set Cao's navy on fire, and came up with the idea of pretending to betray Zhou Yu. With Zhou's connivance, Huang pretended to lose his temper with Zhou, for which Zhou had him tortured, something Cao's spies in Zhou's camp witnessed. Huang subsequently sent a letter pledging himself to Cao, since he obviously could no longer serve under Zhou. He promised to come to him on a certain night, which is why Cao let the "fire boats" approach his navy. —Trans.

Another pair of people who knew and trusted one another are Zhuge Liang and Lu Su. They worked in common to hold the alliance between Wu and Shu together to defend against Cao Wei's strategy. This is a different kind of friendship, but it is also about "righteousness."

In contrast, Cao Wei was full of treachery, exploitation, and deceit. Cao Cao usurped the power of the Han court, and his son Cao Pi completed the conquest of Han. Stories of vengeance followed one after the other, and Sima Yi, who had been charged with weighty matters by Cao Cao and Cao Pi, in subsequent years set himself up as the true ruler of the state before finally usurping power. The generals of Cao Wei were rarely seen to display much "righteousness." In Cao's camp, there was Xu Shu, who was originally a follower of Liu Bei, but he was forced to follow Cao Cao because Cao Cao had kidnapped his mother. However, when Xu Shu left his friend Zhuge Liang, he vowed never to utter a word to Cao Cao for the rest of his life. This was one of the few people in Cao Cao's camp who was a man of righteousness, but his righteousness is ironic, because it had nothing to do with Cao Cao.

All of this suggests that Luo Guanzhong intentionally created a strong contrast between the Cao camp and the Liu family in his writing. The impact of *The Romance of the Three Kingdoms* on the viewpoints of Chinese people in general is that they appreciate Zhuge Liang and Guan Yu of Liu Bei's camp, the former as a symbol of wisdom and strategy, the latter as a representative of righteousness and courage, while Cao Cao's camp is seen as representative of treachery, deceit, and usurpation. The position of the Cao and Liu camps, at least until the Tang dynasty, was not seen as quite so antagonistic. Cao Cao, for example, was always known as "Martial Wei," a posthumous title affiliated with imperial status, an acknowledged strategist and the man credited with ending the chaos of the late Han; in the Tang dynasty, "sons and grandsons of Martial Wei" was still a term of praise. Again, prior to the Tang dynasty, the Shu Han was viewed as the weakest of the three kingdoms, and among the glorious deeds of this era, Sun Wu's heroes, such as Sun Quan and Zhou Yu, were ranked first.

Luo Guanzhong created an unparalleled mastermind in Zhuge Liang, but in fact it is often a case of mistaken attribution, and Zhuge Liang is given credit for things that other people actually did. The idea of the fire attack in the Battle of Red Cliff was planned and carried out by Zhou Yu, while in the novel the credit is given to Zhuge Liang. The stratagem of "using straw boats to borrow arrows" is not found in records from the period, and was borrowed from elsewhere. "Borrowing the easterly wind" is a very dramatic story. Luo Guanzhong describes how Zhuge Liang used magic to summon the southeasterly winds, so that Wu's fire ships could attack Cao's camp on the northern bank. According to the explanation of later generations, the northeast winds are possible in Xiaoyang in the tenth month. In my view, who can predict the wind? Were Huang Gai's fire boats lucky enough to catch the wind?

During the Sino-Japanese war, my family lived in the Jingzhou region, so I am fairly familiar with the geography of the area. When the war ended, the Yangzi River channel had not been dredged for eight years, and there were no navigation markers, so the boat my family took ran aground at the Red Cliff. The main current of the Yangzi in that part of the river flows to meet the Han River after passing Jingzhou, but at this point it is blocked by the hills of Huya and Jingmen, which push the current toward the south. After arriving at the mouth of Dongting Lake, the river turned and merged with the waters coming out of the lake, and flowed northbound until it reached the mouth of the Han River, which is today's Wuhan, before turning eastward. The course of the Yangtze River from Jingzhou to Hankou is in the shape of a "V," flowing south, and then north, and then finally to the east. On the west bank of the Red Cliffs are Huya and Jingmen, and on the east bank is Huang Guai Lake (where Huang Guai's fleet was anchored). Our captain described the landscape as follows: "The fire boat launched by the Eastern Wu from the southeast coast could take advantage of the northern current to directly attack Cao Cao's army north bank, so why did they need the southeast wind?"

As for Zhuge Liang's "Eight Trigrams Foundation," it is very famous in history and literature. Du Fu's 杜甫 (712–770) poem "The Famous Diagram of the Eight Battle Formations" describes Zhuge Liang's achievements. As discussed in Chapter 5 on the *Yijing*, this diagram is a way of setting up camp in terms of four directions and four corners, which gives eight positions occupied by the front troop, the rear troop, the left troop, the right troop, and four auxiliary forces, the idea being to allow the troops to exit the camp quickly following such a strategic arrangement. There is nothing miraculous about it—it is a basic tactic for setting up camp and leaving for battle in an orderly way.

Zhuge Liang is also credited for his "Longzhong Plan,"[6] the grand strategy he put together for Liu Bei, allowing Liu to triumph over his rivals. He traveled to Eastern Wu and discussed with Lu Su the strategy of uniting against Cao Wei, which also established the basic configuration of the Three Kingdoms. When he ruled Sichuan, he combined the essence of Legalism with the Confucian benevolence to govern, a legacy that is still cherished by the people of Sichuan. In his southern expedition to Yizhou, he achieved military victory and brought peace to the people, hence the saying "the southerners have never again risen up." He did not have absolute influence over Liu Bei, whose biggest mistake was that of trusting Guan and Zhang more than Zhuge Liang. The reason Zhuge Liang's "Longzhong Plan" was not finally carried out was that Liu Bei did not follow it to the end. After the death of Liu Bei, Zhuge Liang continued to attempt to achieve the plan, and died at the age of 54 in the heat of battle. In conclusion, Zhuge Liang was a great talent and had great character, but he was not, as described by Luo Guanzhong, a Daoist priest whose magic powers allowed him to foresee the future. But today, the name Zhuge Liang suggests someone who is half immortal, and this is due to Luo Guanzhong's depiction.

---

6   Longzhong was the name of the place where Zhuge Liang was staying when he devised the plan. —Trans.

In contrast with this depiction of Zhuge Liang, Luo Guanzhong was unkind to Zhou Yu. In *The Romance of the Three Kingdoms*, we have the impression that Zhou Yu was a young man, when in fact Zhou Yu was 34 years old at the time of the Battle of Red Cliff and Zhuge Liang was only 27. The author reversed the ages of the two, depicting Zhou Yu as an arrogant youth and Zhuge Liang as a mature gentleman.

Zhou Yu held a high position in Eastern Wu, and was a good friend of Sun Ce, whose younger brother Sun Quan was only 19 years old when he died, after which he relied on Zhou as his main assistant. He was known as the "Zhou lad," which refers to his early fame and great talent. The Song poet Su Dongpo used the phrase "calm and composed" (literally "with feather fan and silk kerchief") to describe Zhou Yu's insouciance, which was later transposed by Luo Guanzhong onto Zhuge Liang. Lu Su was also a leading figure in Jiangdong, but in Luo Guanzhong's version, he was a vacillating type who tried to get along with everyone. The influence that Luo Guanzhong's novel had on readers was such that it actually modified peoples' perceptions of historical figures.

Over the years, Guan Yu evolved to become the god of war. In terms of his own abilities, Guan Yu was a brave and skillful warrior, but not a general with a good grasp of the overall situation. He was assigned to guard Jingzhou, and hence was an important player in Zhuge Liang's Longzhong Plan; Zhang Fei played the same role on the northern frontier between Hanzhong and Guanzhong. The responsibilities of the forces arrayed in the center were to respond to the needs of Guan Yu and Zhang Fei, and Liu Bei sent his adopted son Liu Feng to guard Shangyong, today's Danjiangkou, in the upper reaches of the Han River delta. Guan Yu's armies took Xiangyang and Fancheng, giving him a momentary advantage, but he did not coordinate the movements of the left and center lines, and only the right line advanced, which was a major strategic error.

He was over-confident, and he despised both the Eastern Wu and Liu Feng. He was a believer in heroism and personal glory, and it is hard to blame others for his failures. However, Guan Yu's death was really the result of a plot by the Eastern Wu, and at the time there were people who mourned him. After his death, there was a great plague in Eastern Wu, which many saw as Guan Yu's vengeance. In *The Romance of the Three Kingdoms*, Luo Guanzhong depicts a scene in which, after Guan Yu's death, his head was given to Cao Cao by the Eastern Wu. Every night, Guan Yu's spirit was heard demanding that his head be returned to him. An old monk from Yuquan Mountain asked, "What about the heads of those slayed by Guan Yu at the five passes?" This image of an unhappy ghost was probably already quite popular at the time.

The position of Guan Yu was gradually deified, and he was first posthumously named "Duke" in the Song dynasty, rising one grade from the rank of marquis conferred by the Han. In the Yuan dynasty, he received the title of "King," and in the Ming Dynasty, when the imperial family embraced Daoism, he finally reached the position of "Emperor," and became "Emperor Guan," the highest position among the gods in the heavenly court. Even before entering China, the Manchu dynasty already worshipped Guan Yu, honoring him as the father of the ruling family. Nurhaci 努爾哈赤 (1559–1626), the founder of the Manchu dynasty who began the assault on Ming China, used *The Romance of the Three Kingdoms* as a military textbook to train his generals, and Guan's status rose even higher. Every Qing emperor would add a few words of honor to the name of Emperor Guan, and by the time of the Guangxu period (1871–1908), his honorific title was 26 characters long. Today, in Chinese folklore, Guan Yu is both a Daoist deity and a Buddhist protector. He is not only known as the "god of war"—a status comparable to that of Confucius—but merchants also worship him as the god of wealth. Zhang Fei, probably due to the fame of Guan Yu, is also an emissary of the Daoist gods, who travels around punishing corrupt officials. With all these changes, Guan Yu enjoys an extremely exalted status in the minds of the Chinese people and occupies an important position in their lives.

While we are on the topic of Guan Yu's becoming a god, the 365 gods that appear in another novel, *The Investiture of the Gods*, constitute the *nomenklatura* of the world of folk beliefs. The book was published in the Jiajing period of the Ming dynasty, but there were already some early examples in the Song dynasty, such as the storyteller's version of *King Wu's Battle Against King Zhou* (*Wuwang fa Zhou* 武王伐紂), on the basis of which the Ming-dynasty authors composed their novels. There are many theories as to who the author of *The Investiture of the Gods* was, and by far the most likely possibilities are Xu Zhonglin 許仲琳 (d. 1560) and Lu Xixing 陸西星 (1520–1606). These two authors may both have been Daoists, or even Daoist priests. Regardless of the identity of the author(s), the contents of the book do reflect a strong belief in Daoism, which is not surprising, since Daoism flourished in the Ming dynasty.

The Investiture of the Gods is full of all kinds of strange tales of the gods. The main idea of the story is that the young Shang-dynasty King Zhou, who had just assumed the throne, was a man of uncommon talent and could have been a promising king. The vassals of the Shang were also talented and wise, all of which meant that the kingdom might have continued to build on the foundation of its prosperity. However, King Zhou yielded to his own desires, and invited in temptations from outside, allowing the Nine-Heavens Fox Demon to usurp the queen's soul, and he himself became an unworthy ruler. What might have been a golden age turned into an era of chaos and tyranny. Some of his courtiers and retainers were executed for having dared to remonstrate, while others revolted, causing civil unrest in the country. It was not until King Wen of the Western Zhou led a rebellion against King Zhou that he was finally overthrown, and a new dynasty established. During the civil war, two sects (the Chan Teachings 闡教 and the Jie Teachings 截教) intervened to support Zhou and Shang respectively, becoming rival groups. The two groups shared the same origins and the adepts of both were Daoist practitioners. The Chan (not the same as Chan Buddhism) were orthodox, and virtually all members were Daoists who had practiced to the point of being able to kill evil spirits; the Jie, by contrast, were mostly evil spirits and monsters, who challenged the Chan in their opposition to King Zhou.

In addition to these groups, we also find "the Western teachings" and the "Human teachings," which are mentioned only occasionally and seem to represent Buddhism and Confucianism, respectively. The Zhou were led by Jiang Ziya, who was a disciple of the Chan teachings, and all his fellow soldiers were Daoist practitioners. At the end of the bitter war, the Zhou replaced the Shang and established a new dynasty. The leaders of the three teachings ordered Jiang Ziya to arrange the war dead and assign them their duties in the realm of the gods: 365 people died in the war, counting those on both sides, and all of them were accorded a place in the register (indeed another name for the novel is *The Register of the Investiture of the Gods*).

This approach, which does not discriminate between friends and enemy, is a bit like Lincoln's speech in Gettysburg after the American Civil War, in which he mourned the fallen soldiers of both sides. We find a story of the great war of the gods and demons in the West as well. The earliest of the great battles of the gods and demons is the story of Enuma Elis, the Babylonian creation myth. In medieval Europe, where Christianity was already widespread, Dante's *Divine Comedy* also tells of a great battle between gods and demons. In these two legends, the failed demons are cast into hell, never to be rehabilitated. The difference between the concepts represented by the Western Catholic tradition and the Chinese ideas as seen in the register of the gods is obvious.

The appearance of *The Investiture of the Gods* in the mid-16th century also reflects the political situation of the Ming dynasty at that time. Emperor Jiajing (r. 1521–1567) was a fervent Daoist. He reigned for 45 years, but only in the first decade or so did he cooperate with his courtiers to govern the country. For the remaining 30 years, he indulged in Daoist magic, praying to avoid misfortune and receive good fortune, and taking elixirs to prolong life. Following Daoist counsels, he also engaged in various sexual practices and positions.

At the time, Daoism in China was divided into three main branches, one being the Zhengyi school (the Celestial Masters), which was the sect of the Celestial Masters, located on Dragon Tiger Mountain in Jiangxi province, which practiced talismans and alchemy. The Celestial Masters were the officially appointed leaders of the Daoist church, so this group was very active in the imperial court. Emperor Jiajing had great faith in two Daoist priests, Shao Yuanjie 邵元節 (1459–1539) and Tao Zhongwen 陶仲文 (1475–1560), and gave them high government positions. He spent a large amount of state funds to build various Daoist palaces and temples, and also spent a great deal of time sending "memorials" to the Daoist court in heaven, while turning over affairs of state to Yan Song 嚴嵩 (1480–1567) and his son, who dominated the court for decades.

Following Daoist sexual practices, Emperor Jiajing collected many young girls to be tormented and abused. This led more than a dozen palace women to join together in a (failed) plot to murder the emperor in 1542, an event known as the "palace plot of the Renyin year" in Ming history—a very rare event in Chinese history!

Emperor Jiajing's absurd behavior is closely related to the efforts of the Celestial Masters who assisted the tyrant to commit evil. The other two Taoist sects (Quanzhen in the north and Wudang in Hubei) were both dissatisfied with the Zhengyi religion. These two schools emphasized the accumulation of merit for the benefit of the masses and the cultivation of the inner and external body. The author of *The Investiture of the Gods* was surely making a parallel between Shang and Zhou times; when he praised the Chan school and condemned the Jie school, he was surely making a commentary on Daoism under the Ming. When he told the stories of Bi Gan and Huang Feihu, two ministers who were executed by the tyrannical King Zhou, he was surely thinking of martyred Ming officials such as Yang Jisheng 楊繼盛 (1516–1555), Hai Rui 海瑞 (1514–1587), and Shen Lian 沈煉 (1507–1557).

During the Shang period, the kingdom faced internal unrest and attacks by other kingdoms. During the Jiajing era, China was also plagued by Japanese invaders in the south and Mongol invaders in the north. The author(s) of *The Investiture of the Gods* may have been using the past to mock the present.

The storyline of *The Investiture of the Gods* is that of an initial attempt to impose order, which suddenly slides into chaos, with order ultimately being restored after a period of struggle, a process that was both preordained but which also had many plot twists. In the realm of self-cultivation presented in the novel, the highest attainable level is that of the immortal (*xian* 仙), followed that of god (*shen* 神), and finally human. Spirits and demons (*jingguai* 精怪) can cultivate to a certain level, but they remain outside the mainstream. In the story, the Chan sect sees itself as righteous, while the Jie is full of demons and spirits, and the magic they possess tends toward evil. The main protagonist, Jiang Ziya, is ordered to help the Zhou destroy the Shang. His fellow disciple, Shen Gongbao, is jealous and at every turn incites the spirits of the Jie sect to come out of the mountains to wage war against Jiang Ziya. This is a common phenomenon in China and elsewhere—the conflict between those in the mainstream and those who are not. Those on the margins do their utmost, but still find it difficult to enter the mainstream. They often rant and rave to attract attention, or challenge the norms, just for fun. This is what we saw in the 2016 election in the United States. Perhaps the plot of *The Investiture of the Gods* merely describes the normal state of society.

Many of the characters found in the novel continue to play important roles in today's folk beliefs. For example, the "Third Prince" worshipped in Taiwan is actually Nezha from *The Investiture of the Gods*. Nezha was originally a god reborn as the third son of a military commander named Li Jing, and due to his rash temperament, ultimately clashed with the East Sea Dragon King and his sons and committed a serious crime by cutting the Dragon King's tendons and bones. Li Jing decided to punish him, but Nezha killed himself in anger, returning his bones to his father and his flesh to his mother, putting an end to relations with his parents. His soul wandered off and was left without a master, but luckily, Taiyi Zhenren took pity on him and made him a new body out of lotus leaves and lotus roots, so that he no longer had a human body and was thus saved from destruction. This story is very unique in terms of Chinese ethics: Nezha sacrificed his life and denied his parents for the sake of his principles. And because of his invincible body, he became the nemesis of all demons.

A second character is Yang Jian, the great general of the Chan sect. He was the product of the union of the younger sister of the Jade Emperor and her human lover, and his status was less than pure. On the other hand, he had the blood of the gods, which made him superior to humans. He had special vision, and in folklore is portrayed as having a third eye in the middle of his forehead, which allows him to see the demons' true nature. Yang Jian's appearance is thus also very unusual. The image and behavior of Nezha and Yang Jian seem to deviate from the norm, which shows that the ideal personality of the Chinese people is not entirely in line with Confucian ethics.

The more important value of *The Investiture of the Gods* in Chinese folklore is that after the novel's publication, Chinese folk beliefs ordered the heavens based on what we find in the novel. Today, whenever people think of Emperor Dongyue, they immediately think of Huang Tianhu, the rebellious Shang-dynasty general; when they talk about success in the imperial examinations, they will think of Bi Gan's reincarnation as the Wenquxing—a constellation of stars that yields particular influence over those with literary talent. The God of Wealth must be Zhao Gongming, whose four lieutenants are in charge of accumulating money and treasure. In contrast to the divine courts constructed by other major civilizational systems, the Chinese heavenly court was largely recast after the publication of *The Investiture of the Gods*, which suggests its importance in folk beliefs.

The theme of the great war between gods and demons began in the Middle East, and in Chapter VIII, on secular religion, I mentioned the historical background of the binary worldview of Persian Zoroastrianism, in which opposing forces such as light and darkness, life and death, struggle through a period of chaos before arriving at an eternal harmony. The three great ages imagined in this scenario—the original state, the period of struggle, and the final harmony—inspired the widespread belief in revelation in the Middle East and Central Asia; with the arrival of Buddhism, the concepts of revelation and salvation entered China.

In China, these three stages of change are known as *jieshu* 劫數 (*kalpa* in Sanskrit). The existence of chaos must be resolved, and the return to order is achieved through world-renewing, apocalyptic destruction. This seems to be exactly the theological concept expressed in *The Investiture of the Gods*: The main gods in the story—Hongmeng, Yuanshi, Taishang, and so forth—all represent the original state. The Western Buddhas, such as the Cundi Bodhisattva (*Zhunti pusa* 準提菩薩), are, according to the research of the Chinese-Australian researcher Liu Cunren 柳存仁 (1917–2009), the forerunners of Guanyin, the symbol of salvation. And the Lamplighter Buddha (*Randeng gufo* 燃燈古佛) is surely the god of light from Zoroastrianism. These gods and buddhas oversee the process from a chaotic beginning, marked by desire and temptation, followed by struggle, and the final re-establishment of order.

In the fifteenth chapter of *The Investiture of the Gods*, it is proclaimed that order must be established:

> Heavenly Primogenitor, the Grand Master of Chan Taoism, lived in the Jade Emptiness Palace on Mount Kunlun. As his disciples were destined to experience the vulgar world and break the commandment on killing, he closed his palace and stopped giving lectures on the Way.
>
> The heads of Chan and Jie Taoism and Confucianism held a meeting, at which it was decided to create 365 gods. They were to be the gods of thunder, fire, plague, constellations, stars, sacred mountains, clouds and rain, virtue, and evil. The creation was destined for the downfall of the Shang and rise of the Zhou when immortals would break the commandment on killing. It was not by chance that Jiang Ziya was to enjoy power and wealth as commander and prime minister.[7]

---

7 Gu Zhizhong, trans., *Creation of the Gods* (Beijing: New World, 1992), 280.

This is the main idea of the book. In Chapter 99, "Jiang Ziya's Investiture of the Gods" echoes the preface and explains the ending: "I authorize Jiang Ziya to deify you on my behalf. You shall all be free from transmigration form birth to death. You shall be promoted according to your merits. You must obey the law. Don't commit any new sin or crime."[8]

This passage from Chapter 99 is a summary of the entire book, in which the concepts are a combination of Buddhist and Daoist vocabulary and ideas. A practitioner can start with the human body, or even with an animal body, and gradually cultivate to higher levels of existence. In the middle of this difficult process, he or she will encounter many temptations, the main ones being greed, stupidity, hatred, and anger. In Buddhist thought, in addition to birth, old age, sickness and death, suffering includes having to part from those one loves, having to meet with those one hates, being unable to obtain what one desires, and the suffering arising from the five aggregates of attachment, which is the original source of the above words: greed, stupidity, hatred and anger.

Those people were invested as gods and had to be freed from the calamity of war before they could be elevated through their suffering. Finally, a cosmic order was established, overseeing heaven and earth, with eight divisions of the righteous gods: this was the transition from chaos to harmony. Therefore, the thought reflected in *The Investiture of the Gods* is a synthesis of Buddhism and Daoism, together with the concept of the official Confucian civil system, which became the system of the heavenly court. This novel, in my opinion, is a theological expression of the mixture of the three religions. Some literary historians think that the book is only an allusion to the chaotic times of the Jiajing period of the Ming dynasty. To my mind, in addition to presenting the battle between gods and demons and reflecting the chaos of the Jiajing period, the author was also attempting to construct a new theological system for the three religions.

---

8   Ibid., 457.

The next novel to be discussed is the familiar *Journey to the West* (*Xiyouji* 西遊記). The origin of the story is the well-known tale of Venerable Xuanzang's journey to the West (i.e., Central Asia and India) to seek the scriptures, but the real story of Xuanzang's journey lacks the strange and mysterious stories we find in the novel. Contemporary books such as *Great Tang Records on the Western Regions* (*Datang Xiyouji* 大唐西域記), written by Xuanzang's disciple Bianji 辯機 (619–649), or *Biography of the Tripiṭaka Master of the Daci'en Temple* (*Daci'ensi sanzangfashi zhuan* 大慈恩寺三藏法師傳), written by Huili 慧立 (615–?) and Yancong 彥悰 (627–649), contain no stories about supernatural beings.

Later on, as legends related to Xuanzang gradually emerged in popular folklore, some fragments of a mythology appeared, but there were a limited number of such fragments and would not fill a book. During the Song dynasty, storytelling was very popular, and a number of supernatural plot lines gradually developed. These fragmentary stories were finally incorporated into the novel *Journey to the West*, as composed in the Ming.

There has been considerable debate as to who the author of *Journey to the West* was, but he is now likely identified as Wu Cheng'en 吳承恩 (1500–1582), who composed the volume a few years later than *The Investiture of the Gods*. A good number of the names and images of the gods and Buddhas that appear in *The Investiture of the Gods* are also found in *Journey to the West*, and it is clear that the latter was influenced by the former, although it is unknown whether there was any communication between Wu Cheng'en and the author(s) of the earlier book. However, what the two books have in common is that while they are not religious fables, they are nonetheless grounded in religious viewpoints to a significant degree. The difference is that while religious coloration of *The Investiture of the Gods* is mainly based on Daoism, that of *Journey to the West* is more complicated, as some see it as Daoist while others find more Buddhist teachings, and still others read it as an allegory of the integration of China's three teachings. The late Anthony C. Yu 余國藩 (1938–2015)

translated *Journey to the West* into English. He was a professor of theology, with basic training in Christian doctrine, and from that perspective discussed the elements of Buddhism and Daoism in the book, with some Christian theology thrown in. We were old friends, although our views of religion were not exactly the same. However, we agreed that the message of *Journey to the West* was complex and should be seen as reflecting a variety of religious concepts.

The Monkey King (Sun Wukung) is the main character in the story of *Journey to the West*—many readers will be familiar with this impetuous monkey, and the huge mess he made in the Heavenly Palace. The Monkey King was originally a stone monkey, the stone being left over from the formation of the universe. This meant that the Monkey King himself was of the same nature as the universe. He was part of the universe, but at the same time also a part cut out of the universe. (Incidentally, the origin of the character Jia Baoyu in the novel *The Dream of the Red Chamber* was also this stone!). The place where he learned his magic skills was in the Three Stars of the Slanting Moon Cave in the Fangcun Mountain of Lingtai, where the old master Subhuti (the great disciple of the Sakyamuni) lived. The place names Lingtai and Fancun both are words that can mean "mind," and the "three stars" and the "slanting moon" of the cave name remind one of how the character for "mind" (*xin* 心) is written. This explanation of the Monkey King's origin clearly signifies the theme of the novel. The monkey represents the mind, the same mind that you and I have. (In the famous American movie *Star Wars*, the master who teaches the two main characters is the unassuming Yoda, who also lives in a cave).

In his studies with master Subhuti, Sun Wukong had a number of choices. Among these were "strategic or technical" skills, or "popular" techniques, which were bodies of knowledge like Confucianism or Mohism that were widespread in the world, but neither of these interested the Monkey King. Other possibilities included either "dynamic" or "quietistic" techniques, both of which referred to Daoist practices, which did not interest him either. It was only when the Master finally suggested Buddhism that the Monkey felt that this was the practice for him. The puzzling thing is that the teachings conveyed by Master Subhuti are, at the same time, a statement of Daoist principles.

When the Monkey King took leave of Subhuti, the Master cautioned him, saying that he must be prepared for a great calamity every 500 years. The calamity could include the heavenly wind (*tianfeng* 天風), hellish wind (*yinfeng* 陰風), and the violent wind (*bifeng* 贔風), any of which could destroy the practitioner. The three winds are all different: the heavenly wind arises from outside the body; the hellish wind comes from inside the body, rising from the bottom to the top, and is caused by desire. The most violent wind, *bifeng*, also comes from within the body, but proceeds from top to bottom, and its source is in the mind. If you cannot restrain yourself, you will not be able to control the calamities. The notion of the three *kalpas* is found in both Buddhism and Daoism, but the two winds that damage the body from within represent concepts closer to Daoism.

Later on, when the Monkey King met Guanyin, Guanyin reminded him to pay special attention to the Buddhist concept of the "six thieves" when practicing self-cultivation: "One calls to the eyes to see pleasure, one calls to the ears to hear anger, one calls to the nose to smell love, one calls to the tongue to taste thought, one calls to the mind to desire, one calls to the body to worry." These six items are the six "forms" of the *Heart Sutra* that are perceived by the sense organs. Chan Buddhism specifically indicates that the items to be prevented include having to meet with those whom one hates, having to part from those whom one loves, and being unable to obtain what one desires, which in turn cause happiness, anger, sorrow, and joy. Only by overcoming these emotional temptations and obstacles can one achieve enlightenment and freedom.

In Chapter 19 of *Journey to the West*, after the Monkey King recruited Zhu Bajie (Pigsy, the half-human, half-pig figure that is part of Xuanzang's entourage) at the beginning of his journey, Guanyin told him to recite the entire text of the *Heart Sutra* often. This expresses even more clearly that the point of the journey is to understand that "body is emptiness" and "the mind has no obstructions." The *Heart Sutra* appears frequently throughout the novel, and it is obvious that the theme of the book is basically Buddhist.

Throughout the entire *Journey to the West*, what the monk and his disciples encountered is nothing other than the emotions of arrogance, appetite, lust, anger, resentment. Many of the demons that appear in the book are the embodiment of these emotional disturbances. For example, one great calamity they encountered was the "Flaming Mountain," where "fire" represents anger and violence. Xuanzang was repeatedly tempted by women, represented by the spiders in the Rock Cave (actually women in the form of spider demons who trapped the monk in their web) and the rat in the Trapped Hollow Mountain (another demonic form who also tempted Xuanzang).

The Monkey King and Pigsy are always in conflict and cooperation. Pigsy represents the two desires of food and sex, while the golden headband that the Monkey King wears on his forehead after being brought under control by Guanyin constantly reminded him not to let his "mind" go. In the conflict between the Monkey King and Pigsy, as we saw in our discussion of the five elements in Chapter II, metal overcomes wood, or here, "mind" conquers "desire." All of these "codes" convey the basic principles of the Chan belief of letting go of the "mind." Thus, the religious beliefs explored in *Journey to the West* are mainly Buddhist, with Daoism playing a secondary role.

Sun Wukong learned all kinds of martial arts and was capable of 72 transformations. When he left his master and descended the mountain, he did not know where to go, but he found the Mountain of Flowers and Fruits and became the King of the Monkeys. He and his monkeys seemed to be human but were not, but they wanted equal treatment. In his quest for a weapon, the Monkey King created a great disturbance in the Dragon King's palace in the East China Sea and obtained the Needle that Calms the Seas, a vestige of the Great Yu's having put an end to the great flood. In the same way that he himself was coterminous with the universe by virtue of having been born out of the cosmic stone, this weapon had the same meaning of cosmic oneness. Armed with this weapon, he challenged the Jade Emperor in Heaven saying that he was "The Great Sage who is the equal of Heaven." He proved to be invincible in his attack on the heavenly palace, and this episode shows that the heavenly system of governance was ridiculous and that the gods and generals were incompetent. In the end, it was Erlang Shen (Yang Jian, discussed above in the context of *The Investiture of the Gods*) and his snarling dog who defeated him.

The irony is clear: such a solemn heavenly court was actually not up to the task of confronting a stone monkey. Ming dynasty governance, compared to other major dynasties, was not very good, especially in terms of the character and ability of the emperors and their close retainers. The story the Monkey King's rout of the Great Heavenly Palace is about stripping bare the myth of the seemingly solemn dignity of the imperial court. The gods who are meant to protect the court from the monkey, including Laozi and the Buddha, are also deceiving the emperor with their supposed powers. This satire is a direct accusation of the bureaucrats and Buddhist and Daoist charlatans who were accomplices of imperial power. The critical nature of the rout of the heavenly palace cannot be overlooked.

Before traveling to the West to seek the scriptures, the Monkey King was detained under a mountain, and Guanyin gave him the mission of awaiting Tang Sanzang (as the monk Xuanzang is called in the novel), who would seek the scriptures, and gave the monk the secret of controlling the monkey: the "true words of concentration," manifested physically in the golden headband the Monkey King wore on his forehead. These episodes are about how to control one's "mind" and not to be capricious, arbitrary, or self-indulgent. There is irony in the fact that a compassionate Goddess of Mercy would allow the monkey to fall into such a trap. Of course, we can also explain it by saying that it was out of compassion that he was taught to restrain his mind and not let it run amuck. The name Master Subhuti gave to the Monkey King—*Wukong* 悟空 ("awakening to emptiness")—clearly reflects the *Heart Sutra*'s central message that "form is emptiness." This makes it clear that the search for enlightenment and emptiness is found in both Buddhism and Daoism.

On the surface, the various calamities encountered on the journey to the West appear to be merely the evil spirits that Xuanzang had imagined while crossing the desert on his way to seek the scriptures. Their real meaning, however, is that in the journey of the liberation of the mind, one must face all kinds of temptations. Among the characters accompanying the monk, the Monkey King represents the "mind" and the White Dragon Horse (among other things, the horse that Xuanzang rides) the "intention." Monkey-mind and horse-intention point the direction in which the mind and intention should go, suggesting that they must work together. Xuanzang is a symbol of wisdom, or a symbol of pious pursuit of the Way; he cannot let go of his "intention," and must control it through "mind."

Pigsy, whose dharma name was *Wuneng* 悟能 ("awakening to capacity"), was originally a general of the Heavenly Court who had fallen into the body of a pig because of the temptation of lust. He was capable of at least 36 transformations and was very strong. On their journey to the West, he did not manifest his powers in a positive way, but rather caused trouble. As mentioned, those troubles were the result of either lust or appetite, or else the desire to be strong and victorious. Pigsy often made malicious remarks that confused Xuanzang and frustrated the Monkey King; he is a typical petty character. However, he had his own special "capacity," which had to be controlled by his mind, so that he could follow the direction of wisdom and accomplish his mission of seeking the Way.

Another character in the novel, Sandy, whose dharma name was *Wujing* 悟淨 ("awakening to purity"), was originally the Curtain-Lifting General in the Heavenly Court, but he committed a small error and was banished to earth to live in the Quicksand River, waiting for Xuanzang, whom he was to accompany on his journey. Among the five members of the group, Sandy was the least distinctive of all, yet he followed along, carrying all the burdens on his shoulders. The word *jing* in his name represents purity, the symbol of water. Only with purity can the mind be free from oscillation and can wisdom move forward without hindrance.

Toward the end of the second half of the journey, after having already gone through many difficulties, the five travelers encountered their most serious obstacle: their way was first blocked by the Bull Demon King and his wife, Princess Iron Fan, on Flaming Mountain, and by three other demons on Lion Camel Range, and then again by Red Boy, the Bull Demon King's son. These tests were extremely severe, requiring the intervention of important Buddhist figures such as the Future Buddha (Maitreya Buddha) and Guanyin. The great fire on Flaming Mountain could only be extinguished by the banana leaf fan possessed by Princess Iron Fan. According to Indian concepts, the relationship between wind and fire is double, because wind can both extinguish and fan the flames, thus they can be opposite or complementary. One of the Monkey King's nicknames was "Golden Monkey," and according to the logic of the Five Elements in China, fire can overcome gold (or metal), and the experience on Flaming Mountain was a nearly impossible dilemma for the monkey. The fire was not extinguished until Guanyin's Dragon Girl poured water on it.

The three demons under the Lion Camel Ridge were the Azure Lion (the steed of Manjushri), the Yellow-Toothed Elephant (that the bodhisattva Samantabhadra rides on), and the most powerful, the Golden Winged Great Peng (a huge bird located behind Shakyamuni Buddha). Manjushri and Samantabhadra are the left and right bodhisattvas of Shakyamuni Buddha: Manjushri represents wisdom, and the sword in his hand, together with the roar of the Azure Lion, stand as stern warnings that can bring the world's desires to an end. Samantabhadra represents discipline, and the Yellow-Toothed Elephant's six tusks symbolize the six rules and restrictions that must be observed.

Wisdom and discipline are both necessary qualities for a practitioner, but both can be pushed too far. Excessive wisdom leads to wild speech and behavior, and excessive discipline leads to pedantry. The steeds of these two bodhisattvas are symbolic of going too far, which can be detrimental to one's practice. The origin of the Golden Winged Great Peng is quite extraordinary. He is the great protector of the Future Buddha, who has seen and done everything. Therefore, the speed of his flight greatly exceeds the somersault cloud on which the Monkey King rides (one of his 72 transformations). However, going too fast and being too eager are also taboos for practitioners, and the symbolic meaning of these three monsters, in my opinion, is to remind the Monkey King that exceeding the mark is just as bad as not reaching it—that even the best behavior, if practiced to the extreme, will also end in calamity. Why do these three demons appear on their path to the west? We can understand it as a reminder to all practitioners that they must not go overboard in anything and must be disciplined and vigilant.

The Red Boy also has an extraordinary history, being the child of wind and fire. As mentioned above, the Indian four elements—wind and fire, which are in "motion," and earth and water, which are in "stillness"— complement each other. The Red Boy has the form of a baby, dressed all in red, like Nezha from *The Investiture of the Gods*. Sun Wukong is not very big, the size of a little boy, but he has the face of a monkey, which is a perfect contrast to the fine features of Red Boy. The Red Boy is characterized by his aggressiveness, which matches the unconstrained side of Monkey King. When Guanyin intervened to subdue Red Boy, she similarly used a golden headband, a combination of five circles winding around his head, arms, and legs, only after which Red Boy sits down like a good boy at the foot of the throne, often together with the Dragon Girl. The headbands worn by the Red Boy and the Monkey King kept them under control through a "tranquility spell." It is because of these contrasts that I feel that the two characters are two sides of the same coin, and both represent the Buddhist idea of "constraining the mind."

After these calamities, there is a chapter in *Journey to the West* about being robbed at the estate of Kou Yuanwai. This incident sticks out somewhat in the context of the novels; the thieves have no particular abilities, and simply come in and rob. Nonetheless, the chapter on Kou Yuanwai is quite lengthy. It could well be that these six thieves represent the six "forms" as discussed in the *Heart Sutra*. After Sun Wukong's encounter with Master Crow's Nest, Guanyin taught the Monkey King the passage from the *Heart Sutra* that says, "There are no eyes, no ears, no nose, no tongue, no body, no mind. There is no seeing, no hearing, no smelling, no tasting, no touching, no imagining." These are the *Heart Sutra*'s "six thieves," which may not sound like a big deal, but can have important consequences.

In Chapter 85 of *Journey to the West*, there is a dialogue between Xuanzang and the Monkey King, in which the Monkey King states: "Do not go far to seek the Buddha on Vulture Peak; Vulture Peak is in your heart. Everybody has a Vulture Peak stupa under which to cultivate conduct." He further reminded his master of the truth of cultivating the mind:

> When the heart is purified it can shine alone
> When the heart is preserved all perceptions are pure.
> If there is any mistake then laziness follows,
> And success will not come in a myriad years.
> As long as your will is sincere Thunder Peak is before your eyes.[9]

Sure enough, when they arrived at Vulture Mountain, they encountered another calamity of imprisonment. Vulture Mountain was 800 *li* further on, and if Xuanzang wanted to reach enlightenment, then all demons and devils had to be eliminated. Here, what they needed to pay attention to was the Chan practice of "breaking through the three barriers." The first barrier is penetrating the fundamental investigation, which means awakening to the need for cultivation. The second barrier is breaking the heavy barrier, and seeing one's nature; the third barrier is

---

9 W. F. K. Jenner, trans., *Journey to the West* (Beijing, 1955; Silk Pagoda, 2005), 1186–1187. https://chine.in/fichiers/jourwest.pdf.

breaking the barrier of imprisonment, which means achieving enlightenment. Only by breaking through these obstacles can one become a Buddha. That Xuanzang wound up imprisoned at the point of becoming a Buddha only underscores the difficulty of the undertaking.

Nearing the end of their journey, at the Cloud-Touching Crossing of the River to Heaven, the group of five experienced yet another important relevation:

> Gently and strongly the Buddha pushed off, at which a corpse came floating downstream, to the horror of the venerable elder.
> "Don't be frightened, Master," said Monkey. "That's you."
> "It's you, it's you," said Pigsy. Friar Sandy clapped his hands as he said, "It's you, it's you!"
> The boatman gave a call, then also put in, too, "It's you! Congratulations! Congratulations!" The three of them all joined in these congratulations as the ferryman punted the boat quickly and steadily over the immortal Cloud–Touching Crossing. Sanzang turned around and sprang lightly ashore on the opposite bank. There is a poem about this that goes:
> When the womb–born flesh and body of blood is cast aside,
> The primal spirit finds kinship and love.
> On this morning of actions completed and Buddhahood attained
> The thirty–six kinds of dust from the past are washed away.
> This was indeed what is meant by great wisdom, the boundless dharma of crossing to the other bank.[10]

After passing through the gate of death, they were freed from everything and finally reached the realm of Vulture Mountain. In view of the monk's sincerity in seeking the sutra from afar and his ability to pass the many tests, Shakyamuni Buddha allowed them to bring the true sutras back to the Eastern Land. Ananda, who was in charge of the scriptures, asked them if they sought the scriptures without words. Xuanzang replied, "I have

---

10   Ibid., 1368–1369.

travelled a long way to seek the scriptures in the hope of bringing back to the Eastern Land the scriptures *with* words. What is the use of bringing back the scriptures *without* words?" Ananda gave them the scriptures, but in the middle of the journey, they found that the scriptures were blank.

The difference between "with words" and "without words" in this passage is a very important analogy in Chan Buddhism: those without words are the scriptures that one has understood oneself; those with words are the scriptures that have been passed down by others. The true meaning must come to you through your own experience. At the same time, the *Diamond Sutra* also says, "If one sees me in form, If one seeks me in sound....He cannot see the Future Buddha." Form, sound, and words are all mediums of expression, and not meaning itself. Hence the famous verse of Huineng, the Sixth Patriarch of the Chan school, which says: "Fundamentally there is not a single thing. Where could dust arise?" Laozi's *Daodejing* also says, "A Dao that may be spoken is not the enduring Dao. A name that may be named is not an enduring name."

In the preceding paragraphs, I have repeatedly raised the question of whether the religious concepts expressed in *Journey to the West* were more Buddhist or Daoist. My conclusion is that in the era when Wu Cheng'en lived, there were two schools of Daoism in China, namely the talismanic school and the alchemical school. The talismanic Celestial Masters catered to the preferences of the royal family and the high and mighty and advocated the use of divine power to achieve immortality and to avoid calamities. The Quanzhen alchemical school, in contrast, was based on inner alchemy—in other words, the use of specific methods of internal cultivation designed to elevate one's character. In addition, many Buddhist schools of the Tang and Song dynasties had already become quite scholastic, with only Chan, Vinaya, and Pure Land remaining as popular schools of mass practice. The doctrines of Chan and the beliefs of the Quanzhen school of inner alchemy actually echo each other.

Some of the Daoist concepts discussed in *Journey to the West*, especially the terms used, such as beautiful maiden (mercury), infant, primordial spirit, etc., are all terms of the inner alchemy school. Beautiful maiden and infant are not real things outside of the body; "infant" refers to the pure yang of the human body, and "beautiful maiden" refers to the true yin. The duality of yin and yang must cooperate with each other to develop the "primordial spirit," that is, the true self. As for the theory of the five elements, in the *Journey to the West*, it appears as the golden male and the wooden female, and, as explained above, this relates to the mind over-coming desire. Several people have attempted to identify the five members of Xuanzang's entourage with the Five Elements, but it never made much sense. Judging from the totality of *Journey to the West*, Wukong's master Subhuti should be a Buddhist figure, but the poems taught convey Daoist meanings; after learning from Master Crow's Nest and Guanyin, the Monkey King finally learned the lessons of the *Heart Sutra*.

In *Journey to the West*, the Jade Emperor's heavenly court is not stately and dignified, but instead merely a posturing bunch of bureaucrats. The Supreme Lord Laojun heads a Daoist system outside of that of the Jade Emperor, while the Future Buddha and Guanyin represent a third system, Buddhism. As mentioned above, the Jade Emperor's heavenly court in *The Investiture of the Gods* was Daoist, and gave over the administration of everything in the universe to Daoist gods. When comparing the two divine orders of Buddhism and Daoism, it is obvious that *Journey to the West* respects the Buddhist order more than the Daoist one.

To sum up, I agree with Anthony Yu: *Journey to the West* is a journey of the mind. Slightly revising his conclusion, I would argue that *Journey to the West* is an allegory of Chan Buddhism, but also includes some ideas of the Daoist inner alchemy school that were popular at the time. Such coor-dination was possible not only because Chan Buddhism and Quanzhen Daoism shared many ideas, but also because the evolution of Quanzhen was much influenced by Chan. Moreover, the Confucian thinker Wang Yangming's study of the mind is deeply steeped in Chan. Wang Yangming is not mentioned in *Journey to the West*, but the convergence of

Confucianism, Daoism, and Buddhism is an important feature of modern Chinese thought.

Looking back at this chapter, we have explored four popular novels as a reflection of the spiritual world of the Chinese people. In terms of the historical period they represent, we noted both continuity and change. Shi Nai'an's *Water Margin*, written during the Yuan-Ming transition, reflected the cultural catastrophe of the collapse of Confucian rites and music after the Mongol conquest of China. This was followed by the tyranny of Ming rule, when the contemporary world was ruled by violence. Shi Nai'an wanted to create an ideal world, so that those who were oppressed could rise up and install a new order. However, contrary to expectations, the world of Mount Liang was not so beautiful, and, like the real world, was full of cheating, scheming, and violence. Consequently, the effort to create this ideal world could only end in the destruction of the dream of Mount Liang: Lu Zhishen escaped to another world through death, Li Jun fled to Siam, and Yan Qingyun wandered off to no one knows where.

The Romance of the Three Kingdoms is set in the period at the end of the Han marked by an era of upheaval and national division, which the author depicted in two extreme forms: orthodox characters and usurpers. We see the orthodox side especially in Guan Yu's heroism and Zhuge Liang's wisdom; their counterparts are Dong Zhuo and Cao Cao, who are depicted as treacherous rather than righteous, and deceitful rather than wise. Because of their depiction in the novel, Guan Yu and Zhuge Liang became immortal gods. The spirit that runs through the entire novel stresses the idea of "righteousness," a virtue practiced within interpersonal relationships chosen by the individuals, and not as a part of existing social status and ethics. Yet reading *The Romance of the Three Kingdoms* inevitably raises certain questions: Why is the friendship between Liu, Guan, and Zhang so lacking in tacit understanding? For example, why could Liu and Zhang not coordinate properly with Guan Yu in his efforts to retake the central plains? Why was Zhuge Liang, who saw the big picture so clearly, unable to build a functioning team—to the point that he wound up taking care of everything, working himself to death in the process?

The third novel, *The Investiture of the Gods*, portrays the two worlds of gods and demons. These two forces, however, originate from the same source. The rivalry between gods and demons is resolved through death, and the various grudges in the period of rivalry have resolved into a particular cosmic order. The bureaucracy of the divine realm may symbolize the notion that everything in the universe should exist as a whole; therefore, the gods and the demons finally bury the hatchet and enter a network of mutual dependence.

The fourth book, *Journey to the West*, following on concepts we find in *The Investiture of the Gods*, turned the order of the universe inward, presenting it as a world of the "mind." As the main component of the human spirit, the "mind" must go through various obstacles, constantly renew itself by overcoming difficulties, and finally rise to a greater level, where it transcends the agitation of the senses, and through enlightenment come to grasp that there is no difference between "form" and "emptiness." As expressed in the *Heart Sutra*:

> All things are by nature void.
> They are not born or destroyed.
> Nor are they stained or pure.
> Nor do they wax or wane.
> [...]
> So know that the Bodhisattva
> Holding to nothing whatever,
> But dwelling in Prajna wisdom,
> Is freed of delusive hindrance,
> Rid of the fear bred by it,
> And reaches clearest Nirvana.[11]

---

11 Translation taken from "The Heart Sutra as recited in the Triratna Buddhist Community," https://thebuddhistcentre.com/system/files/groups/files/heart_sutra.pdf, 1.

The 81 difficulties encountered on the westward journey are all the karma of the individual mind, and having overcome these 81 difficulties, the individual rids himself of the difficulties of his own making. This "journey of the mind" probably also represents the gradual integration of the three schools of Confucianism, Daoism and Buddhism in China, the process of arriving at a cultural and spiritual consensus.

If we string these four novels together in a series, we can then see them as a four-part movement of a tragedy and comedy commenting on the ideal state of humanity. *Water Margin* sought to translate a "righteous revolt" into an ideal world, but the failure of the experiment left people embarrassed. *The Romance of the Three Kingdoms* modeled several typical characters out of "righteousness;" they failed to accomplish their missions, yet the ideal of their personalities continued to shine through the ages. *The Investiture of the Gods* is a dialectical process of confrontation, transcendence, and liberation against all kinds of oppositions and struggles such as good and evil, success and failure, after which a harmonious coexistence finally emerges. And finally, *Journey to the West* depicts many of the hardships of the human world as an individual's interior struggles to understand and overcome desire, perfecting oneself, and finally reaching an enlightenment in which liberation results from seeing that everything is emptiness. Therefore, the series of novels shows us a life path, being both sad and happy, jointly composing a lasting human comedy.

These authors are not great Confucian scholars or eminent monks, nor were they well-known figures in their societies. Yet because of their rich content, lively plots, and vivid character descriptions, countless readers have been attracted to their novels for hundreds of years. Some of the ideas they conveyed unconsciously found their way into readers' hearts. Therefore, whenever people gather to talk in villages and towns, they will bring up their heroes: Jiang Ziya, Zhuge Liang, Guan Yu, Wu Song, Third Prince, Monkey King. The gods appearing in *The Investiture of the Gods*—the Jade Emperor, Dongyue, Guanyin—became the gods that rule our lives. In polite and even less polite society, "righteousness and loyalty" remain important personal values, and "conscience" is the foundation of life and conduct. These works may not come from the people, but they have been integrated into the mentality of common people and constitute an important part of Chinese folk culture.

Conclusion

A New Life for Chinese Culture

For the past 20 years, the United States economy has experienced violent ups and downs. Several major disasters have been caused by the corporate and financial worlds' disregard for credibility and the overall interests of the marketplace, and their preoccupation with their own self-interest, to the point of falsifying records to hide their errors. Modern capitalism is based on the idea of "trustworthiness." In the absence of this, all securities, deeds, and loans become mere instruments of deception.

According to Max Weber's theory, the relationship between modern capitalism and Protestant ethics is that the success of the individual is a reflection of God's grace. Modern economic development has produced many successful entrepreneurs who have returned some of their wealth to society. Unfortunately, modern capitalism has been in existence for a long time, and the original Protestant spirit has faded. The way things look now, its return seems unlikely.

Western civilization is the foundation of modern civilization, and the economic prosperity and material abundance of the modern world is driven by capitalist self-interest. Sadly, if the hunger for gain gets out of hand, people's greed becomes excessive, so that the rich get richer while the poor get poorer. In the United States today, the concentration of wealth has reached the point that the richest one percent of the population owns half of the nation's wealth, while the poorest 30 percent live below the poverty line. Such an inequitable distribution of wealth will sooner or later lead to chaos. Thus problems are bound to arise in the economic dimension of modern civilization. Problems with American democracy were particularly obvious in the 2016 election: the rich control the media with their money, and the media in turn influence and even manipulate public opinion, so that votes are determined by money, and wealth controls politics, turning the "United States of America" into the "Disunited States of America."

Industrial production is another pillar of modern civilization. This system relies on the capitalist marketplace to concentrate capital for the distribution of products, as well as on rapid advances in science and technology, especially in the last half century, when digital and Internet technologies have had a huge and far-reaching impact on the efficiency of production and the spread of information. However, the system of mass production works its miracles at the expense of nature, which is being drained dry. As we strive for comfort in our daily lives, the balance of the universe is disturbed as we forcibly modify our ecology and ignore the laws of nature. Moreover, the technologies that have underwritten economic growth in the past few decades are gradually developing artificial intelligence and robots, which means that the production work and perhaps even intellectual work will be taken away from the workers and entrusted to machines. We can already see this trend: the workers of the future will require skills beyond those supplied by primary and secondary education, and today's manual laborers will have no place in the coming economy. Many working-class people have been at the bottom of the social ladder for 200 years. What will happen to them when high tech jobs take over?

Digitalization and Internet technology have shortened the distance between people, making us all neighbors in cyberspace. However, at the same time, we are becoming more and more lonely and isolated, with no one to turn to. Alienation is already obvious in urban life, despite the virtual intimacy promised by the Internet. Nowadays, in both urban and rural areas, the ties between individuals in local communities are weak, to the point that communities barely exist. The mobility of work and the ease of transportation mean that work opportunities are increasingly dispersed, making it difficult for individuals to experience a sense of belonging. Individual independence has affected the institution of the family and even the institution of marriage. Scattered people with no sense of belonging cannot care for one another, which means that the goal of their work and effort has returned to the most primitive, immediate desires for food and comfort. From these perspectives, modern technology has enriched our lives materially, so that individual life is better and more comfortable than it was in the past. The price one pays for this kind of life is, as stated above, a loss of a sense of direction and belonging.

Modern civilization is changing rapidly; we can throw away the past, and we certainly don't have to worry about tradition. Since everyone's life is only concerned with today, and family life has lost its centrality, one does not have to be worried about what comes after or about children and grandchildren. Life is all about today, with no thought to the past or the future. The "line" of time has finally been reduced to the "point" of the present moment.

Personal alienation has broken the bonds between people; focusing on the present has broken the continuity of time. People used to be social animals, but now we are simply lonely individuals. Faced with the complexity of society and the extreme power of the state, these lonely individuals are mere ants. We have opened up outer space, but cannot preserve our own earthly resources. We have an abundance of goods to consume, but we cannot control our desires.

The word "progress" teaches us to think only about moving forward and not about preserving, and we do not give a thought to the resources available. If this trend continues, modern civilization, which was once the blessing of humankind, will become its curse. Signs of the curse are already visible: the threat of nuclear war between great powers, and Islamic terrorism, which is the hopeless rebellion of the weak against the strong— both wind up at the same end. After more than 300 years of development, today we cannot help but wonder: what is the future of this civilization?

I noted in the Introduction to this book that the place of the individual in modern civilization, which is built on ideals of Protestantism, could have been united with all of humanity through God's grace to the whole of humankind, equally blessed by God. Yet the scientific part of modern civilization has gradually reduced the position of God, his place having been taken over by mathematics. Individuals are no longer connected through God's grace, but rather wander through life with no connection to each other. If "profit" is all that matters, then people fight over it, and have difficulty arriving at a harmonious coexistence. With the great disparities between rich and poor and the lack of justice in today's world, how are we different from animals?

In the past three to four centuries, Europe underwent a long period of change, and under the aegis of the Christian faith, capitalism, and modern science developed so that Western civilization became the most powerful cultural force in the world, and indeed swept the world. Christian civilization overwhelmed the Islamic world and defeated the Eastern civilizations of China and India. The pillars of modern civilization are capitalism and democracy, coupled with the pursuit of the only truth in the universe (the modern scientific quest). In the age of Western domination, modern civilization has unconditionally embraced the West. For better or for worse, Western civilization has provided everything we associate with modern life, unfortunately also including the spirit of dogmatism and individualism. As mentioned above, the predicament of modern civilization is also due to this cultural orientation.

It was only 15 or 20 years ago that the American political scientist, Francis Fukuyama, wrote an essay declaring that the civilization of the world had reached a point of near perfection. In particular, in terms of democracy and individual freedom, only minor revisions were needed for history to reach its final destination. While these words were still ringing in our ears, the turmoil and changes that took place in the world over the past decade or so, from September 11 to the present day, seemed instead to confirm the warnings of Samuel T. Huntington, Fukuyama's teacher, that a great conflict between civilizations was imminent. As we know today, history did not end, but has continued to evolve. Recently, Fukuyama modified his theory, arguing that the recent rise of China can be attributed to China's strong government. I thought yet again that he had missed the point. In the past two or three decades, the term "universal values" has become a common slogan referring to the Anglo-American concept of human rights and democracy. Indeed, as we have said before, modern democracy and individualism have their merits, but they are not perfect. Not long after the founding of the United States, Alexis de Tocqueville pointed out that American ideals and institutions, might, over time, become so degenerate as to be utterly divorced from their origin, like the changes that occurred in the Greek city-states. Now it seems that his prophecy is coming true.

The universe is always in flux, as is the human world; there are no eternal truths, no universal principles. All truths and principles are contingent on "proper" conditions. Moreover, all things are subject to the principle that going too far is as bad as coming up short. Coming up short means that you did not get the job done; going too far means that you exceeded proper limits, either in quantitative terms, or by assuming that a good job will remain forever good, so you refuse to change, which leads to rigidity.

Because of different natural environments and contacts with other groups, human societies have faced many different conditions, and consequently acquired different "cultural genes" that developed into unique civilizations. Human experience is multifaceted and diverse, and human beings need not struggle to follow a single path. In today's globalized world, many other civilizations that have been overcome by Western civilization still have something valuable to offer and deserve to be revisited as intellectual resources that might be useful in responding to the predicament of modern civilization. In today's world, Islamic civilization suffers from the same flaw as Christian civilization: dogmatism. Indian civilization has declined and is too class-riven internally to truly achieve the equality of all beings that the Buddha insisted upon many centuries ago.

Among the world's complex civilizational systems, Chinese civilization had its own unique development process, which produced its own particularities. One should of course be humble about one's own achievements, but to my mind there are few choices available to the world outside of China's system of civilization. Many Chinese historical experiences have, of course, been pushed aside by the influx of Western influence. However, it appears from the topics discussed in this book that while China's cultural elite embraced the West, some elements of traditional culture remained at the level of folk culture. This book has returned to these cultural elements found in folklore, in the hope that the legacy of Chinese culture can be reinterpreted and used as a reference for the reconstruction of world culture today.

The order of the Chinese universe is multifaceted and interactive, with the "five elements" complementing and replacing one another, and a process engaged in by the dual elements of yin and yang. In the *Yijing*, changes are constantly taking place, with every change triggering yet more changes as the universe remains in eternal balance. All these features are not so much a matter of looking to God's divine dominion, but instead one of relying on one's own efforts in the pursuit of eternal balance within a larger system. Equilibrium is a goal to be pursued, but it is not permanent, so any state is merely a moment in the process. This kind of world imagined here is very different from the European and American conceptions of a perfect universe.

These two traditional Chinese views of change and equilibrium permeate the lives of Chinese people, whether in the food they eat, the medicine they take, or the *fengshui* which tells them how to set up their homes and offices, or even broader principles concerning how to live in the world, all of which reflects the cosmology and epistemology mentioned above.

In terms of the concept of time, Western civilization focuses on the present, while the Chinese emphasize the continuity of the past, the present and the future, without beginning and without end. The Chinese view of life does not separate life and death; life and death are seen as continuous, and it is only by linking the generations together that we can be respectful of our origins, and incorporate the life of the individual into the life of the group, thus transcending the life of the individual. In this sense, the death of an individual is merely a step in the transformation of life. The overarching Chinese concept of life imagines two lines: one hopes for the continuation of life into the future, and the other remembers the past; the two are parallel streams. Thus, for the Chinese, the realm after death and after life is a continuation of the realm of life before death, and interpersonal relationships that existed before death will continue after death. These two parallel lines—life and death—combine the future, the present and the past in an eternal engagement. Such ideas are also very different from the traditional concepts in European and American culture, where these three stages of past, present, and future are cut off from each other.

Because the Chinese emphasize the interconnectedness of nature and people, they have a special sense of intimacy with nature. In a lifestyle based on farming, spring plowing, summer planting, autumn harvesting, and winter storage are all closely related to the changing seasons. Spatially, a farming community is different from a herder's tribe; a farm community continues from generation to generation, and the people all live, age, get sick, and die in the same village or town. Agricultural people are attached to the land and reluctant to move, and the surrounding environment, the mountains, rivers, forests and fields, are all one with the life of the people. In the life of Chinese people, natural space-time is not an exterior object but a whole that is integrated into themselves and their lives. This characteristic is fundamentally different from the division of nature and human beings into opposing "subjects" and "objects" in Europe and America.

The mountains, rivers, land, and creatures of the natural world are all sentient beings in the Chinese view of the world. Mountain gods, water gods, tree spirits, and demons are all reflections of our human life. This is part of Chinese nature worship: the gods and spirits are all connected with human beings, and the power of the supernatural realm is interwoven into the lives of human beings. Therefore, the gods of the mountains and water, transformed by the power of nature, can penetrate into the human world. Humankind is grateful to all beings. The spirits that become demons can also transform into human beings and enter human life. The intermingling and fusion between people and nature are in fact a projection of their philosophy and wisdom, a reification of nature. Humans are, after all, the subject of everything. The aesthetics of the Chinese, whether in literature or in art, are also an emotional experience. Feelings about nature and the expressions of those feelings are intimate and interactive. Nature and human beings are not polar opposites, but joined and inseparable. In Chinese landscape painting, people walk into nature, rather than standing outside and looking at the objects in the frame. In poems and lyrics in languages throughout the world, anthropomorphic descriptions are everywhere. However, in Chinese literature, especially in poetry, there is hardly a natural object that does not appear as a human emotion or appearance.

According to Confucianism, the ethical relationship of the self to a group is to put oneself in another's place, to practice empathy, although this diminishes with the distance of the relationship. This structure is like a concentric circle: after cultivating oneself, the goal is to pacify the people and then the world. Empathy and a feeling of oneness with all things can be extended to the world beyond the human being. On our ancestral timeline, one's own self is only one point of connection in a long-range continuum, which extends to future generations. Yet without your existence, the space-time continuum in the universe would not exist. It is inevitable that people imagine that the future will be better. If we use the language of "modest prosperity" and "great harmony" from the "Liyun Datong" chapter of the *Book of Rites*, while great harmony is more difficult to attain, the Confucian assumption was that it existed in the past, and the Confucian goal was its revival. I have already talked about how, in the society of the Wuxi of my youth, people worked together to provide welfare services to the community and to take care of the poor, the old and the weak—in other words, to realize the continuity of the community and the self by "putting oneself in the place of others." Today, folk beliefs in Taiwan encourage the faithful to help one another, based on exactly the same principle.

⁓

The dream of a better world is a dream shared by people the world over. The Euro-American idea already existed before humankind left the Garden of Eden, and shines forth as well after the final judgment, when God promises a return to infinite beauty. In the Middle Eastern Zoroastrian and Manichaean versions, there is a struggle between good and evil, and in the end, good overcomes evil, becoming eternal light. In the Indian Buddhist tradition, a "Pure Land" can be a distant paradise somewhere far to the west, or more likely, a blissful world Maitreya will establish after his return. Modern evolutionary theories of society, such as Marxism, envision a future in which there are no classes and no rich or poor. The ideal of a perfect world is the goal for which we strive.

The Chinese dream of a great harmony is not very different from that of the rest of the world, except that the path to this dream is not one of continuous struggle, but of continuous self-perfection. In folk religions, this longing for another world is expressed in the concept of the "three *kalpas:*" the past, the present and the future. In the future world of Manichaeism, we see the total victory of light; in Buddhism, the future Pure Land is the realm freed of all care and worry. In Chinese folk religions, however, the future world has been gradually transformed into a type of self-cultivation, a way to move from anxiety to peace in one's mind. To my mind, this self-cultivation is an extension of the very similar Confucian ideas to religious sentiments.

In order to uphold this ideal, Chinese folklore and legends have deified figures who have contributed to the well-being of humankind. These characters tried their best to do good for humankind, worked hard and suffered, experienced injustice and slander, and even sacrificed their own lives. In a general sense, they were failures, but in the eyes of the Chinese people, these failures are cherished. In reality, there are many injustices in the world, and many things in life that are not as we would wish, but in legends, the Chinese have long recorded these disappointments, and in remembering them, there is also a tacit denunciation of injustice. In popular sacrificial rituals, there are festivals and temple fairs in which all local people participate, reminding them year after year of the people they should remember and the mistakes they have made in the past. The same regrets are expressed in opera, in popular songs, and in other media, and the audience sighs and weeps, yet another expression of their judgment of the past and a reminder to remain vigilant.

The system of Chinese thought is grounded in Confucianism, which in turn is based on humanity. Confucianism sacrifices unite the gods and humans from a human perspective. Although Confucianism claims that it does not talk about strange forces and malevolent spirits, Confucianism's respect for nature and the recognition of merit to those who deserve it also display a very sincere religious sentiment.

Outside of Confucianism, the two most important sources of Chinese thought are Buddhism and Daoism. Buddhism came from India, but it was transformed in Central Asia, incorporating many of the ideas of Zoroastrianism and Manichaeism, which were nurtured in ancient Persia. The evolution of Daoism was stimulated by the arrival of Buddhism, which inspired Chinese "masters of techniques" (*fangshi* 方士) to combine the theories of *yin* and *yang* and the five elements into something that became an institutional religion. In the Middle Ages, the revealed faiths of the Middle East, which also originated in ancient Persia, entered China, bringing their beliefs of apocalypse and ultimate liberation.

The Chinese people's beliefs are the result of a continuous integration of various factors: the three religions merged to form a number of popular religions, which gradually incorporated the humanism of Confucianism; in modern times, almost all of these religions have become increasingly secular and engaged with the world. In Taiwan today, not only are religions more engaged with the world, but for some people, this engagement has become a process of "self-cultivation," a quest for self-improvement and self-restraint leading to a state of peace and tranquility. This is how the sacred returns to life and how the profane is elevated to become sacred. To sum up, all of this means that the spiritual life of the Chinese people is centered on the human being and is directed towards the human being, and even in its transcendent form, it places the human being in a pivotal position. What is even more remarkable is that these ideas developed gradually among the people, seemingly without the intervention of religious professionals or scholars.

Here, I would like to particularly mention Chapter 10, because this chapter represents a synthesis of what was discussed in the preceding nine chapters, reflected in the novels that people enjoy reading. My guess is that Chinese readers who only finished high school may not be familiar with the material presented in the first nine chapters, but they can understand the interaction between folk behavior and the textual world through the four novels presented in Chapter 10. In my view, Shi Nai'an drew on existing legends to tell the story of Mount Liang, which, on the one hand, is a story of the people at the bottom of the social order pursuing their ideals and dreaming of a building new world of equality in which they can participate. Yet on the other hand, the reality was that the tyranny of the Ming dynasty and the separation of the upper and lower classes finally left them discouraged. Hence the second part of *Water Margin* describes the destruction of Mount Liang. Of the important characters who helped to build the dream world, some died, some took up the religious life, some fled to other countries, some wandered aimlessly.

Luo Guanzhong's *The Romance of the Three Kingdoms* is set against the backdrop of the political machinations following the fall of the Han dynasty. In the midst of the rivalry between orthodox and heterodox, loyal and treacherous, the author constructed two idols: the sincere and wise Zhuge Liang, and the righteous and brave Guan Yu. To shore up these two almost perfect images, the author attributed all things worthy of admiration to them. What Luo Guanzhong was imagining here was probably another kind of "other world:" he took the "righteousness," which is an individual choice, as the fundamental link between people. The whole of *The Romance of the Three Kingdoms* boils down to the contrast between "righteousness" and "injustice," and while the representatives of righteousness fail, the glory of righteousness shines through the ages.

In the mid-Ming, the dispiriting institutions and behavior of the time also stimulated the author of *Investiture of the Gods* to compose his work. In this novel of gods and demons, the presupposition is that conflict, compromise, and order will emerge. Before the end of the struggle, we will witness the conflict between orthodoxy and heterodoxy, gods and demons, loyalty and treachery, and love and hate; when the struggle is over, all the people and monsters involved are brought together in a new court of the gods, where they divide up the responsibility for everything in the universe. The result of the battle between the gods and demons is not the overwhelming victory of one side over the other, but the emergence of a new, orderly universe under the pre-determined ideals of Buddhism and Daoism.

The fourth novel is *Journey to the West*, in which Wu Cheng'en adapts the story of a Tang monk's journey to the west to seek scriptures into a story of humanity's quest for liberation. In the novel, he combines the teachings of Buddhism and Daoism, as well as elements of Confucianism, and uses the 81 difficulties encountered on the journey as a symbol of the trials one has to endure in the course of one's spiritual cultivation, the temptations and mistakes one must overcome before reaching the state of perfection and liberation. The outcome, however, is the highest state of Chan Buddhism—the realization that what is experienced by the senses and the mind is an illusion—and the attainment of "ultimate nirvana," and complete liberation. At that moment, words and language are no longer needed.

Taken together, these four books, together with their characters and plot lines, provide many resources for the thought of the Chinese people. The heroes of the novels remain the objects of our worship and admiration today. The gods of Chinese folk imagination, or the gods of *Investiture of the Gods*, govern our present life and our future release. The magnificent characters and stories of *Journey to the West* are still alive for ordinary people today. The authors of these four books were not entirely at the bottom of society, but were instead intellectuals and marginalized members of the middle and lower strata of society. Their educational backgrounds and knowledge enabled them to convey the ideas of Confucianism, Daoism and Buddhism to the people. Through storytelling and drama, the people were able to absorb these originally quite subtle concepts into widely accepted explanations of the changes occurring in the world. Mircia Eliade once took the difference between "sacred" and "profane" as an important precondition for the doctrine of the one true God in the West. However, in the development of Chinese religion, the sacred could be incorporated into the profane, and the profane could be absorbed into the sacred. It is particularly noteworthy that the *Journey to the West* presents a "journey of the mind," which returns a transcendent divinity to the mind of humanity and opens up the possibility for mortals to seek liberation on their own.

Summing up the contents of the chapters of this book, we can see that the spiritual life of the Chinese people is multifaceted and interactive, and the contact between diverse elements leads to fusion. This gives rise to the dialectical transformation of many oppositions. In the course of this transformation, there is always a concern not to overdo it (because exceeding the mark is the same as not achieving it), to swing too far on either side of the pendulum—that is, to subvert the dialectical process. The spiritual life of the Chinese people is internal; that is to say, we observe, we feel, we investigate, we absorb and we finally reach our inner enlightenment. This kind of spiritual life is characterized by the fact that one can finally reach a state of perfection. It is unlikely that all these characteristics evolved over a short period of time. The gradual evolution of such a spiritual state in China is probably due to the fact that since the Neolithic period, a large cultural community has encountered different cultures at each stage of development, and these contacts have led to adjustments, coexistence, and ultimately fusion. As mentioned above, different regions in China have developed different beliefs and customs due to differences in the natural environment. The fusion of these diverse regions formed a major part of

Chinese culture. Later on, constant contact with the outside world—the Middle East, India, and Europe—brought in cultural elements from those regions that became nutrients enriching Chinese culture.

Major cultural systems elsewhere have also had the same experience. Today's modern culture is best seen as a period in the long transformation of globalization. If we look back to the origins of antiquity, we see a similar process of multiple origins in constant contact and interaction with other nearby cultures. Central Asia, South Asia, the Middle East, the Mediterranean and continental Europe have all experienced a similar process of integration. Modern culture itself is a synthesis of these many sources, and the dramatic international, intercultural exchanges in modern times, especially with the development of a common global community, have combined the elements of these many different civilizations into a modern global culture that envelops the world.

Compared to the Chinese experience, the process of building a modern civilization has not been particularly smooth. Struggles between ethnic groups, between religious beliefs, and between different types of economies have marked the process, all of which has meant that the institutions of scientific civilization are not necessarily compatible with those of the older civilization on which they have been built.

As I said at the beginning of this chapter, modern civilization is entering a very tense period of change, perhaps even a crisis of survival. Western civilization has dominated the world for 300 years. Over this long period of time, due to its exclusivistic tendencies, Western civilization has weakened and even destroyed many other civilizations. Therefore, we have to look for new elements to revive them. At present, if you look around the world, you may find that China is the only cultural system that can point out the errors of Western civilization.

However, China has also experienced nearly two centuries of turbulence and frustration. Chinese civilization itself has lost many of its precious elements. The purpose of this book is to reflect on the situation of Chinese civilization itself, and to determine if there remains enough richness to nourish a modern civilization in crisis. Discussions in this volume suggest that it does: namely, the relationship between humans and nature as described in various chapters of this book, the multifaceted and interactive search for equilibrium in nature, each individual's concern for others, the common desire for an ideal state, and justice and fairness as a reflection of one's moral needs, all of which are interconnected and mutually supportive.

In the Introduction, I mentioned Fei Xiaotong's notion of a "differential mode of association" and C. K. Yang's work on market interactions. Both of these are models built on the basis of fieldwork in society, the former reflecting the extension of individuals to groups at various levels, the latter representing the state of multiple interactions in a network system. I also mentioned Feng Youlan's *Purity Descends, Primacy Ascends*, his *A New Treatise on the Nature of Man*, *New Philosophy of Principle*, and *A New Treatise on the Nature of Dao*, in which he arrived at his conclusions in the process of developing Chinese philosophical thought. His conclusion, in short, is that we must pay attention at three levels: the individual and himself, the individual and the group, and the individual and nature.

In the chapters of this book, China's three main philosophical systems of Confucianism, Daoism, and Buddhism, and particularly the successful efforts to combine the three, generally followed the line of development from "self-cultivation" to interaction with the group, and finally to a more important effort to combine the individual and humanity in a continuous web of connection. Similarly, the relationship between humans and nature is nothing more than the overlapping of the three layers of heavenly principles, the way of the world, and the minds of humans, and the continuity and resonance between these three layers bind them together as a whole in a multi-directional space. In addition, remembering one's ancestral roots and revisiting the past, while simultaneously assuming the past and looking toward the future, extends time so that it becomes an unbroken line, all creating a vast universe in which the individual is a central point in a huge network.

This is a spiritual state of mind in which individuals both respect themselves and have respect for all sentient beings of the universe. This is how one's conscience, or "mind," is developed. Beginning from this central point, the individual can merge with other structures with other people at their center. Since the universe and human beings are one, people should not exploit the universe and take whatever they want for their own enjoyment, ultimately damaging the natural environment in which they live. Everyone talks about "sustainable development" these days; sadly, the human heart is endlessly greedy, demanding more abundance and comfort instead of embracing moderation, and modern technology is based on the massive consumption of energy and resources. This Faustian spirit is, unfortunately, leading humankind to destruction.

Modern industrialization and capitalism are the products of the modern industrial revolution of the 18th and 19th centuries. At that time, the mentality was one of Newtonian absolutism, the belief that human knowledge could fully grasp everything. The concepts of relativity and quantum mechanics of the 20th century, however, have forced us to ask ourselves: could we not be a little more humble? Or at least acknowledge that what we see and know is only one very small corner of the great unknown? Moreover, how much of our knowledge of this little corner of the world reflects our subjectivity? Or how much is due to the limitations of our tools of observation? To my mind, this kind of intellectual modesty might be a remedy that the two cultural systems of ancient India and China could offer today's world as a word of caution.

In sum, this book describes the spiritual life of the Chinese people as tending toward a state of total integration and mutual response, after thousands of years of absorption, tempering, and digestion. In comparison to the dilemma facing modern Western civilization depicted above, we should believe that the unique spirit of Chinese culture may well compensate for the deficiencies of modern civilization, and that the fusion of the two would lead to the development of a truly global civilization. The Chinese understanding of the relationship of individual and the group, the individual and nature, and the individual as one point in a connected universe, can still capture the emphasis we find in Western individualism on the dignity, freedom and equality of the individual. Perhaps Chinese and Western civilizations can complement one another, inspiring individuals to respect and value themselves, so that the work of "self-cultivation" and self-improvement can achieve a more secure place in the modern world, and then finally through "putting oneself in the place of others," we can make progress toward the ultimate goal of universal harmony, where "heaven and humans are one" and people and nature live in peaceful coexistence.

The process of reasoning behind this book is different from that of Feng Youlan's *Purity Descends, Primacy Ascends*. As a philosopher, Feng's interpretations are based on the history of ideas. By contrast, I have drawn my conclusions based on the daily life of ordinary people and their behavior in various situations. Beginning from the end of the 19th century, when the Western tide was at its zenith, the Chinese people had to find their own way forward. Feng's *Purity Descends, Primacy Ascends* came into being at a time when China was on the brink of defeat, and the Chinese people were still searching for solutions despite the destruction of war. More than half a century has passed since the 1940s, and some of the phenomena described in this book no longer exist; for example, the state has now taken care of social welfare in small districts. In addition, some of the poetry discussed in the aesthetics section is no longer familiar to today's youth. However, the hopes and dreams of the common people, as reflected in their beliefs concerning making the world better, as well as in their operas and legends, have not changed much. In their daily lives, Chinese people still attach great importance to diversity and harmony in their diet, medicine, and architecture, and they still think and act in a way that seeks equilibrium and avoids extremes. In this sense, I hope, the conclusions at which I have arrived may not be far off the mark. Now old and in declining health, I have written this in haste, my only hope being to make my small contribution to today's world, to inspire others to continue the conversation as modern civilization faces disaster.